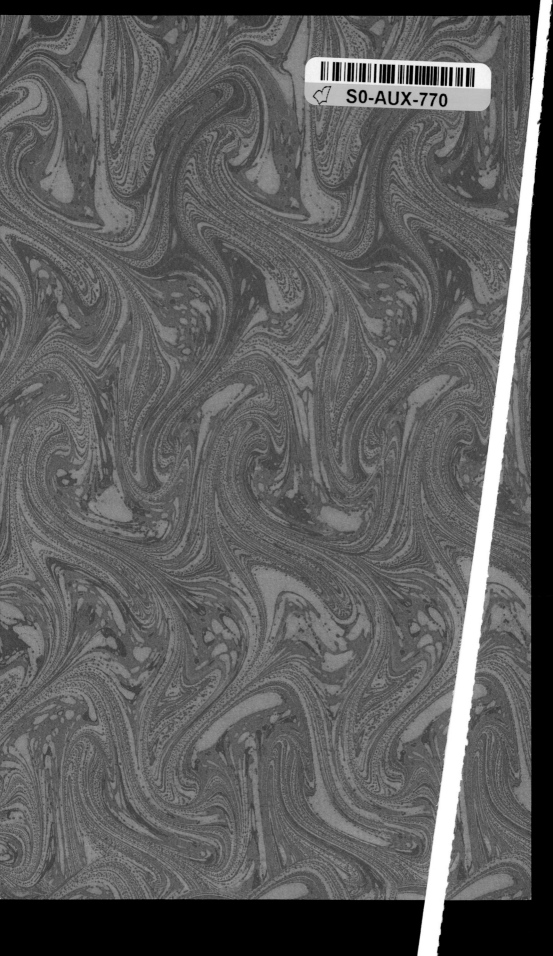

HEROES OF ISRAEL

HEROES OF ISRAEL

Profiles of Jewish Courage

CHAIM HERZOG

STEIMATZKY LTD.

CONTENTS

INTRODUCTION

THE SUBJECTS chosen for this tribute to Jewish courage range from the biblical period to modern times, from Joshua to Hannah Szenes and from Bar-Kokhba to Yoni Netanyahu. National leaders have been included, as well as individual fighters; commanders in addition to ordinary soldiers. The choice is a personal one and makes no claim to being comprehensive.

Bravery, rather than success, has been the criterion for inclusion. Those who died courageously, like Samson, Bar-Kokhba and Hannah Szenes, are included together with such victors as Deborah, King David and David Ben-Gurion. There are many other figures who might have been included, and possibly the reader will be disappointed to find his own special hero omitted.

Only those who actually fought on behalf of the Jewish people, or led them in a military or paramilitary campaign, have been chosen.

Each of the subjects illustrates a special type of courage: Deborah led an army long before any other woman fulfilled a similar role; Samson pursued a lonely and defiant struggle to his death; Bar-Kokhba dared to defy the awesome power of Rome; Hannah Szenes revealed hidden strength in the body of a young woman; Mordechai Anielewicz led the Warsaw Ghetto revolt in a display of grit and steadfastness that went far beyond bravery; Ben-Gurion took far-sighted and fateful decisions under intense pressure.

The personalities and groups selected have been described within the framework of a continuous narrative, so that, although each portrait is complete in itself and can be read as an individual essay, it is advisable to read the chapters in chronological order. In this way each figure can be seen both in the context of his or her times and within the continuum of Jewish history as a whole.

It will be noted that no single heroic figure between the death of Bar-Kokhba and the modern era has been described. Deprived of their land, the Jews did not produce a military leader of the stature of King David or Judah the Maccabee for almost 2,000 years.

It was, nevertheless, a time of great moral courage, during which the Jews maintained their religious and cultural identity against overwhelming pressures, and a special linking chapter has been written to pay tribute to these spiritual heroes, as well as to provide chronological coherence.

The reader will notice that, whereas in the early chapters, individual personalities have been depicted, many of the later chapters deal with groups. In the historic period, individual figures, such as King David and Judah the Maccabee, came to symbolize a heroic period, whereas, in the modern era, outstanding individuals, such as Mordechai Anielewicz and Yigal Allon, are seen as the leaders of the forces they commanded. Joseph Trumpeldor, Avshalom Feinberg, Dov Gruner and Avigdor Kahalani are other modern heroes who led forces or groups; but there is one man in the modern period who towers above his contemporaries in a biblical fashion.

David Ben-Gurion was the man with the ultimate responsibility for the modern Jewish revival, who took the crucial military and political decisions and led Israel to statehood. Like Joshua, King David or Bar-Kokhba, he resolutely ensured the unity of the nation.

Although not an army man, he made himself a military expert, prepared the nation for war and took all the major strategic decisions in the War of Independence, Israel's most difficult conflict. Subsequently he consolidated the nation he had created from a military, political, social and economic point of view.

Finally, it is my belief that, apart from showing courage and resolution, each of the personalities and groups described has played a vital role in ensuring the survival and security of the Jewish people.

1

Joshua: Man of Faith and Loyalty

Despite the burning heat of the Jordan valley, Joshua Bin-Nun, commander of the Israelite tribes, may well have felt a shiver of apprehension as he regarded the formidable walls of Jericho, for his moment of truth had arrived. Alone, without the support of Moses the great leader, he was charged with guiding the Children of Israel across the River Jordan into Canaan, the promised land.

Moses, the towering figure who stood face-to-face with God and received His Holy Law, who led the twelve Israelite tribes out of slavery in Egypt, who held them together through their desert sojourn, sustaining their faith and sense of purpose, defusing their discontent, was no more. Joshua, who had carried out the orders of Moses, now had to make the decisions, not only execute them, to devise and plan as well as lead.

He faced a task to daunt the bravest man, for his followers, although toughened by forty years of wandering in the desert, were not equipped to tackle the massive walls of the Canaanite towns. They had no heavy slings or battering-rams, no tunnelling equipment, no experience in conducting a siege. Nor had they faced well-trained forces like the Canaanites, equipped with iron weapons and backed by horse-drawn chariots.

True, they had waged a successful campaign against the Amorites, led by their kings Sihon and Og, and established themselves east of the Jordan; but then Moses was still alive. Furthermore, the Amorites, who had only recently arrived in the area, were not protected by walled cities as were the Canaanites across the river.

Joshua's nomads were tough skirmishers, daring and resourceful, who had proved themselves against the desert tribes. They had shown themselves capable of carrying out sudden raids and lightning attacks, but never before had they faced a challenge to compare with the one facing them now.

Joshua had long known about the walls of the Canaanite towns. Many years previously, he was one of the twelve men — one from each of the twelve tribes — sent by Moses to spy out the land of Canaan. Ten of the spies had returned with unfavorable reports; but Joshua and the representative of the tribe of Judah, Caleb, had mastered their fear and insisted that the land could be conquered.

Despite the furious opposition of the people, who accepted the majority report, Joshua and Caleb stuck to their views, even to the extent of facing down a stone-throwing mob. The biblical account depicts God's fury at the people of Israel for their lack of faith, and the intercession of Moses with the Almighty.

God, the Bible tells us, agreed not to destroy the Israelites, but resolved that only Joshua and Caleb of the generation which left Egypt would enter the promised land. The others, including Moses himself, were fated to wander in the desert; only their descendants would survive to reach Canaan. This would be a new generation of Israelites, free of the slave mentality of their fathers.

Facing Jericho, Joshua knew that the moment of decision could not be postponed again. He had already despatched two spies across the river, who reported that the people of Canaan were in a state of panic. Lodging with Rahab, the wife of a local innkeeper, they heard of the impression made on the population by the successful Israelite campaign against the two Amorite kings.

The tel of Jericho showing the excavations of the 6,000-year-old town. To the north lies a large, but mostly abandoned refugee camp. (*David Rubinger*)

Relying on the archaeological evidence that Jericho was severely damaged by an earthquake in the fourteenth century B.C., a hundred years before Joshua's arrival, it is legitimate to speculate that the spies had also told the Israelite commander that the walls of Jericho were not as strong as they seemed to be; but with an outer wall six feet thick, and an inner wall twice as massive, they looked formidable enough. Anyone who has visited the ruins of Jericho has seen the incredible width and strength of its walls.

Before launching his attack, Joshua took three crucial steps: he assumed supreme power, including the right to pass the death sentence; he ensured the participation of the tribes which were to settle on the east side of the river; and he ordered the circumcision of the entire male population.

The Jewish people is a difficult people, with a tendency to divisiveness. The account of the exodus from Egypt makes it clear that their ancestors were very much the same. It took all of the tremendous authority of Moses to hold them together; now Joshua had to wield a similar authority. The right to inflict the supreme penalty ensured discipline.

The tribes of Reuben and Gad, and half the tribe of Menashe, had already reached their territory in Transjordan. Self-interest did not compel them to participate in what promised to be a long and arduous campaign to conquer Canaan, but Joshua invoked the authority of Moses:

> Your wives, your little ones, and your cattle shall remain in the land which Moses gave you on this side of the Jordan; but ye shall pass before your brethren armed, all the mighty men of valour and help them;
>
> Until the Lord have given your brethren rest, as he hath given you, and they also have possessed the land. . . . (*Joshua 1:14–15*)

The mass circumcision symbolized the ancient covenant between God and the Children of Israel; but it was also a covenant between man and man, a shared spiritual and physical experience irrevocably binding all who carried it out.

The subsequent action is well-known: the Israelites marched around the city every day, carrying the ark of the covenant, led by priests blowing trumpets of rams' horns:

... Thus shalt thou do six days ... and the seventh day ye shall compass the city seven times ... and when ye hear the sound of the trumpet, all the people shall shout with a great shout; and the wall of the city shall fall down flat. ...   (*Joshua 6:3 – 5*)

Many scholars have sought a rational explanation for what happened. The most convincing seems to be the theory that the repetitive action by the Israelites lulled the defenders into a false sense of security, upon which the attackers struck suddenly and forcefully.

In the event, Jericho was destroyed and burnt and its population massacred; but here Joshua demonstrated his characteristic loyalty. He did not forget Rahab, the innkeeper's wife, the source of his intelligence. He saved her entire family from the slaughter. According to the account in the Book of Joshua, the household of Rahab continued to live at peace among the Israelites.

BEFORE PROCEEDING with our narrative, let us pause to consider the character of Joshua, the man who took over the leadership of the Israelites from Moses, arguably the greatest figure in all of Jewish history.

A brilliant military commander, Joshua was also an inspiring leader, a wise administrator, a nation-builder and a man of profound faith and vision. When he took over the leadership of the people of Israel, they were a homeless tribe of wanderers, fired only by a vision. On his death, he left them a unified nation settled on its own land.

Israel, a small people among the nations, needs faith and optimism in order to survive; but these qualities must be tempered with a realistic assessment of what is attainable. Too little faith will limit achievement, but overconfidence can lead to defeat. Joshua possessed the correct balance of vision and realism. Without his pragmatic leadership, the nation might not have survived.

However, in considering this man who grew up in the shadow of Moses, it is the quality of loyalty that springs most readily to mind: loyalty to his leader, loyalty to his principles, loyalty to his word, loyalty to his people and faith.

It was Joshua who stood by Moses when he went up on Mount

The oasis of Jericho leading to the River Jordan and the mountains of Trans-jordan. (*David Rubinger*)

Sinai; Joshua who possessed the inner faith to continue believing in his people's ability to occupy the promised land; Joshua who stood by his word to the Gibeonites and came to their aid against the powerful alliance confronting them; Joshua who never forgot his commitment to God and who, on his death-bed, urged his people: "Put away the strange gods which are among you, and incline your heart unto the Lord God of Israel." (Joshua 24:23)

We do not know a great deal about Joshua's origins, except that he was the son of Nun and a member of the tribe of Ephraim; but he was already demonstrating his military prowess some two months after the Israelites left Egypt, when they were attacked by the Amalekites, a tribe of desert nomads, at Refidim in the Sinai desert. Appointed by Moses to conduct the defence, Joshua launched a successful counterattack and routed the enemy.

Subsequently Joshua was in constant attendance on his leader, approaching Mount Sinai with him, accompanying him to the camp of the golden calf–worshipping Israelites after his descent from the mountain and present with him in the tabernacle when Moses first communed with God.

As we have seen, Joshua was one of the two spies who recommended going ahead with the invasion of Canaan. Apart from the physical bravery of being prepared to press forward into the "land of giants," Joshua showed the moral courage to oppose the majority of his colleagues.

Backed only by Caleb, he insisted that Canaan was "an exceeding good land. If the Lord delight in us, then he will bring us into this land, and give it us; a land which floweth with milk and honey." (Numbers 14:7–8)

The real test of a leader is whether he is prepared to maintain his opinion in the face of strong opposition, whether he is prepared to stand by his judgement, even against his own friends and colleagues. Measured by this yardstick, Joshua early on emerged as a true leader.

Joshua's conquest of Canaan, which was carried out in three stages, clearly illustrated his ability as a strategist. First he established a bridgehead west of the Jordan; then he secured a base in the hills across the river, from which he moved south and then north.

The strategy was well thought out; but the military plan, however brilliant, was not enough. He needed an enthusiastic and united fighting force. A national leader as well as a general, his first concern was to ensure national unity, to weld the twelve tribes into one unit that would act together. Like David Ben-Gurion more than three millennia later, he brooked no partisan behaviour, no private armies fighting for their own sectional interests.

Joshua's task was both easier and more difficult than that of Moses, his illustrious predecessor. It is true that he was able to show his people a tangible aim and a practical plan of action; but the dangers before them were far greater than the mere hazards of desert climate and topography, or skirmishes with nomads.

HIS BRIDGEHEAD in Jericho secured, Joshua aimed for the hills to the west, defended by the town of Ai. The two battles for this town demonstrate another facet of Joshua's character: his ability to recover after a setback, because the first attack, made with a relatively small force, was beaten back.

Joshua was concerned about the effect of this defeat on the morale of his own people, but even more on the morale of the enemy. The myth of Israelite invincibility had to be maintained.

A new attack was swiftly launched, with different tactics. One force marched by night and concealed itself in low ground to the southwest of Ai. The main force, under Joshua's personal command, launched a frontal attack on the city from the north, pretending to retreat in the face of a counterattack.

With most of the fighters pursuing the main Israelite force, the concealed fighters stormed Ai and set the buildings alight. The pursuing Canaanite force turned back towards the burning town, but was caught between the two Israelite units and destroyed.

According to the biblical account, the initial defeat at Ai was the result of one man's disobeying the divine commandment not to plunder Jericho. The man was duly executed and victory achieved.

Traditionally the ban on plundering Jericho has been explained not as a general moral principle, but because Jericho, as the first city to be conquered, and conquered on the seventh day — the Sabbath, belonged to God.

Nevertheless, the ban indicates the high degree of discipline expected from the Israelite fighters, and also established the principle that plunder was not the inevitable consequence of conquest.

Later interpretations of the biblical account indicate a remarkably humane attitude on the part of Joshua. According to the tradition, before embarking on a battle Joshua offered peace: "Whosoever desires to go, let him go; and whosoever desires to make peace, let him make peace; whosoever desires to make war, let him make war." (Midrash, legends of the Bible)

Although the offer of peace or flight is not in the biblical account, we do find Joshua making a pact with the Gibeonites, who inhabited the hill country north of Jerusalem, which indicates that he was not irrevocably set on conquest if different means were available.

Again and again we see Joshua striving to unite his people before moving on to the next phase of the campaign. After the fall of Ai, he built an altar on Mount Ebal above Shechem (today's Nablus), sacrificed to the Lord and read out to the entire congregation the laws handed down by Moses.

Archaeologists recently found an altar on Mount Ebal, believed to be the one built by Joshua. The stones, unhewn according to the biblical commandment, were of a type found in the Jordan valley.

Following the fall of Ai and the alliance with the Gibeonites, a powerful federation of five Canaanite kings resolved to nip the Israelite invasion in the bud by launching an attack against their new allies. The Gibeonites called for help and, faithful to his word, Joshua hurried to their aid, once again marching at night to gain the advantage of surprise.

Stampeding the enemy, the Israelites pursued them through the pass of Beth Horon and the Ajalon valley. At this point, according to the biblical account, Joshua asked God to stop the sun and the moon in their tracks:

Then spake Joshua to the Lord in the day when the Lord delivered up the Amorites before the children of Israel, and he said in the sight of Israel, Sun, stand thou still upon Gibeon; and thou, Moon, in the valley of Ajalon.

And the sun stood still, and the moon stayed, until the people had avenged themselves upon their enemies.   (*Joshua 10:12–13*)

What this indicates is that Joshua pursued his enemies without letting up, consolidating his initial victory. In a remarkable demonstration of mobility and stamina, the Israelite forces traversed some thirty miles in two days, most of them under battle conditions. If Jericho and Ai were conquered by ruses, the victory in the battle against the five kings was apparently achieved by sheer speed.

Again Joshua utilized the courage, resourcefulness, flair and mobility of his fighting men to prevail over a far stronger enemy. This was the model for subsequent Israelite — and Israeli — commanders in the years to come.

The victory was, of course, limited. The king of Jerusalem was among those killed; but Jerusalem, along with several other strongly fortified cities, stood out against the Israelites for many more years.

Furthermore, Joshua kept his people in the hills, not venturing into the coastal plain where the chariots of the Canaanites would have given them the advantage, and where he might have provoked the intervention of Egypt, the nominal ruler of Canaan. The Egyptians seem to have turned a blind eye to the Israelite advance; but this might not have continued to be the case if the invaders had occupied the sea route between Egypt and Syria.

Joshua here showed a fine sense of judgement. He was level-headed and self-disciplined. He was not intoxicated by his spectacular victories, but knew when to stop. He persisted against Ai in the face of an initial defeat and pursued the five kings remorselessly, but he was ready to reassess his objectives in the light of Canaanite power.

It is not fanciful to compare him again to Ben-Gurion, who, in our time, accepted the United Nations partition plan for Palestine, tempering his desire for the whole land with an intelligent pragmatism, which judged coolly and correctly what could be achieved in the circumstances.

Indeed, when the tribes of Ephraim and Menashe complained that they did not have enough land, that the hill country was insufficient for the tribes, Joshua replied that they should clear the woods to make more room. His message was unequivocal: make do with what you have and utilize it fully. Thus, in our own day, did Ben-Gurion urge his people to settle the Negev desert.

The Israelites now turned north, against Jabin, King of Hazor, where they overcame the chariots of their enemies in the narrow valley by the waters of Merom, before they were able to deploy in open ground. The fact that the chariots were destroyed indicates that the Israelites had no use for them. Several centuries were to pass before they achieved a sufficient sophistication to use such equipment.

The role of Joshua the warrior was over. He now entered a new phase of his career, that of administrator who divided the conquered land among the tribes. But before this, Joshua once again laid emphasis on the unity of the nation: "And the whole congregation of the children of Israel assembled together at Shiloh, and set up the tabernacle of the congregation there." (Joshua 18:1)

Only after this act of national unity did Joshua turn to the task of dividing up the land. The fighters of Reuben, Gad and half the tribe of Menashe were permitted to return to their homes east of the Jordan. The parts of Canaan which had been conquered were divided up among eight and a half of the remaining tribes, the exception being the priestly tribe of Levi.

The Levites were expected to perform religious duties for the whole nation, so they were granted a number of cities in the area of each of the tribes. Six of these cities — three on each side of the Jordan — were designated "cities of refuge," where someone who had killed accidentally could find sanctuary from those seeking to avenge the killing.

Again Joshua proved himself ahead of his time: the primitive custom of the blood feud was tempered with mercy and restrained with the principles of self-control and the rule of law.

Joshua's task was almost accomplished. The enemies had been vanquished; the tribes settled in their territories; the land was at peace. In fact, as we have seen, large parts of Canaan remained unconquered, but the Israelites had won a breathing space.

The aged leader, however, was still concerned for the unity of his nation. He called an assembly of the people in Shechem and reminded them of their history and their unique traditions. They were living in a land for which they had not laboured, he pointed out, dwelling in cities they had not built, eating produce that others had planted. For this they had God to thank: "Now therefore fear the Lord, and serve Him in sincerity and in truth: and put away the gods which your fathers served on the other side of the flood, and in Egypt; and serve ye the Lord." (Joshua 24:14)

Joshua's final covenant with his people was a renewal of the ancient covenant made with God by Abraham and Moses. It was a wonderful conclusion to a lifetime of achievement.

The victorious commander in battle, the administrator who built the nation and allocated its territory, the supreme judge of his people's disputes, was also the one who established a firm foundation of unity around a new sanctuary in the heart of what had now become the land of Israel. Joshua, the man of faith and loyalty, had completed his mission.

2 🦢

Deborah: Woman of Valour

🦢 IT MUST have been with a deep feeling of dread that Deborah, the judge and prophetess, answered the call of her people to lead them in war against their enemies. It was unusual enough in ancient times for a woman to fulfil a leadership role, and Deborah had already broken the mould dramatically by serving as a judge and arbiter of her people's problems.

She was certainly a remarkable personality to be accepted as such by the people of Israel, with its patriarchal traditions and distinctly masculine deity; but, even taking her character into account, the position of commander-in-chief must have been a daunting challenge for a woman.

We have seen that Joshua, when commanding the tribes of Reuben, Gad and Menashe to take part in the invasion of Canaan, permitted them to leave their women and children on the eastern side of the River Jordan: the battlefield was not considered to be a suitable place for a woman.

Twelve centuries were to pass before the legendary Queen Boadicea led her Britons against Rome, and a further fourteen centuries until Joan of Arc became the leader of France. Many years would also pass before another woman became a leader in Israel; but the emergence of Deborah is a singular demonstration of the Jewish ideal of equality before God. Deborah was chosen as the most suitable leader, regardless of the fact of her sex.

EARLY IN the twelfth century B.C., the Israelites found themselves in serious trouble. Only a few generations after Joshua's conquest, there had been something of a Canaanite revival. Jabin, the Canaanite king of Hazor—presumably a descendant of the Jabin who was resoundingly defeated by Joshua—was in control of northern Canaan.

The Bible, in fact, contains two accounts of the situation. A rather terse prose account is followed by a surging lyric poem, the Song of Deborah. The first, in the Book of Judges, relates:

> And the Lord sold them into the hand of Jabin king of Canaan, that reigned in Hazor; the captain of whose host was Sisera, which dwelt in Harosheth of the Gentiles.
>
> And the children of Israel cried unto the Lord: for he had nine hundred chariots of iron; and twenty years he mightily oppressed the children of Israel.   (*Judges 4:2-3*)

The Song of Deborah gives us more details of the nature of that oppression: " . . . in the days of Jael, the highways were unoccupied, and the travellers walked through byways. The inhabitants of the villages ceased, they ceased in Israel. . . ." (Judges 5:6-7)

The northern Israelite tribes, then, lived in fear of the oppressive rule of King Jabin, unable to pursue their daily lives without interference. His chariot forces patrolled the main routes, which the Israelites were not permitted to use. Cut off from each other, they were forced to use paths and tracks to communicate.

Deborah lived farther south, between Ramah and Beth-el in the territory of Ephraim north of Jerusalem, and was probably not directly affected by Jabin's domination of the north. However, the people of Israel turned to her because she was a judge.

The unity of the Israelites had not entirely survived the death of

Joshua. As he had feared, the dispersal of the tribes to their individual territories had weakened the links between them, with each tribe looking to its sectarian interests. A series of "judges" exercised varying degrees of authority over the loose confederation.

Deborah, in fact, was the only one of the biblical judges who was actually described as judging the people, dispensing justice under a tree. Trees have traditionally been holy places in many religions and Ethiopian Copts hold services under them to this day.

Deborah settled the disputes that were brought to her out in the open, rather than behind closed doors. The Jewish tradition suggests that she sat in judgement outside to avoid being alone in her house with a man. Even if this were the case, it was also one of the earliest instances of ensuring that justice was not only done, but seen to be done.

As a judge of proven integrity therefore, Deborah was a figure of authority. She immediately demonstrated her fitness for the role of national leader by summoning Barak to be her general. Barak was from Kedesh in the territory of the tribe of Naphtali farther north, one of those directly threatened by Jabin.

Although she presented him with a detailed plan of battle, Barak, no doubt mindful of Deborah's tremendous prestige among the people, insisted on her presence by his side: "And Barak said unto her, If thou wilt go with me, then I will go: but if thou wilt not go with me, then I will not go." (Judges 4:8)

Mention has been made of the French heroine Joan of Arc; but Deborah surely surpassed her in the way she led her people in battle, planning the campaign, deciding on tactics and strategy and leading them to a magnificent victory.

DEBORAH ORDERED Barak to mobilize 10,000 men and station himself atop Mount Tabor. Her own role was to draw Sisera, the commander of King Jabin's forces, towards the valley of the River Kishon to the west, giving Barak the chance to attack from the rear.

When Barak made it clear that he wanted her by his side, Deborah accepted; but the battle plan, which showed a keen sense of military strategy and made allowances for the potential superiority of the enemy—in particular of his chariots—remained unaltered.

Deborah developed a three-phased campaign. Phase one was the concentration of 10,000 men from the tribes of Zebulun and Naphtali on Mount Tabor, a looming, bulbous mountain which towers over the Jezreel valley. Its steep sides were a sure defence against the chariots of the enemy. It was also a superb look-out post, with excellent visibility in all directions and an obvious base for a sudden attack on an enemy below.

Phase two, which Deborah initially intended to lead, concentrated fighters in the hills of Ephraim to the southwest, to draw Sisera's forces away from Tabor.

Phase three was a move on the part of the Ephraim-based Israelites westwards towards the Haifa bay area, enticing Sisera's forces into the Kishon valley, where they were simultaneously attacked by both Israelite armies.

The biblical account suggests that Heber the Kenite, an ally of the Israelites, was part of this ruse. Heber seemed to ally himself with Sisera, separating himself from the rest of his tribe, and informing Sisera about the ascent of Barak and his forces on to Mount Tabor.

Sisera fell into the trap, moving his "nine hundred chariots of iron, and all the people that were with him, from Harosheth of the Gentiles unto the river of Kishon." (Judges 4:13) At this point Barak descended from the mountain and launched his assault. The first account merely records Barak's total victory over the powerful army of Sisera, backed as it was by a huge force of chariots.

Deborah's subsequent paean of praise gives us more details: "The river of Kishon swept them away, that ancient river, the river Kishon." (Judges 5:21)

Sisera's chariots were obviously bogged down in the swampy land of the valley. Probably the river was swollen by a rainstorm, a common enough event in the land of Israel to this day. At all events Sisera's forces were utterly routed, and he was forced to flee on foot. His subsequent death at the hands of Jael, the wife of Heber, only serves to confirm that Heber was part of the plot. Jael gave him shelter in her tent, fed him and then drove a spike through his head as he slept.

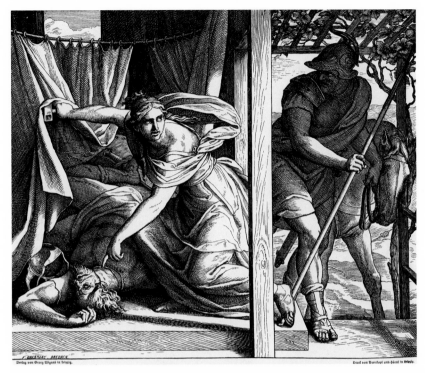

"Then Jael Heber's wife took a nail of the tent, and took an hammer in her hand, and went softly unto him [Sisera], and smote the nail into his temples. . . ." (Judges 4:21). From *Die Bibel in Bildern* by Julius Schnorr von Carolsfeld, Germany, 1860.

One of the most important sections of Deborah's song relates to her failure to mobilize the different tribes to participate in her campaign. She is full of praise for those who rallied to the national cause:

> Out of Ephraim was there a root of them against Amalek; after thee, Benjamin, among thy people; out of Machir [Menashe] came down governors, and out of Zebulun they that handle the pen of the writer.
>
> And the princes of Issachar were with Deborah.
>
> (*Judges 5:14 – 15*)

However, the prophetess pours out her scorn on those who failed to respond to her call:

Why abodest thou among the sheepfolds, to hear the bleatings of the flocks? For the divisions of Reuben there were great searchings of heart.

Gilead [Gad] abode beyond Jordan: and why did Dan remain in ships? Asher continued on the sea shore, and abode in his breaches.

(Judges 5:16 – 17)

Judah and Simeon are not mentioned in the song. One may assume that these southern tribes were not called. This can be taken as an early indication of the split between the northern and southern tribes, which became permanent after the reign of Solomon, several centuries later.

Of particular note, however, is the fact that the tribes which settled east of the Jordan, Gad and Reuben, which Joshua had made such strenuous efforts to keep in the national fold, failed Israel in its hour of need.

In this Deborah, the Israelites' singular woman leader, failed, and her bitterness is manifest. Her achievement, however, is no less notable, securing peace for her people which lasted for forty years.

One should be wary of historical comparisons, particularly of events separated by millennia; but the parallel between Deborah and Golda Meir, Israel's Prime Minister during the Yom Kippur War of 1973, is remarkable.

Moshe Dayan, Israel's most famous general, Minister of Defence at the time, plays a role similar to that of Barak, who insisted that Deborah remain at his side. In the same way, Dayan relied on the authority of Golda Meir, who, already in her seventies, was forced into making operational decisions that would affect the very survival of her people.

In the early hours of the morning of the Day of Atonement on October 6, when it was learnt that the Egyptians and Syrians would launch a simultaneous attack, Dayan argued with David Elazar, Chief of General Staff of the Israel Defence Forces (IDF), whether to mobilize two or four reserve divisions to meet the threat, compelling the elderly grandmother to make the fateful decision.

Instinctively, Golda backed Elazar, calling up four divisions, and thereby ensuring a sizable mobilization to deal with the subsequent threat to Israel's security.

Her military secretary recorded in his diary that she later remarked bitterly: "They were the experts; I was a civilian, I don't even know what a division is. What do I understand of such matters?"

If Deborah had a military secretary, his diaries have not survived, so we do not know whether the biblical leader was similarly troubled by conflicting advice and assailed by doubts. The record is one of decisive leadership.

The picture that emerges is one of a vibrant, inspired national commander, ready to take the mantle of leadership, sufficiently self-confident as a woman to share that leadership with a man, wise enough to enlist a general from one of the tribes more directly involved in the confrontation.

Deborah was the first leader after Joshua to take up arms against the Canaanites; but unlike Joshua, who led his people through a number of campaigns, Deborah fought only one battle.

It was, however, a decisive one. After her stunning victory in the Kishon valley, the power of the Canaanites was permanently broken. Peace was achieved and the people of Israel prospered until a new power—that of the Philistines—arose to challenge their hegemony over the promised land. Meeting this threat was to be the task of future leaders.

3

Samson: The Lonely Hero

THOUSANDS OF people were crowded into the vast temple of Dagon. The Philistine leadership was present in force, having called the assembly to rejoice over the final degradation of their greatest enemy. The supernatural strength of the Israelite hero, Samson, had been neutralized; it was a victory for their god, Dagon, over the formerly invincible God of Israel.

Now, at last, they would be revenged for the repeated humiliations inflicted on them by the Israelite champion. Savouring their triumph, the lords of the Philistines called for Samson to be brought before the multitude.

Led by a boy, the blinded fighter was brought into the temple. The cheers of the crowd turned to jeers as the people mocked the enemy, whom they had formerly feared. The mighty warrior, whose very name once struck a chill in Philistine hearts, had become a figure of fun and ridicule.

Unlike Joshua and Deborah, Samson did not lead his people

against their enemies. His acts of valour and daring were performed without the help of others. All his life, he had been a man alone; but he could never have felt so lonely as on that day in the temple of Dagon, surrounded by his jeering enemies.

In this, his moment of shame, he resolved to perform his final, magnificent act of bravery and defiance. He asked the lad who was guiding him to set his hands on the main pillars of the temple. The crowd went wild: the pitiful strongman, deprived of his strength, actually seemed to be trying to pull down the temple.

Samson is far from being a virtuous figure, in the pattern of other biblical heroes. He acted impulsively, instinctively, without regard to the consequences. He sought his pleasures with self-indulgence; but he acted according to his nature, with a rough honesty. Furthermore, he never asked anything for himself.

He had sinned, he knew that. Above all, he had broken his covenant with the Almighty, symbolized by his unshorn hair. He had betrayed the secret of his strength, thereby forfeiting it; but, humbly, fearfully, he made his first and last agonizing plea to his maker: "O Lord God, remember me, I pray thee, and strengthen me, I pray thee, only this once, O God, that I may be at once avenged of the Philistines for my two eyes." (Judges 16:28)

The jeering and laughter reached a crescendo, as the former hero strained ridiculously at the massive pillars that supported the vast building. And then, with a chilling suddenness, the shouting ceased, for, incredibly, the huge stones had begun to shift.

Pandemonium followed, as the panicking Philistines trampled on each other in their haste to escape from the crowded temple. It was to no avail. Samson succeeded in moving the supports and the temple collapsed, destroying the Israelite hero together with his enemies.

A COLOURFUL, swashbuckling rebel, who defied the conventions, Samson is unlike any other figure in Jewish history. His troubles were largely of his own making, a result of his unbridled sensuality, which was combined with a dangerous innocence. In every incident described, he was betrayed by a Philistine woman, yet he always repeated his mistake.

More than the other historical personalities of the time,

Samson, with his miraculous birth and superhuman strength, possesses the aura of a mythological hero; but the tales of his exploits are sufficiently circumstantial to suggest that he was a historical figure. Moreover, his weaknesses are poignantly human.

He is an essentially tragic man, in some ways more typical of Greek than Jewish legend, moving inexorably towards his doom. Yet there is nothing mean or petty about him: he is a titanic figure, larger than life, with a generosity of spirit, a superb recklessness that reaches a towering climax in his final gesture of ultimate defiance.

When Samson made his appearance towards the end of the twelfth century B.C., the Canaanites had been defeated; but the Philistines, a seafaring people from the Aegean, were starting to threaten the hegemony of the Israelites in their land.

The two peoples reached Canaan together. The arrival of the Philistines from the sea was more or less simultaneous with the Israelite incursion from the desert. The Philistines were originally traders; but, settling in the southern coastal plain, where they created five city-states, they took advantage of the fertile soil to become farmers. The development of their agriculture was clearly assisted by the iron tools which they used.

Their mastery of iron, like that of the Canaanites, made them formidable fighting men, as the Canaanites had been, and there is evidence that they were expanding their sphere of influence beyond the five towns. In particular, their presence increasingly cramped the small tribe of Dan, most of which migrated to a new territory farther north. Most — but not all — for Samson the Danite, with his gigantic strength and unlimited resources, waged a one-man campaign against the Philistines for two decades.

Despite their covenant with God, the Israelites did not always live up to the high standards that they set themselves. Indeed the biblical account attributes their troubles largely to their habit of forgetting their covenant and failing to observe their side of the accord between them and the Almighty. The story of Samson, in fact, begins: "And the children of Israel did evil again in the sight of the Lord; and the Lord delivered them into the hand of the Philistines forty years." (Judges 13:1)

Until Samson, the Israelite heroes from Moses to Deborah were, unlike their people, righteous figures who saved them from the results of their transgressions. In Samson, we have by contrast a hero who himself transgressed, and transgressed frequently.

He was born miraculously, after his mother had suffered many years of barrenness. According to the biblical account, an angel visited his mother and told her:

> Now therefore beware, I pray thee, and drink not wine nor strong drink, and eat not any unclean thing:
>
> For, lo, thou shalt conceive, and bear a son; and no razor shall come on his head: for the child shall be a Nazarite unto God from the womb: and he shall begin to deliver Israel out of the hand of the Philistines.   (*Judges 13:4 – 5*)

Samson, in other words, would be pure, untainted by drink or unclean food, dedicated to God and His purpose. In view of his subsequent actions, which are far from holy, this appears to be a paradox; but Samson's great strength was from God and performed the divine purpose, even if he did not always understand exactly what he was doing or why.

His single-handed rebellion against the Philistines was occasioned by personal quarrels; but resistance against foreign domination served the interests of his people. The epic of Samson must be seen in this context.

Samson, with his great physical strength, is different from other Jewish heroes, whose success inevitably resulted from daring, initiative, speed and resourcefulness against stronger enemies. Jewish history for the most part is the story of the triumph of the weak against the strong.

However, Samson's strength was not a result of his size or muscularity, but rather from his faith in God. When his bond with the Almighty — his uncut hair — was broken, he lost his strength. The divine gift is usually manifested in moral, spiritual or intellectual power. The story of Samson indicates that it can also be transmitted in the form of physical might.

As soon as he reached adulthood, Samson expressed the desire to marry a woman of the Philistines, despite the disapproval of his parents, who urged him to take a bride from his own people. The Bible makes it clear that this was God's purpose: "But his father

". . . behold, a young lion roared against him. And the Spirit of the Lord came mightily upon him, and he rent him as he would have rent a kid. . . ." (Judges 14:5 – 6). Stone relief of Samson from the Bezalel Arts and Crafts School, Jerusalem, early twentieth century. (*Israel Museum*)

and his mother knew not that it was [the purpose] of the Lord, that He sought an occasion against the Philistines: for at that time the Philistines had dominion over Israel." (Judges 14:4)

On his way to visit his future bride, Samson was attacked by a lion, which he killed bare-handed. On his way home, he discovered that bees had nested in the carcass of the animal, and he extracted the honey. At the subsequent wedding feast, Samson quizzed his Philistine guests with a riddle, promising to supply them with thirty sets of clothes if they managed to solve it.

The riddle was based on the paradox of the bees nesting in the lion's carcass and producing honey, the fact that the eater had produced food, and the strong animal had created sweetness. The wedding guests were unable to solve the riddle, but they persuaded Samson's new wife to entice the secret from her husband.

When the wedding guests solved the riddle, Samson, realizing what had happened, was infuriated; but he had to pay his debt. He chose to do so in a damaging manner, killing thirty Philistines and giving their clothes to their fellows in payment.

Despite her betrayal, Samson was not able to shake off his fascination with the Philistine woman and, after first leaving her, returned to claim her, only to find that her father had given her to someone else. This time he vented his rage on the Philistine crops, catching 300 foxes, tying flaming torches to their tails and setting them among the fields, burning the wheat, olive trees and vineyards.

The conflict escalated, with the Philistines taking revenge on Samson's wife and her father, and Samson retaliating by killing large numbers of Philistines. Unable to capture Samson, the Philistines marched up into the territory of Judah, demanding that their troublesome enemy be handed over. Faced with this demonstration of strength, 3,000 men of Judah came to Samson and pointed out that his actions had put their security in jeopardy: "Knowest thou not that the Philistines are rulers over us? What is this that thou hast done unto us? And he said unto them, As they did unto me, so have I done unto them." (Judges 15:11)

Despite justification of his actions as legitimate retaliation, Samson appeared to accept his fate, stipulating only that the men of Judah (against whom he was not prepared to fight) did not attack him themselves. He allowed himself to be delivered bound into his enemies' hands, but then broke his bonds and, seizing the only weapon that came to hand—the jawbone of an ass—he slaughtered 1,000 of his captors. That this was still part of the divine purpose is illustrated by the fact that a spring miraculously appeared to quench his thirst after the battle.

Samson's thirst for drink was satisfied, but not his thirst for Philistine women. He promptly repaired to Gaza, where he spent the night with a Philistine whore. When he realized that, in

"And he found a new jawbone of an ass, and put forth his hand, and took it, and slew a thousand men therewith." (Judges 15:15) Bronze of Samson by Pierino da Vinci, Florence, c. 1550. (*The Metropolitan Museum of Art*)

entering the walled city, he had walked into a trap, Samson broke out of Gaza by night, dismantling the gates of the city and carrying them away.

It was apparently God's purpose to continue pitting Samson against the Philistines. On a human level, the hero seems to have been driven by uncontrollable self-destructive urges, because he could not stay away from his enemies. He became involved with yet another Philistine woman, Delilah, who was to cause his defeat and humiliation.

Right from the start, Delilah, handsomely bribed by the Philistine leaders, was determined to pry from Samson the secret of his great strength. At this point Samson's naivety is so staggering that it defies belief, further strengthening the assumption that he was driven by forces beyond his control.

Delilah openly asked him the secret of his strength and he tested her with three false replies. He told her that, if he were bound with "green withs" (creepers), he would be helpless. She accordingly tied him up, having first ensured that a Philistine detachment was waiting to take him prisoner: "And she said unto him, The Philistines be upon thee, Samson. And he brake the withs, as a thread of tow [flax] is broken when it toucheth the fire. So his strength was not known." (Judges 16:9)

Subsequent attempts to bind him with new ropes, and to plait his hair and peg it to the ground, achieved the same results. Even the fact that Samson was infatuated with the beauty and charm of Delilah cannot adequately explain the extent of his subsequent folly. He revealed that his uncut hair was the source of his strength: "There hath not come a razor upon mine head; for I have been a Nazarite unto God from my mother's womb: if I be shaven, then my strength will go from me, and I shall become weak, and be like any other man." (Judges 16:17)

Delilah, first taking care to secure her reward, put Samson to sleep, had his head shaved and called up a Philistine detachment, which captured him, put out his eyes and set him to work grinding wheat in prison.

The scene was now set for the final act of supreme drama, the cathartic gesture which completed the saga:

"And Samson said, Let me die with the Philistines. And he bowed himself with all his might; and the house fell upon the lords, and upon all the people that were therein." (Judges 16:30). From *Die Bibel in Bildern* by Julius Schnorr von Carolsfeld, Germany, 1860.

> And he bowed himself with all his might; and the house fell upon the lords, and upon all the people that were therein. So the dead which he slew at his death were more than they which he slew in his life.   (*Judges 16:30*)

This scene has been so misinterpreted in modern times that it is important to clarify what happened. Samson committed suicide, taking his enemies with him; but there is not so much as a hint of universal destruction either in the biblical text or in the later interpretative commentaries.

The Jewish tradition is distinctly pro-life; suicide is, in fact, forbidden by Jewish religious law and almost unheard of in Jewish history. In most cases the Jews fought on, even when the odds against them were hopeless, as in the various sieges of Jerusalem, the Warsaw Ghetto revolt, or in the uprisings in the various Nazi concentration camps.

The story of Samson symbolizes the obstinate refusal of the Jewish people to submit to tyranny. While forbidden to take their own lives, the Jews have often been prepared to make the ultimate sacrifice and fight to the end, dying as free men, rather than agreeing to live as slaves.

Samson, the simple man, whose strength was given to him by God in order to serve his people, revived the fighting spirit of the Israelites at a time when they were cowed by oppression. He was a true hero of his time, carrying on his lonely battle against almost overwhelming odds. Inspired by his bravery and defiance, the people of Israel were to continue their struggle against the Philistines until they achieved ultimate victory.

4 ≋

David: Warrior, Poet, Nation-Builder

≋ F ROM THE time that he is anointed as King of Israel, late in the eleventh century B.C., David's story is one of continuous, unremitting action: single combat, battles, jealousy, intrigues, escape, flight, rebellion, success, treachery, adultery, incest and vengeance follow each other with dizzying speed.

Soon after being secretly appointed as King Saul's successor by the prophet Samuel, the youthful David was facing Goliath, the giant Philistine champion, in single combat. Subsequently, as a soldier in the service of the King, and then as the leader of an armed band, he experienced many brushes with death.

King before he was forty, David was only beginning: he won spectacular victories north, south, east and west, creating an Israel larger than it had ever been. He forged alliances, put down rebellions and ruled for four decades.

He was the builder of his nation, moulding its army, defending its frontiers, establishing its institutions. He brought the ark of the covenant to Jerusalem, laid the groundwork for the Temple and unified the people around their faith.

After David, Jewish history acquired cohesion and consistency. His dynasty ruled a united Israel for less than a century; but even when the kingdom subsequently split into the two nations of Israel and Judah, the Jewish people remained the dominant force in the land for over a thousand years.

Moreover, the Davidic dynasty remains enshrined in the hearts of the Jewish people until today, in the form of belief in a Messiah from the house of David, who will establish a universal reign of peace and justice.

This would certainly be enough to make him one of the most important figures in Jewish history, but David was far more than a warrior, ruler and man of action. As a singer and poet with a deep religious faith, he was responsible for some of the finest and most lyrical verses ever written.

A man of human weakness, who repeatedly sinned and transgressed, he was nevertheless a person of profound love and compassion. Although he was capable of base treachery, his vilest acts were redeemed by genuine repentance and an ultimate acceptance of moral standards.

THE ACHIEVEMENTS of our three previous heroes are in no way diminished by the observation that David operated on an entirely different scale to them. With his conquest of most of Canaan, Joshua laid the foundations of a nation; Deborah, winning a splendid victory over the Canaanites, continued his work; Samson bravely refused to submit to the emerging power of the Philistines; but it was David who finally ensured Israelite hegemony in the land, and established the national and religious identity that was to survive across the millennia.

The biblical account of the emergence of the Israelite monarchy is intriguing. The people asked Samuel the prophet, at that time the supreme authority in Israel, for a king. Hostile to the idea, Samuel consulted with God, who ordered him to warn the Israelites against the institution, but to accept the popular demand.

Historically we can see the need for a strong, central authority if the Israelites were to survive against their enemies. Morally, it is difficult to justify the concept of a supreme ruler over a people which was supposed to be ruled by God alone.

The result was a compromise: a king with full executive powers, particularly in time of war, but subject to moral principles. Uniquely in the world of the eleventh century B.C., the kings of Israel were constantly called to order by the prophets, who were said to express the divine will.

Saul, the first king, unified the tribes and won notable victories over the Ammonites, Philistines and other enemies of Israel; but he lacked the ability to administer the nation. Samuel the prophet, who apparently still retained enormous prestige, constantly criticized the King for his shortcomings, eventually breaking with him entirely and secretly anointing the young David as the chosen successor.

David, a simple shepherd boy, entered history in a spectacular fashion. Visiting his brothers, who were serving with King Saul against the Philistines, he found the Israelite and Philistine armies deadlocked.

The Israelites, positioned in the hills, were reluctant to descend to the plain, where the chariots of their enemies would have given them a distinct advantage. The Philistines for their part refused to venture into the hills, the home ground of the mobile, lightly armed Israelites.

In this situation, a giant Philistine warrior, Goliath, proposed single combat to settle the issue:

> . . . Choose you a man for you, and let him come down to me.
>
> If he be able to fight with me, and to kill me, then will we be your servants: but if I prevail against him, and kill him, then shall ye be our servants, and serve us.   (*I Samuel 17:8–9*)

It does not seem likely that this was a serious suggestion, rather that the Philistines sought a psychological advantage to break the deadlock. As Goliath was a formidable figure, and no Israelite was prepared to risk fighting him, they were already gaining the upper hand.

David swiftly concluded that the Philistine champion, mighty as he was, could be beaten with the right tactics. Realizing that he stood no chance against Goliath in straightforward combat, and consequently refusing Saul's offer of his armour and equipment, David stepped forward to meet the giant, unencumbered and armed only with a sling.

The subsequent combat, in which David felled his opponent with a stone and cut off his head with his own sword, can be taken as a model for Jewish history throughout the ages: faith, imagination, speed and daring prevailed over physical might. The armies of Israel, almost always smaller and weaker than their opponents, refused to play by the accepted rules.

David's victory over Goliath prompted a Philistine flight, which swiftly turned into a rout, as they were pursued by the jubilant Israelites, and the young hero was enlisted in Saul's army.

The subsequent relationship between Saul and David veered chaotically between love and hatred. The King, subject to fits of melancholy, was soothed by the young man's singing and playing on the harp; but his jealousy at David's military success became paranoid.

After failing to kill the youngster with a javelin, Saul tried a ruse, promising the hand of his daughter, Michal, in marriage, but demanding a dowry of "a hundred foreskins of the Philistines." David, reasoned the King, would certainly meet his death trying to collect such a dowry.

When this plot was foiled by David's success, Saul tried to persuade his son Jonathan to kill the young man; but Jonathan's friendship for David stood the test and he warned his friend to flee. David's wife Michal also saved him from the schemes of her father.

David was joined in his wanderings by other fugitives, in due course leading a band of some 600 men. He sent his parents across the River Jordan into Moab, out of harm's way, and based himself in Keilah, south of Hebron; but Saul pursued him, and he was forced to withdraw into the Judean desert to the east.

David made numerous attempts to prove his loyalty to the King. More than once, he had the opportunity to kill Saul, but desisted. On one occasion, when he found him sleeping in a cave, David cut a piece off Saul's cloak, afterwards showing it to the King as proof that he could have killed him.

Saul was filled with remorse:

> Thou art more righteous than I: for thou hast rewarded me good, whereas I have rewarded thee evil.
>
> And thou hast showed this day how that thou hast dealt well with me: forasmuch as when the Lord had delivered me into thine hand, thou killedst me not.   (*I Samuel 24:17–18*)

However, the King's paranoia got the better of him, and the young fighter was again forced to flee for his life. Unable to find safety in the territory controlled by Saul, David sought refuge among his former enemies, the Philistines. He enlisted with his band in the service of Achish, the King of Gath, who made him governor of the southern desert town of Ziklag.

From his new base, David conducted frequent raids against the southern tribes, while managing to avoid conflict with his own people. However, another Philistine campaign against the Israelites was launched, and Achish asked for David's help. Fortunately for the Israelite fighter, the other Philistine leaders did not share their colleague's trust in him. They expressed doubts about his reliability, and he led his band back to Ziklag, before battle was joined.

The Israelites, led by Saul and Jonathan, were soundly defeated at Mount Gilboa. Jonathan was killed and Saul fell on his sword. David composed a lament of thundering eloquence:

> The beauty of Israel is slain upon thy high places: how are the mighty fallen!
>
> Tell it not in Gath, publish it not in the streets of Ashkelon; lest the daughters of the Philistines rejoice. . . .
>
> Saul and Jonathan were lovely and pleasant in their lives, and in their death they were not divided: they were swifter than eagles, they were stronger than lions. . . .
>
> How are the mighty fallen, and the weapons of war perished!
>   (*II Samuel 1:19–20, 23, 27*)

There is no reason to doubt the sincerity of David's grief, for he had consistently tried to achieve a reconciliation with Saul, and Jonathan was his loyal, proven friend; but he lost no time in taking advantage of the new situation.

He had taken care to maintain good relations with the leaders of his own tribe, Judah, during his exile, and was therefore promptly accepted as their king; but the other Israelite tribes did not at first accept him as their ruler.

Saul's son Ishbosheth, backed by his general Abner, was for a time king of the other Israelite tribes; but, after their victory over Saul, the Philistines were dominant in the north and Ishbosheth exercised his limited authority from a base across the Jordan.

Up to this point, David had proved himself as a daring and resourceful military commander; but now he began to show signs of the political skills that would become increasingly apparent. Rather than wage war against the other tribes, David reached an accord with Abner, whereby he would become ruler of all the tribes.

Joab, David's general, a brilliant but primitive soldier, failed to understand the subtleties of the new situation and killed Abner. David, although unable to dispense with the services of so able a general, cursed Joab and gave Abner a public funeral.

When two of Ishbosheth's officers murdered him and brought David his head, he showed no such inhibitions and immediately had them executed. This dramatically demonstrated both the principle that it was wrong to kill a king, and achieved a reconciliation with the house of Saul, which he further strengthened by renewing his marriage with Michal, who had not accompanied him on his wanderings.

He also showed great generosity towards Mephibosheth, the lame son of Jonathan, restoring his grandfather's lands to him and inviting him to stay with him.

Like all the great leaders of Israel — Moses, Joshua, Judah the Maccabee, David Ben-Gurion — King David placed great emphasis on achieving national unity.

David's next move — the conquest of Jerusalem — is a further indication of his developing talent for statecraft. With a single campaign, he completed the conquest of Canaan started by Joshua, acquired a strategic centre, and established a capital which was not associated with any of the tribes and could therefore be a symbol of unity.

Jerusalem, which had remained under control of the Jebusites,

Excavations at Ophel — the City of David, Jerusalem. (*Zev Radovan*)

a small Canaanite tribe, was centrally situated both on the road linking Transjordan and the coast, and the north-south watershed route. On a ridge surrounded by valleys, it was easy to defend, as the Jebusites had proved. Possessed of a pleasant hill climate, Jerusalem had enough rainfall in winter to fill its cisterns through the summer and also had access to a perennial spring at the foot of the ridge.

Faced with these formidable features, David once again achieved the unexpected, sending Joab at the head of a commando force to penetrate the city by means of a rock-hewn passage that led up the eastern side of the ridge.

The Philistines had apparently not objected to their one-time ally ruling the tribe of Judah, particularly in view of the split with the other tribes; but faced with a king at the head of a united nation, with a new, powerfully defended capital, they determined to attack.

Allowing the Philistines to penetrate deep into the territory of Judah, David defeated them twice. The second battle was decisive:

David attacked through a forest southwest of Jerusalem, where his forces had an important advantage over his adversaries. Knowing the terrain and unencumbered by heavy equipment, they attacked and routed the Philistine army. David established his authority from the hills to the coastal plain, confining the Philistines to a narrow strip between Gaza and Ashdod.

He now moved to establish Jerusalem as a unifying symbol for the nation by bringing the ark of the covenant to its final resting place there. David was told by the prophet Samuel that, as a man of war, he was not fit to build the Holy Temple. This task was to be left to his successors; but he made all the necessary preparations for the permanent tabernacle, which, more than anything else, established Israel as a lasting entity.

The new King proceeded to strike out in all directions, mopping up the Canaanite remnants in the Jezreel valley, defeating the Moabites in the east, the Edomites in the south and the Arameans in the northeast. His forces pushed north beyond Damascus, where he placed a garrison, extending the area under his control from the River Euphrates (in today's Iraq) to "the brook of Egypt" (generally believed to be Wadi el-Arish in Sinai).

The kingdom of Israel now controlled the three main routes between Egypt and Mesopotamia: the coastal road, the watershed route via Jerusalem and the central mountain range, and the King's Highway, which skirts the edge of the desert through Transjordan.

With regard to the seacoast, David was more cautious, permitting the Philistines, as we have seen, to remain in their enclave and forging an alliance with the Phoenician king Hiram of Tyre. Apparently recognizing the fact that the Israelites were not a seafaring people, he preferred to rely on the Phoenicians and Philistines for the sea trade.

The army was reorganized, with universal conscription supplemented by mercenaries, and divided into units of thousands, hundreds, fifty and ten. The idea of separate units, rather than an undisciplined mass, was well in advance of its time.

Both Joshua and Deborah had split their forces in certain battles; but it was David who created permanent separate units, each with their own commander, who were capable of operating independently and adapting their tactics to meet the developing situation on the battlefield.

Furthermore, David made use of the special fighting skills of the various tribes. The Book of Chronicles tells us that the Benjaminites were armed with bows and slings, the tribe of Gad were fast-moving fighters armed with shield and buckler, Judah and Naphtali were mainly spearmen, the tribe of Issachar, across the Jordan, possessed talented scouts, and so on.

To lessen the influence of tribal loyalties, a reserve force was set up, based on military service for one month per year, which meant that David had a continuous pool of troops from all the tribes. At the same time every able-bodied man could be mobilized in an emergency.

Around his original band which had been with him in exile, David formed two regular divisions of professional troops. He also conscripted a unit of foreign mercenaries, including Philistines. Except for the presence of foreign mercenaries, the resemblance to the system in modern Israel, with its professional forces, conscript army and trained reserves, is obvious.

Continuing with the guerrilla tactics used by Joshua — and by himself during his exile — David developed other skills in his army to supplement these. In addition to the continuing use of swiftly moving forces to harass the massed troops of his opponents, he made use of his spearmen, deploying them as heavy infantry in more direct confrontations.

BACK IN Jerusalem David established a court to replace the military camp that had served Saul. Reorganizing both the civil government and the priesthood, he needed a larger central administration to rule the more complex society that had resulted from his conquests.

He ordered the building of a luxurious palace, which later became known as the City of David, a name also used for Jerusalem as a whole. Fascinating archaeological excavations in this area provide a link between today's capital and the ancient centre built by the King.

The palace was to be, albeit indirectly, the cause of one of his most important moral lapses. Strolling on its roof one night, he

". . . David arose from off his bed, and walked upon the roof of the king's house: and from the roof he saw a woman washing herself; and the woman was very beautiful. . . ." (II Samuel 11:2). Rembrandt van Rijn, *The Toilet of Bathsheba,* oil on wood. (*The Metropolitan Museum of Art, Bequest of Benjamin Altman, 1913*)

saw a beautiful woman bathing on a neighbouring roof. Told that she was Bathsheba, the wife of Uriah the Hittite, one of his mercenary commanders who was away fighting the Ammonites, David nevertheless made love to her.

When she became pregnant, the King summoned Uriah from the front, hoping that the Hittite would sleep with his wife and consequently accept the child as his own. He was foiled, however, by the integrity of the mercenary soldier, who refused to sleep with his wife while his comrades were out in the field.

The King now adopted an uncharacteristic ruse to rid himself of Uriah and keep Bathsheba for himself. He ordered Joab to send Uriah to the most dangerous part of the front and to leave him stranded there. Uriah duly met his death, and David married Bathsheba.

In behaving as he had, David was clearly acting the role of a normal despot of his time. In fact, another king would probably have taken any woman he desired and had her husband killed, without resorting to a ruse; but David was no normal king. Despite his victories and the power he had achieved, he was still, as an Israelite monarch, subject to moral laws.

The prophet Nathan, appearing before him, told him about two men, one rich, the other poor. The rich man possessed many flocks; the poor man had only one ewe lamb, which he cherished and raised with care. However, when the rich man received a guest, he took the poor man's lamb and killed it for the meal, instead of one of his own.

His sense of injustice aroused, David stated that the rich man should be sentenced to death:

> As the Lord liveth, the man that hath done his thing shall surely die:
> And he shall restore the lamb fourfold, because he did this thing, and because he had no pity.
> And Nathan said to David, Thou art the man.
>
> (*II Samuel 12:5 – 7*)

Because of his sin, continued the prophet, "the sword shall never depart from thine house." Not only would David be continuously at war, but the warfare would embrace his own family. Furthermore, Bathsheba's son, conceived as he was in sin, would die.

David acknowledged his sin and fasted in repentance, hoping thus to save the life of his child. When the boy died, David refused to mourn him:

> While the child was yet alive, I fasted and wept: for I said, Who can tell whether God will be gracious to me, that the child may live?
> But now he is dead, wherefore should I fast? Can I bring him back again? I shall go to him, but he shall not return to me.
>
> (*II Samuel 12:22 – 23*)

David, the loving, indulgent father, can also be seen in his overly tolerant attitude to his other sons, Amnon and Absalom. Amnon fell in love with his half-sister, Tamar, and tried to seduce her. When she resisted him, he raped her and threw her out of his house. The humiliated Tamar was taken in by her brother Absalom, who swore revenge.

The Bible tells us that when David heard about the incident "he was very wroth." It seems a remarkably mild reaction to the rape of his own daughter, particularly as there is no evidence that he took any steps to discipline his son.

Two years later, Absalom did the job for him, ordering his servants to kill Amnon, after first getting him drunk. After the murder of his brother, Absalom fled from his father's anger; but, once again, there is little evidence of any determination on the part of David to set his house in order. On the contrary, it is clear that David desperately missed his son.

The sophistication of David's court, probably necessary for ruling a large kingdom, brought with it many disadvantages. The atmosphere of intrigue is no better illustrated than by the way General Joab secured his permission for Absalom's return.

Joab, the simple, brave fighter, who formerly had not understood his master's political calculations and had killed General Abner, perceiving him as yesterday's enemy rather than tomorrow's friend, had become an intriguer and used a cunning ruse to bring Absalom back to Jerusalem.

Instead of asking David outright, he persuaded a woman from Tekoah to come to David with a trumped-up tale of her own two sons. Unlike the subtle Nathan, Joab was no match for his sovereign. David immediately saw Joab's hand in the scheme, but approved Absalom's return. Another two years would pass, however, before he agreed to a complete reconciliation.

There is no indication that Absalom felt any gratitude towards his father. On the contrary, he began at once to build up a power-base, declaring that he would give better judgement to the people than David, and mobilizing a force of horsemen and charioteers to guard himself.

One of David's most endearing qualities was that he refused to harm those he loved. Even when Saul pursued him ruthlessly and did everything in his power to have him killed, David would not lift his hand against him. Now, when his son Absalom openly planned insurrection, he refused even to believe it until it was too late.

Deserted by some of his leading counsellors, David fled to the other side of the Jordan, leaving Absalom in command of Jerusalem. Departing from the capital, which he had created, David was further humiliated by Shimei, a man from the tribe of Benjamin (Saul's tribe), who reviled him as "a man of blood." In his deep depression David would not even let his followers take action against the man.

The great King seemed to have reached the end of the road, but his remarkable resilience and courage were not exhausted yet. As many of his men had deserted to Absalom, it was not difficult to plant another, Hushai, among his son's advisers.

David needed time to regroup, and Hushai won it for him by advising Absalom against an immediate attack. Instead he persuaded the young man to mobilize a large army against his father.

Dividing his forces into three, David acceded to the request of his commanders not to lead his forces, but asked them to be merciful towards his rebel son: "And the king commanded Joab and Abishai and Ittai, saying, Deal gently for my sake with the young man, even with Absalom. And all the people heard when the king gave all the captains charge concerning Absalom." (II Samuel 18:5)

At this point, the loyal Joab clearly took the initiative. After leading the King's forces to victory, he hunted down Absalom and killed him. Desolate at the death of his son, David went into deep mourning: "O my son Absalom, my son, my son Absalom! Would God I had died for thee, O Absalom, my son, my son!" (II Samuel 18:33)

Storming into his presence, Joab reproached his leader for "loving his enemies and hating his friends," and demanded that he appear before the people. In fact, David's troubles were far from over. His own tribe, Judah, accepted him again as king, but the other Israelite tribes refused to accept him and launched another revolt. David was forced to go to war against them to regain the kingship.

Shortly after this, David bought the threshing floor of Araunah the Jebusite and built an altar to God there. This later became the site of the Temple, the permanent resting place of the ark of the covenant.

Another conflict broke out with the Philistines, and David, de-

The Ark of the Covenant. Fresco from Dura Europos, Macedonia, third to fourth century A.D.

spite his advancing years, insisted on personally leading his army against them. A curious incident in this battle harked back to David's youth.

An enormous Philistine, armed with a gigantic spear and sword, attacked him. David was not the same swift, strong youth who had felled Goliath with a stone from his sling. Preparing to defend himself, he nearly passed out and was saved by his nephew Abishai, who killed the Philistine. Ishbi-benob, the huge soldier, may well have been the son of Goliath, David's first opponent — he is described as "one of the sons of the giant."

After that incident, David was told in no uncertain terms by his own soldiers that his fighting days were over; but his very presence on the battlefield illustrates that his remarkable physical courage had not deserted him, even though his speed and stamina had. Thus it was that David ended his military career as he had begun it, facing a giant Philistine soldier.

In his later years, David apparently played a less active role in conducting the affairs of state. During this period he drew on his childhood memories to compose many of the beautiful psalms that bear his name.

> The Lord is my shepherd; I shall not want.
> He maketh me to lie down in green pastures: he leadeth me beside the still waters.
> He restoreth my soul: he leadeth me in the paths of righteousness for His name's sake.
> Yea, though I walk through the valley of the shadow of death, I will fear no evil: for Thou art with me; Thy rod and Thy staff they comfort me.
> Thou preparest a table before me in the presence of mine enemies: Thou anointest my head with oil; my cup runneth over.
> Surely goodness and mercy shall follow me all the days of my life: and I will dwell in the house of the Lord for ever.   (*Psalm 23*)

Even as a poet, David surely commands immortality, but he was not to be permitted to rest from court intrigues. Adonijah, his oldest surviving son and official heir, was showing visible signs of impatience, in view of David's interest in Solomon, the son Bathsheba bore him after the death of their first child.

Despite his many wives and concubines, Bathsheba seems to have been the love of his life, and he clearly felt a special affection for her son; but he was chiefly concerned to secure an orderly succession and to ensure capable government after his death. Solomon possessed the quality of wisdom, which made him suitable to be the ruler of the relatively large nation that Israel had become.

General Joab and Abiathar, one of the two high priests, openly threw in their lot with Adonijah, who held a celebratory feast and offered up sacrifices. The assembled guests hailed him as king.

Apprised of this by Bathsheba and the prophet Nathan, David ordered Nathan, Zadok, the other high priest, and Benaiah, the captain of his personal guard, to take Solomon to the spring of Gihon in the Kidron valley and to anoint him king.

Faced with this pre-emptive action, Adonijah quickly gave up his claims and sought sanctuary, later submitting to his brother, who spared his life. The smooth succession of Solomon to the throne of the united kingdom was now assured; but, although the wise King successfully administered his father's nation, its unity would not survive his death.

After securing the succession of Solomon, David died. He had transformed the people of Israel from a loosely linked tribal confederation into a united nation. He had routed his people's enemies, won them extensive territory and established them as the dominant force in the region.

He had forged an effective army, established an administrative framework and created a cultural and religious entity that would survive into the future. Commander, warrior, king, nation-builder and poet, a human being with very human weaknesses, David is the most complex and interesting character in the Bible, and second only to Moses as a leader of the Jewish people.

5

Judah the Maccabee:
Fighter for Freedom

THE SLAVE merchants from the coast would do a brisk business: a whole people was about to be sold into slavery. The orders of Emperor Antiochus Epiphanes had been quite specific: the Jews were to be defeated, and then deported or killed. Others were to be settled in their place. The problem of Judea was to be settled once and for all.

The huge Seleucid army, commanded by no less than three generals, Ptolemy, Nicanor and Gorgias, had been supplemented by forces from Idumea and the coastal region. Antioch was not going to repeat the mistake of underestimating Judah the Maccabee, commander of the Jewish guerrillas. No more ambushes! This time the Seleucid army would set the rules.

The generals chose their route with care. Avoiding the perilous Judean mountains, where two previous armies had been ambushed and routed, they marched south down the coast and established their base at Emmaus, in the foothills fifteen miles to the west of Jerusalem. The relatively level ground favoured the well-trained Seleucid army and provided few opportunities for the Jewish irregulars.

Gorgias, an experienced commander, resolved to turn the tables on the Jews by leading a force up into the hills under cover of darkness and taking their camp by surprise. It was the last thing that might have been expected from the vast Seleucid army, as it advanced through Judea.

Judah's intelligence, however, must have been excellent, for he heard about the plan. By the time Gorgias reached the Jewish encampment, the irregulars had already left, although they had lit numerous camp fires to give the impression that they were still in place. A small Jewish detachment, which had been left behind for the purpose, drew Gorgias's forces through the valley of Shaar Hagai (Bab al-Wad), where today's main road to Jerusalem runs, where they were harassed by other Jewish fighters.

The main Judean force under Judah prepared to attack Nicanor's base at Emmaus, but it was now their turn to be surprised. The Seleucid soldiers had been alerted and were drawn up ready for battle. The Seleucid phalanx was a formidable fighting force, and hitherto Judah had carefully avoided direct confrontations with it.

A tactical force of some 2,000 heavy infantry, drawn up in close formation, the phalanx advanced towards the enemy in a tight mass, 120 yards wide and fifteen yards deep. The first five ranks held their spears horizontally, while the next eleven held them vertically. Protected on its flanks by cavalry and light infantry, it could inflict a crushing defeat on a weaker enemy.

Judah's tactics had been to lure the heavily armed troops into narrow valleys and gorges and to ambush them, but this was not possible now. Forced to deal with the surprise night attack of Gorgias, Judah had already changed his normal tactics once; faced with the phalanx, deployed and ready for battle, he had to change them again. For the first time, the Jewish irregulars were going to face the Seleucid army in an open fight.

This, resolved Judah, did not mean a head-on confrontation. Dividing his forces into three units of 1,000 each, he sent one against the cavalry and the two others against the flank of the powerful formation. Unused to such unorthodox methods, the phalanx started to crumble under the impact of fierce hand-to-hand fighting.

At this point, another Judean force launched an attack on the Seleucid camp, taking it by surprise and routing the defenders. Gorgias, meanwhile, was still chasing the small detachment he had found in the Judean camp towards Jerusalem. By the time he gave up the pursuit and returned to Emmaus, it was to witness the defeat of the forces there. The entire Seleucid army now fled to the coast, pursued by the jubilant irregulars.

Judah had shown that he could think on his feet, twice changing his tactics to cope with a developing situation. The Jewish guerrillas had proved that they could take on the Seleucid army, even when the topography favoured the regular troops and the element of surprise was lacking.

Far from rooting out the Judean irregulars and destroying the Jewish people, the empire of Antioch had been handed a humiliating defeat. The Jews, for their part, had ensured their survival and taken a giant step on the road to religious and political freedom. They were a fighting people again, after a pause of nearly four centuries.

THE UNITED nation bequeathed by King David to his son Solomon did not survive. Even in David's time, divisions had occasionally appeared. After the death of Solomon, the split into two kingdoms became permanent: the ten northern tribes became Israel; the two southern ones, Judah.

In the eighth century B.C., Israel was conquered by the Assyrians and much of its population was scattered. Judah lasted on its own for more than a century, only to be conquered and its people exiled in their turn by the Babylonians, who had succeeded the Assyrians.

Although Jerusalem was captured and the Temple destroyed, the people of Judah, who became known as the Jews, remained together in Babylon, and when the Persian Empire conquered that of the Babylonians in 539, they were permitted to return to Jerusalem and rebuild the Temple. Their exile had only lasted some fifty years, but they left a large part of their people behind in Babylon.

The Judean province of the Persian Empire was an area of about 1,000 square miles around Jerusalem, considerably reduced from the kingdom built by David; but within it the Jews lived according to their religious beliefs, both in Jerusalem and in their farming villages in the Judean hills.

In the fourth century B.C., Alexander the Great conquered the Persian Empire and Judea came under his control. Alexander was a man with a mission. His aim was more than mere conquest: he was determined to spread the Greek way of life throughout his empire.

Wherever he went, Alexander built Greek-style cities, where he settled Greeks, who intermarried with the local people. In the cities he built temples for the worship of Greek gods, theatres for the performances of Greek plays, gymnasia for sport and exercise. Local customs were adapted to, or integrated with, the Greek ways, forming a universal Hellenism throughout the empire; but Alexander made an exception in the case of Judea, permitting the Jews to maintain their religion and traditions.

There is a legend that the high priest of the Temple of Jerusalem predicted Alexander's conquest of Persia, and consequently the youthful general spared Judea his Hellenizing zeal. Probably the shrewd commander realized that trying to force a foreign culture on this small, but obstinate people was more trouble than it was worth.

Since the time of Abraham, the Jews had been forbidden to erect statues, or to worship gods other than the supreme invisible deity with whom they believed they had a covenant. According to the Torah, the Law of Moses, they were not permitted to eat food regarded as unclean, to view plays and certainly not to exercise naked (as was the Greek custom) in the gymnasia.

Alexander did not interfere with any of this. He established some Greek communities in Samaria, in what had once been the territory of Israel, but the Jews of Judea were left in peace to live their own lives.

When Alexander died, his empire was divided among three of his generals, Judea coming under the rule of the Ptolemies of Egypt, who continued with a laissez-faire policy towards the Jews. Judea remained a Jewish cultural island in the Hellenist sea.

Silver tetradrachm of Antiochus IV, obverse and reverse; minted in Acre. (*Israel Museum*)

However, among the Jews there were some who regarded the practices of the majority as backward. The richer families — including even some of the priestly line — who wished to develop trading links with other parts of the empire felt that they were held back by the Jewish isolationism. A Hellenizing movement developed in Jerusalem, which encouraged Jews to adopt the Greek way of life, although for some years it represented only a small minority.

The situation changed somewhat when, as the result of a power struggle between the Egyptian and Seleucid (Syrian) parts of Alexander's former empire, Judea came under the rule of the Seleucids of Antioch. The Seleucids were more inclined to encourage the development of Greek culture in Judea, assisted by the local Hellenistic movement, but this continued to be resisted by the Temple establishment.

The real problems began when Antiochus Epiphanes became emperor. More ambitious than his predecessors, he dreamt of restoring the empire of Alexander. He advanced into Egypt and planned campaigns to the east, but came up against the newly emerging power of Rome.

Still an oligarchy ruled by the Senate, Rome was consolidating its power slowly and carefully. The Romans had already taken over much of the Macedonian part of Alexander's former empire and had compelled the Seleucids to sign a treaty promising, among other things, not to use their war-elephants. Now a Roman legate abruptly ordered the Seleucid Emperor out of Egypt.

Meanwhile, Antiochus, concerned to maintain his position in Judea, determined that in the Hellenizing party there were more reliable allies and so appointed one of them to be high priest in the Temple of Jerusalem, with the purpose of spreading Greek culture and suppressing Jewish traditions.

This was a shock for the Jews. The high priesthood was a hereditary position, and certainly not an appointment to be made by the Seleucids, even if they were the temporal power in Judea. This action set Antiochus on a collision course with the majority of Jews, who still favoured their ancient traditions.

An account of the humiliation of Antiochus in Egypt seems to have reached Judea in a garbled form, suggesting that the Emperor had been killed. This news triggered off a full-scale attack by the traditionalists against the Hellenizers. Antiochus heard about the rebellion in Jerusalem as he was on his way back to Syria. Smarting from the Roman insult, he was in no mood for compromise.

He sent more troops to Jerusalem with strict orders to enforce its Hellenization. After killing large numbers of Jews, the Seleucid soldiers broke into the Temple, stealing its ancient treasures, defiling it and converting it into a shrine of Zeus. As a crowning insult, a pig, regarded as unclean by the Jews, was sacrificed on the holy altar of the Temple. Dominating the Temple, a massive fortress, the Acra, was constructed.

In what is believed to be the first case of specifically religious persecution in history, the Law of Moses, the Jewish religion, was made illegal: observing the Sabbath, circumcising the male children and celebrating the festivals became capital offences.

The Seleucid forces now fanned out into the Judean countryside, forcing the villagers to set up heathen shrines and to perform sacrifices which they regarded as sacrilegious. A small, passive resistance group known as the Hassidim sprang up, most of whom retreated to the desert.

Disgusted by the earlier moves towards Hellenization in Jerusalem, a priest called Mattathias had withdrawn to the village of

Mattathias the Maccabee, a priest in the village of Modi'in. He and his five sons rose in revolt against the Greeks, founded the Hasmonean dynasty and eventually captured Jerusalem and rededicated the Temple. Bronze by Boris Schatz, founder of the Bezalel Academy of Arts and Crafts in Jerusalem, 1894. (*Israel Museum*)

Modi'in in the Judean foothills. When a Seleucid detachment arrived in this village and set up a heathen altar, Mattathias refused to perform the required sacrifice.

Another villager moved to carry out the will of the soldiers and the old man killed him on the spot, upon which the villagers, led by the five sons of Mattathias, set upon the troops and killed them all. It was the first act of resistance since Jerusalem had been subdued, and it triggered a religious revolt, which was to develop into a full-scale national uprising.

THE VILLAGERS of Modi'in fled northwards to the region of Gophna, in the hills of Samaria, where they organized themselves as a guerrilla force, under the command of Judah, one of the sons of Mattathias. He was called the Maccabee (hammer) of the Greeks, and his followers came to be known as the Maccabees.

For more than a year, Antioch left them alone, possibly unaware of what was happening in the Judean countryside. The Maccabee irregulars, armed initially only with slings, maces and adapted farm implements, would visit villages, conduct Jewish ceremonies such as circumcision and recruit fighters. As their strength, experience and confidence grew, they began ambushing the small Seleucid patrols, which were charged with ensuring compliance with the anti-Jewish decrees.

The primary sources for our knowledge of the Maccabean rebellion are the two Apocryphal books of the Maccabees. The first book was written during the reign of Alexander Yannai, a later Maccabean monarch, some fifty years after the events it described. The second book was written in Egypt much later.

According to the first book, Mattathias, in calling on his fellow villagers to follow him, said: "Whosoever is zealous of the law, and maintaineth the covenant, let him follow me." (I Maccabees 2:27)

Thus the Maccabean struggle was the first war in history to be waged for an ideal — that of religious freedom — rather than for national or political motives. In taking on the mighty Seleucid Empire, the Judean farmers were not aiming to conquer territory or defeat a rival army. In the early stages of the struggle, they did not think about political independence or even national identity. They were fighting in order to be able to observe the Torah.

After an incident in which large numbers of the pious Hassidim were killed by Seleucid troops, whom they refused to resist on the Sabbath day, Mattathias persuaded his followers (who now included the Hassidim) that they must be prepared to defend themselves on the Sabbath, if they did not want to be wiped out: "At that time therefore they decreed, saying, Whosoever shall come to make battle with us on the Sabbath day, we will fight against him; neither will we die all, as our brethren that were murdered in the secret places." (I Maccabees 2:41)

(More than 2,000 years later, when Jerusalem was under siege by the Arabs in 1948, the rabbis granted special dispensation to permit Sabbath work on the "Burma Road," a secret dirt-track linking Jerusalem with the coastal plain. Like Mattathias, they ruled that saving life takes priority over observing the Sabbath. Orthodox volunteers from Jerusalem were among those who worked on the road, dug fortifications and unloaded supplies on the Sabbath.)

MATTATHIAS DIED and was succeeded by his son Judah, who soon had to face his first real challenge. Apollonius, the Seleucid Governor of Samaria, led an army of some 2,000 men into Judea. Judah, who by now commanded a guerrilla force of several hundred men, was more or less in control of the countryside outside Jerusalem.

He had followers in almost every village, which meant that he possessed an effective intelligence network. Although his supply of weapons had been supplemented by the ambushing of Seleucid patrols, his guerrillas were no match for the Seleucid phalanx in a direct conflict. However, he was operating in hill country, and this terrain was more suitable for swift-moving fighters than for heavily armed troops, no matter how well trained.

There is no record of any military activity by Judah and his brothers before the killing of the Seleucid detachment in Modi'in. Apparently Judah simply worked things out for himself and learnt how to fight as he went along. In the few short years of his leadership, he proved to be one of the most daring and effective guerrilla commanders in history.

Using his knowledge of the countryside, and taking advantage of the speed and mobility of his followers, Judah changed the rules of war. Refusing to meet his enemies head-on, he resolved to attack them on the march, when they would not be prepared for battle, nor able to deploy as they had been trained.

As the Seleucid columns marched south through the hills of Judea, Judah decided that a valley just north of Gophna, where the route wound uphill through a narrow defile, was the best place to meet the invading army. He therefore divided his forces into four units. One unit sealed the gorge to the south; two other forces took up positions on the hillsides to the east and west; and the fourth detachment stood ready to seal off a possible retreat to the north. Marching in two formations of 1,000 men each, the Seleucid soldiers walked straight into the trap.

Attacked first from the south, then from the east and west, and finally from the rear, they were unable to fight their usual battle. Apollonius himself was killed early in the encounter and his forces were completely wiped out. Their equipment and weapons were taken by the victorious guerrillas. Judah himself took the sword of Apollonius; he was to use it in all the subsequent battles.

Determined to put an end to the trouble in Judea, Antiochus despatched an army twice as large under another commander, called Seron. Noting that his predecessor had been ambushed in the hills, Seron brought his forces down the coastal plain, only turning east when he reached Jaffa.

He was compelled to ascend to Jerusalem through the narrow pass of Beth Horon, but he was on the alert for ambushes and, accordingly, dispersed his forces so that they could not all be surprised at once. Despite their earlier victory, Judah's men were afraid and openly expressed their doubts about attacking so large a force.

Here Judah emerged as more than a brilliant tactician. Exhorting his forces with a stirring speech, he proved that he had become an inspiring leader:

> They come against us in much pride and iniquity to destroy us, and our wives and children, and to spoil us:
>   But we fight for our lives and our laws.
>   Wherefore the Lord himself will overthrow them before our face: and as for you, be ye not afraid of them.   (*I Maccabees 3:20–22*)

Beth Horon, a strategic plain some twenty miles west of Jerusalem where Judah the Maccabee conquered the forces of the Seleucid General Seron, *c.* 166 B.C. (*Ronald Sheridan*)

Wielding the sword of Apollonius, Judah himself led a furious charge at the advancing Seleucid column. Falling back, the retreating soldiers were pelted from the hillsides. Seron was killed and his forces panicked. The jubilant guerrillas pursued them all the way to the coastal plain.

WE HAVE now reached the point at which we started this account, when Antiochus sent a formidable army to settle the Judean problem once and for all. The Book of Maccabees says that he despatched 40,000 infantry, backed by 7,000 cavalry, into Judea, and that they were reinforced by Idumean and other detachments.

It seems an exaggerated figure, particularly taking into account that Antiochus himself was embarking on a campaign to restore Seleucid hegemony in Persia; but it was certainly a large army, possibly as many as 20,000 troops.

His orders were chillingly explicit: not only were Judah's guerrillas to be defeated, but the very memory of the Jews was to be obliterated, and strangers were to be settled in Judea. The struggle for religious freedom had become a war for national survival.

After Judah's third great victory, at Emmaus — already described — Lysias, the cousin of the Emperor, personally led an equally large army into Judea, despite the fact that a power struggle was developing in the Seleucid Empire. He marched south down the coastal plain and hooked round to approach Jerusalem via Hebron from the south.

Lysias established his camp at Beth Zur, north of Hebron. Judah was by now in command of 10,000 men, many of whom had already proved themselves in battle.

Once again, Judah dictated the form of battle, engaging the forces of Lysias as they were marching through the ravines north of Beth Zur. Keeping half his troops in reserve, Judah attacked the flanks of the powerful Seleucid formation, killing some 5,000 of the enemy.

Observing the poor performance of his soldiers, and worried about the power struggle back home, Lysias withdrew. This time Judah did not order his men to pursue the retreating enemy.

In control of the Judean countryside, he now determined to carry the fight to Jerusalem and to cleanse the Temple. The first Book of Maccabees has a moving account of the grief of the Jews, when they saw the desolation that had been wreaked on their most sacred shrine.

Deploying a force to prevent interference from soldiers stationed in the Acra fortress that still dominated the Temple, Judah selected priests who had remained faithful to the Jewish religion and set them to cleaning the sanctuary and restoring the desecrated building.

The altar on which pigs had been sacrificed was dismantled and rebuilt from fresh stones, holy vessels were refashioned, incense was burnt on the new altar, lights were lit and the Temple was dedicated once more to God. The Temple, the centre of Jewish identity and faith, had been restored. "Then all the people fell upon their faces, worshipping and praising the God of heaven who had given them good success." (I Maccabees 4:55)

According to Jewish legend, a single cruse of oil, enough for one day, was found in the Temple as fuel for the sacred lamps; but when the lamps were lit, they burned for eight days. This miracle is celebrated by the Jewish festival of Hanukkah in the Hebrew month of Kislev, which usually falls in December, when candles are lit for eight days, starting with one on the first day and ending with eight on the last.

In Israel today, Hanukkah has become a holiday that inspires the modern nation, as it commemorates the ancient struggle for independence. Today's Israelis see themselves as the successors of the Maccabees: the few who won their freedom and independence by daring to face the many.

AFTER THE withdrawal of Lysias, the Maccabees had won a respite from Antioch, but they were not to enjoy a rest from their struggle. The successes in Judea had caused resentment among the Hellenist neighbours of Judea, resulting in persecution of Jewish communities in Galilee and in Gilead, across the Jordan.

Judah called an assembly of the people and received authorization to mount rescue missions, thus establishing the principle that the Jewish nation was responsible for the welfare of Jews everywhere.

One of Judah's brothers, Simon, led a force of 3,000 to western Galilee, where he defeated local forces near Ptolemaïs (today's Acre) and brought the Jewish community back to Judea. Judah himself, accompanied by his younger brother Jonathan, crossed the Jordan with 8,000 fighters on a much more ambitious campaign.

Travelling light, with minimal supplies, they moved with incredible speed to the town of Bosora, some sixty miles northeast of today's Jordanian capital, Amman, reduced it and rescued the local Jews. Fighting their way from town to town, and collecting the Jewish communities on the way, they eventually reached Dathema, the main Jewish centre in Gilead, where the Jews were besieged by their enemies. Arriving just as the attackers were storming the walls, Judah's forces took them in the rear and defeated them.

Returning to Judea, leading large numbers of Jewish civilians, the forces of Judah and Jonathan were blocked by the town of Ephron, east of the Jordan, opposite today's Beit Shean. Trying the

Candelabrum depicted on a bronze coin bearing a Greek inscription, "Of Antigonus the King," 40–37 B.C. (*Hebrew University, Jerusalem*)

Plaster fragment with an incised seven-branched candelabrum, discovered in the Old City of Jerusalem excavations. (*Israel Government Press Office*)

path of diplomacy, Judah appealed for safe-conduct through the town, only to be denied. Scaling the walls of Ephron, the Jewish forces sacked the city. They then passed through Ephron, crossed the Jordan and brought the Jews of Gilead to Jerusalem.

These spectacular rescue operations bring to mind the rescue of Jewish hostages in Entebbe on July 3, 1976, when an Israeli commando force was flown unexpectedly to the Ugandan town and freed over a hundred captives, who were being held by Palestinian and German hijackers (see chapter 16).

On his return, Judah launched punitive operations against the hostile Idumeans in the Negev and against Jaffa, where the members of the small Jewish community had been taken out to sea and drowned.

Antiochus died in the year 163, and a struggle for succession broke out between Lysias and Philip, the general who had accompanied the Emperor on his eastern campaign. Taking advantage of the fluid situation in Antioch, Judah laid siege to the Acra in Jerusalem.

It was his first serious mistake: Lysias led a vast army to attack Jerusalem, including for the first time — in breach of his treaty with Rome — a detachment of war-elephants, which caused complete panic among the Judean fighters. One of the Maccabee brothers, Elazar, in a valiant attempt to show that the beasts were not invincible, killed one of them by stabbing it in the stomach with his sword; but he was crushed to death when the huge creature fell on him. At Beth Zur, south of Jerusalem, Judah's forces suffered their first defeat.

Lysias pressed on and besieged Jerusalem, and he might well have ended the Maccabean fight for freedom there and then, if not for his need to return urgently to Antioch to confront his rival, Philip. Before leaving, he offered a truce, annulling the anti-Jewish decrees of Antiochus, which Judah was relieved to accept. Lysias also executed the renegade Hellenistic high priest, as a gesture to the Judeans.

At this point, many Jews felt that they had achieved enough. After five years of bitter struggle against enemies far more powerful than themselves, they had won more than they had dared to believe was possible. They were free to practise their religion and to worship in their restored Temple.

The Maccabees had started their struggle without clearly defined aims, but, as we have seen, Judah was characterized by a remarkable ability to learn as he went along. Having attained so much, he was confident that he could achieve even more. The decrees of Antiochus had been rescinded, but, in different circumstances, they could be re-enacted. Judah resolved to settle for nothing less than political independence. Only this, he argued, would guarantee Jewish survival and continued religious freedom.

That this was attainable was proved by later events. The Maccabees did eventually win national independence, but it seems that Judah tried to achieve too much too soon. He had managed to mobilize his people to support his struggle; but now a majority of the people — including the Hassidim, who had been among his first supporters — were tired of the ceaseless warfare and rejected his plea to continue the fight.

Further power struggles in Antioch brought a new emperor, Demetrius, to the throne. Demetrius appointed a new high priest in Judea, Eliakim. One of his first actions was to execute a number of Hassidim, members of the faction who (unlike the Maccabees) were prepared to accept Seleucid domination. Demetrius also despatched Bacchides, a ruthless general who killed large numbers of Jews in the area of Gophna, where the Maccabees had first raised the standard of revolt.

These gratuitous actions by the new Emperor restored support for the Maccabees among the general population. Judah reacted by harassing Eliakim and his Hellenist supporters, who appealed to Antioch for support. Demetrius immediately despatched an army under Nicanor, who had been defeated by Judah at Emmaus three years earlier.

Nicanor's plan was to link up with the garrison in Jerusalem, and then to come out and subdue the Judean countryside. He reached Jerusalem without incident; but when he moved his combined forces northwards, he was yet again ambushed by the Jewish guerrillas near Beth Horon, scene of an earlier Judean victory.

Nicanor now called for more reinforcements from Antioch and, joining up with them, led the united force back towards Jerusalem. It seems most unlikely that Nicanor, who had already been in action against the Maccabees, was careless; but possibly he felt safer, once he had linked up with his extra forces. If Judah was about to attack, he might have reasoned, he would have attacked the armies before they merged.

Again managing to surprise his enemies, Judah launched an assault on the combined Seleucid army at Adasa, five miles north of Jerusalem. Nicanor was killed early in the engagement, and the result was another stunning victory for the Jews.

Once more in control of Judea, Judah sent emissaries to Rome to enlist the support of this growing regional power. Realizing that Judea, despite its military successes, was a small nation, he wisely sought international backing.

He also established another important principle: independence did not mean isolationism. Judah wanted to preserve the Jewish national identity and to secure freedom for the Jews to perform their religious customs, but he also ensured that Judea was a member of the international community.

However, in his overtures to Rome, Judah may again have acted too hastily. His emissaries secured a promise of Roman support, but Demetrius clearly felt compelled to react. He sent Bacchides with a force of some 20,000 directly to Jerusalem. Judah was unable to recruit successfully from the war-weary population, mobilizing only 3,000 men, many of whom deserted when they saw the size of the opposition.

Left with a minuscule force of 800 fighters facing Bacchides's 20,000 at Elasa north of Jerusalem, Judah was urged by his comrades to avoid conflict and wait for better times; but he insisted on fighting. Leading a frantic attack on the enemy's right flank, he seemed for a time to be succeeding; but Bacchides, unlike his predecessors, refused to be panicked. He brought his left flank around, catching Judah's valiant few in the rear.

The Maccabees were defeated and Judah himself was killed. Jonathan, Johanan and Simon, the three remaining brothers, retrieved his body and managed to bury him in their village of Modi'in before withdrawing to the desert.

Coins minted by the Hasmonean kings. *Left:* Aristobulus II (67–63 B.C.); *Right:* Hyrcanus II (63–43 B.C.). (*Israel Museum*)

The Maccabees eventually achieved Judah's dream of national independence, but without Judah. First under Jonathan, later under Simon, the Maccabees restored their fortunes. Jonathan used a combination of fighting, diplomacy and intrigue to regain power in Judea. After his death, Simon took over and founded a dynasty that ruled the independent Jewish nation until Roman forces under Pompey conquered Jerusalem in 63 B.C.

There can be no doubt that Judah made some bad mistakes; he should certainly have avoided that last hopeless battle at Elasa. Indeed it is difficult to see why the careful, prudent commander rejected the sensible advice of his followers and refused to withdraw so that he might fight another day.

One can only conclude that Judah was simply worn out by six years of exhausting, unremitting struggle. Possibly he was discouraged by his failure to mobilize more supporters, depressed by the lack of stamina of the Jewish population, which so clearly signalled that it had fought enough.

However, this remarkable man—freedom fighter, national redeemer, statesman—did not sink into indecisive inaction. He led his followers in a final, valiant battle and met death head-on, with his honour intact.

Judah the Maccabee developed in six years from a farmer into a brave guerrilla fighter, subsequently becoming an effective commander of large forces and an inspiring national leader. Later still he moved into the sphere of diplomacy and politics, showing a remarkable awareness of the balance of regional forces.

His achievements lived on after his death. Judah died, his forces were defeated, his struggle suffered a setback; but the seed he nurtured would never die: the imperishable ideal of freedom had been implanted in the minds and hearts of the Jewish people for ever.

6 🔁

Bar-Kokhba: Taking on
the Invincible

🔁 JUDEA WAS desolate, its fortresses reduced, its villages destroyed, its people massacred or sold into slavery, Jerusalem, its eternal capital, ploughed under. What Antiochus had failed to do, Hadrian the Roman Emperor seemed to have accomplished: the small but obstinate Jewish people had been utterly defeated and dispersed.

By the end of the 132–135 A.D. Judean revolt—according to the Roman historian Dio Cassius—fifty of the main Jewish strongpoints and almost 1,000 Judean villages had been razed; 580,000 men, women and children had been killed in battle, with countless others sold as slaves or dead from hunger and disease.

A Jewish legend recounts: "They slew the inhabitants until the horses waded in blood up to the nostrils, and the blood rolled along stones the size of forty measures and flowed into the sea, staining it for a distance of four miles."

Simon Bar-Kokhba, autocratic, determined and cruel, managed —like King David and Judah the Maccabee before him—to unite the Jewish people under his leadership. The Romans were forced to mobilize legions from as far away as Britain and Spain to crush the rebellion. Judea remained free for less than four years; but, by the time it had been defeated, the foundations of the mighty Roman Empire had been shaken.

In Jerusalem and all over Judea, the Jews fortified towns, strongholds, villages and caves, from which they made devastating raids against the Roman occupation forces. Inspired by Bar-Kokhba, the Judean irregulars held out against all the forces that Rome sent to crush them.

The scale of the uprising reflects the fact that Bar-Kokhba rapidly established himself as the unchallenged leader of the Jewish people. He was clearly a brave fighter and skilled general, as well as a powerful and inspiring personality; but it was his proclamation as the promised Messiah, or redeemer, by Rabbi Akiva, the leading sage of the era, that fired the national imagination and rallied the masses to his cause.

Recruits to Bar-Kokhba's forces were required to show evidence of a remarkable strength and stoicism. According to one legend, they were ordered to cut off one of their fingers as a demonstration of their steadfastness and dedication. When the rabbis objected that this mutilation was contrary to Judaism, they were then expected to uproot a young cedar while riding by on horseback.

As for Bar-Kokhba himself, the legends say that "he used to catch the missiles from the enemy's catapults on one of his knees and hurl them back, thus killing many of the foe."

Despite a campaign of savage ruthlessness, Tineus Rufus, the local Roman ruler, failed to suppress the uprising with the troops at his disposal, and the Emperor Hadrian was forced to despatch Julius Severus, the Governor of Britain, to do the job.

Mobilizing at least three extra legions, Severus went about his task in a methodical manner, destroying the points of resistance one by one and massacring the survivors. When it was necessary, Severus laid siege to the fortresses, villages or caves, until the defenders perished from hunger and thirst.

As Jerusalem had been destroyed by the Romans sixty years earlier and its massive walls razed, it was not able to hold out for long against the Roman legions; but, after it fell, the Jewish fighters mobilized for a last stand at Betar, five miles to the south-west.

Betar fell after a long and arduous siege in the summer of 135, and Bar-Kokhba himself was killed. Hadrian, so the legend says, had the head of the Jewish commander brought to him and declared: "If his God had not slain him, who could have overcome him?"

Unfortunately the accounts of the Bar-Kokhba revolt are somewhat fragmentary. There is no history of the struggle, merely brief mentions by Roman historians, supplemented by legends from the post-biblical Talmud and Midrash. Modern archaeological discoveries have done something to fill the gap, but there are no accounts comparable to the Books of the Maccabees.

However, the scale of the struggle is indicated by Dio Cassius, who graphically describes the destruction of Judea and the slaughter of its inhabitants, adding:

> Many Romans moreover perished in this war. Therefore Hadrian in writing to the Senate did not employ the opening phrase commonly affected by the emperors, "If you and your children are in health, it is well; I and the legions are in health."

The omission of this phrase suggests a campaign of unusual toughness.

The historian also recounts that Jews outside Judea and "many outside nations too" were joining in the rebellion, "and the whole world, so to speak, was shaking." So, despite the absence of first-hand accounts, it is clear that we are not talking about a small-scale revolt, but of a major conflict that threatened the stability of the empire.

THE BAR-KOKHBA uprising was the culmination of two centuries of struggle between Rome and Jerusalem, and the third major conflict between the two in the space of seventy years.

There was only one way that a confrontation between a small people and a mighty empire could end. The Jews were totally defeated; but, whereas heaps of stones are all that remain of the Romans in the deserts of Israel today, the Jews are building their new nation there.

Any one of a number of patriotic leaders could have been the subject of this chapter, but in the earlier wars against Rome the leaders of the various Jewish factions spent as much time fighting each other as they did fighting the enemy.

Bar-Kokhba was the only one who achieved undisputed national leadership and led a united struggle against Rome, and has therefore been chosen as the chief representative of those who dared to take on the invincible. However, a brief description of the previous struggles will help put the Bar-Kokhba rebellion in perspective.

As we have seen, it was none other than Judah the Maccabee who brought Rome into the affairs of Judea by seeking the backing of the Senate in 161 B.C.; Jewish-Roman relations were cordial enough for many years, but it was only a question of time before the two peoples were set on a collision course.

The Maccabean dynasty lasted for a century, to be usurped by a family of Jewish converts from the southern territory of Idumea, the most famous of whom was Herod the Great. The Herodian rulers were essentially Roman vassals, and, following their demise, Rome ruled Judea directly with procurators.

The Jews, who had from time to time rebelled against the Herods, became increasingly restive under the procurators, who were drawn from the lower middle classes and therefore collected taxes for their own purses on top of the already severe imperial levies.

During the period of Roman hegemony, many Jews started to believe in the coming of a Messiah, a saviour or redeemer of the house of David, who would deliver them from foreign rule and usher in an era of peace and justice on earth.

The belief was based on a biblical passage where Nathan tells King David that his rule will be eternal: "And thine house and thy kingdom shall be established for ever before thee: thy throne shall be established for ever." (II Samuel 7:16)

Combined with messages from the prophets Isaiah and Micah predicting "the End of Days," which would be an era of universal peace, when people would "beat their swords into ploughshares and their spears into pruninghooks," the belief in Messianic redemption became increasingly important during the Roman era.

A partially unrolled sheet from the "Thanksgiving Scroll," one of the Dead Sea scrolls, Qumran, first century B.C. (*Israel Museum*)

The famous Dead Sea scrolls, discovered in caves near Qumran in the Judean desert east of Jerusalem in 1947, show that Jesus of Nazareth was not the only patriotic Jewish leader whose followers thought he was the Messiah. Qumran was the centre of a sect, which most scholars identify with the Essenes described by the Roman historian Pliny.

It was one of many that existed in Judea at that time. The scrolls show that the members of the Qumran sect, who had something in common with the early Christians, also believed that their leader, an unnamed "Teacher of Righteousness," was the Messiah.

As the Roman administration under the procurators became more oppressive, the Jews became increasingly rebellious. A dozen years of anarchy and bloodshed in Jerusalem culminated in the Jewish War against Rome, chronicled in great detail by the

The Temple candelabrum borne into captivity by the Romans. Detail from the Arch of Titus, Rome, first century A.D. (*Museum of the Diaspora*)

Roman-Jewish historian Flavius Josephus, which lasted from 66 – 73 A.D.

A Jewish rebel leader in Galilee at the outset of the war, Josephus became convinced of the futility of fighting the awesome power of the Roman Empire and went over to the enemy. Traditionally regarded as a traitor to the Jewish cause, Josephus has nevertheless been valued as a recorder of events.

His epic history *The Jewish War,* while replete with atrocity stories, criticism of internecine Jewish strife and some gratuitous toadying to his patrons, the Roman Emperor Vespasian and his son Titus, pays no little tribute to the heroism of the Jewish resistance.

According to his account, the Jewish defenders, known as the "zealots," indulged in vicious faction fighting even as the Romans besieged Jerusalem; but they nevertheless defended their city and their Temple with a ferocious obstinacy and dedication. And even

The Temple before its destruction in 70 A.D. Model in the grounds of the Holyland Hotel, Jerusalem. (*Werner Braun*)

after the fall of the Temple, the Jews fought on heroically at the fortresses of Herodium, Macherus and — most memorably — Masada.

The rock of Masada is a section of cliff in the Judean desert southeast of Jerusalem overlooking the Dead Sea, 1,000 feet below. It is cut off by steep ravines on all sides, which makes it practically inaccessible. On it, Herod the Great had built an impregnable fortress as a retreat from his rebellious subjects.

One of the Judean zealot groups seized it from its Roman garrison at the outset of the war and, having secured a base there, proceeded to Jerusalem, where, for a time, they took over the leadership of the Jewish forces. Losing out there in the bitter infighting among the different rebel factions, they were forced to withdraw to their desert fastness.

Under their new leader, Elazar Ben-Yair, they waited out the war at Masada. Elazar and his zealot followers were joined by other rebel groups, particularly after the fall of Jerusalem. When the Roman Tenth Legion arrived at the foot of the rock with its auxiliary forces early in 73 A.D., there were just under a thousand men, women and children living in the fortress.

Despite the imbalance of forces, capturing Masada was not a simple matter, for the Jewish defenders had more than adequate supplies of food and water. The largest ravine had been dammed, and from it an aqueduct fed a line of cisterns cut into the side of the rock. The Romans destroyed the aqueduct, but there was plenty of water in the cisterns from the winter's rainfall. Herod's storehouses were crammed with grain, oil, dried fruit and vegetables.

The Romans set about their siege in typically methodical fashion, building small forts at every possible point of egress and joining them with a wall circumventing the rock. They then constructed a gigantic ramp of earth and wood in the valley to the west.

A remarkable engineering feat for those days, the ramp is still there, pointing like a sword at the fortress. On top of the ramp, the attackers constructed a siege tower under cover of which they battered the defensive walls.

They broke through the stone walls, only to discover that the defenders had constructed an inner wall of wood and earth, which was impervious to their battering-rams. In due course, the Romans set alight this inner wall.

The attackers were surprised at the speed with which the fire spread to the whole fortress. The following morning they discovered why: when they entered the charred remains of the stronghold, they found the bodies of the defenders laid out in neat rows. The men had first killed their own families and then drawn lots for a final ten to kill the men, upon which one man had killed the others and then himself.

Masada became a place of pilgrimage for modern Israelis and an exploratory archaeological dig was conducted there in the 1950s. In 1963–64, Yigael Yadin, the soldier-archaeologist, led two seasons of spectacular excavations at Masada.

Fragments of biblical scrolls and documents of the Dead Sea sect were discovered there, as well as numerous inscriptions, jars with the remains of food (preserved in the dry climate for almost two millennia), mosaics and wall paintings.

Herod's incredible palaces were uncovered; but the most moving discovery was of the zealot living quarters in the casemate wall surrounding the fortress, their ritual baths, synagogues, the traces of the fire they ignited and, in some cases, the very remains of their final meals. Weapons used by the defenders, including stones ready to roll down on the Roman attackers, were also uncovered.

The most dramatic find was of a collection of inscribed pottery fragments, which might have been the lots drawn by the defenders to decide which of them would kill the others. One of them was inscribed "Ben-Yair."

Masada is rightly a symbol in Israel today, an inspiring monument to heroic ancestors who preferred death to slavery. Young soldiers of the armoured corps swear their oath of allegiance atop the bleak mountain with the vow, "Masada shall not fall again!"

Even after Masada fell and Jerusalem and the Temple were no more, the Jews were still not cowed. A series of uprisings and rebellions against the Emperor Trajan surged through the Jewish communities in Egypt, Mesopotamia, Cyrene and Cyprus in 115 A.D., eventually spreading to Judea. Thousands of Jews were killed, and order was only restored in 117 at the start of Hadrian's reign.

THIS, THEN, is the background to the defiant uprising led by Simon Bar-Kokhba against the legions of Rome. There are, however, contradictory versions as to the specific causes of the Bar-Kokhba revolt.

One account suggests that the spark was provided by Hadrian's order to start building a Roman city on the site of Jerusalem, and a temple to Jupiter on the site of the Temple; but another version says that construction only started after the defeat of Bar-Kokhba. Yet another account suggests that an imperial order banning mutilation — which also applied to circumcision — was the cause of the rebellion.

It seems probable that a combination of such circumstances sparked off the confrontation, which rapidly escalated. Hadrian was in the region shortly before the conflict. He is well-known as an enthusiastic builder, and it is possible he gave orders for the construction of a new city and temple, the execution of which was interrupted by the fighting.

An unpopular imperial order may have provided the tinder of the revolt, but it was a passionate religious conviction that fanned the flames that set a whole nation alight.

Rabbi Akiva, the remarkable man who, according to the Midrash, said of Bar-Kokhba, "This is the king Messiah!" must be regarded as largely responsible for the initial success of the uprising.

Akiva started life as a simple shepherd, but was persuaded by his wife in middle age to go and study the Torah at the academy of Lod in the coastal plain. He became the leading sage of the era. His approval of Bar-Kokhba and his struggle constituted the moral underpinning of the revolt.

Apart from his one declaration, there is no account of the relationship between the two men. Their careers seem to have taken parallel paths, with Bar-Kokhba leading the armed struggle and Rabbi Akiva continuing to teach the Torah in defiance of the Roman authorities.

Akiva was arrested and imprisoned by the Romans for teaching the Law. When one of his followers visited him and suggested that he should desist for a time, he replied that a Jew could no more exist without the Torah than a fish could exist without water. He

The Roman Emperor Hadrian, 135–138 A.D. Bronze statue found at Tel Shalem near Beth She'an in the Jordan valley. (*Department of Antiquities*)

Hoard of coins dating from the time of Bar-Kokhba found in the Hebron hills,
132–135 A.D. (*Israel Museum*)

was tortured to death for his belief; but, according to the legend, he welcomed the martyrdom.

The name Bar-Kokhba, which means "son of a star," also indicates the belief in his Messianic nature, based on the biblical passage,

> . . . there shall come a Star out of Jacob, and a Sceptre shall rise out of Israel, and shall smite the corners of Moab, and destroy all the children of Sheth.
>
> . . . and Israel shall do valiantly.
>
> Out of Jacob shall come he that shall have dominion. . . .
>
> *(Numbers 24:17 – 19)*

A later rabbi, Shimon Ben-Yochai, quotes Rabbi Akiva as referring to the above passage in relation to Bar-Kokhba; but, in fact, the name Bar-Kokhba was preserved only in the sources of later Christian writers. The Jewish sources give his name as Bar-Kosiba, or Ben-Kosiba.

The famous Bar-Kokhba letters, discovered by Yadin in a Judean desert cave in 1960, are headed by the name "Shimon Bar-Kosiba, President over Israel." The whole matter is further complicated by the fact that Bar-Kosiba means "son of a liar." After the failure of the revolt, some sages did indeed regard him as such. Interestingly, nowhere in the letters discovered by Yadin's team is there any indication of Messianic claims.

The revolt began in Judea, but it spread as far as Galilee and Gilead, across the Jordan; Jews outside Judea and other nations also joined the fight.

Faced with the legions, the Jews did not seek open battle, but fortified their villages and dug tunnels and cellars. The explorations of Yadin in the caves by the Dead Sea have confirmed that the rebels lived in caves, holding out against the Romans after the larger centres fell — possibly even after the fall of Betar.

The Roman advance was slow but remorseless. The Talmud and Midrash contain many accounts of the mass slaughter of civilians, including children, who were wrapped in Torah scrolls and burned to death. One passage describes how "the brains of three hundred children were dashed upon one stone."

Letter from Bar-Kokhba to a certain Ben Galgoula threatening to bind him in fetters. Found at Wadi Muraba'at, Nahel Hever, 132–135 A.D. (*Israel Museum*)

The letters discovered by Yadin describe an autocratic commander giving orders for supplies and sequestrations of crops, and threatening dire punishment if he is not obeyed. However, there is also a picture of increasing desperation as the situation deteriorates. A particularly poignant passage reads: "From Shimon Bar-Kosiba to the men of Ein Gedi to Masabala and Yehonathan Bar-Be'ayan, peace. In comfort you sit and drink from the property of the House of Israel, and care nothing for your brothers."

There is no indication that Bar-Kokhba attempted to fortify Jerusalem or rebuild the Temple. It is probable that he did not have time. Before the Yadin explorations, there had been some doubt as to whether he even occupied Jerusalem. However, coins found in the Dead Sea caves were inscribed on one side "Shimon," and on the other "of the Freedom of Jerusalem," which indicates that Jerusalem must have been for a time his centre of operations.

Silver tetradrachm, 133–134 A.D. One side shows the façade of the Temple and the reverse carries the inscription "Year Two of the Freedom of Israel." (*Israel Museum*)

Betar, where Bar-Kokhba gathered his supporters for their final stand, is a village surrounded by the steep-sided valley of Sorek. No serious excavations have been conducted there, but inscriptions nearby mention three of the Roman legions which besieged the stronghold.

The location has a spring, still flowing today and used by the Arab villagers of Battir. The Romans surrounded Betar with a wall, and the siege — by now apparently commanded by Hadrian in person — must have been similar to that of Masada. Unfortunately, there was no Flavius Josephus to write an account of the epic.

The Jewish sources are mostly hostile to Bar-Kokhba at this stage, because of his killing of Rabbi Elazar of Modi'in, who was with him during the final siege. According to the Midrash, a Samaritan soldier, serving with Hadrian, deliberately deceived Bar-Kokhba by talking to Rabbi Elazar and making it look as if he were collaborating with the enemy. The conversation was duly reported to Bar-Kokhba.

Challenged by the commander to disclose the contents of his conversation with the Samaritan, the rabbi pointed out that, as he was praying, he had not heard what was said to him. Upon which the Jewish commander assumed that the venerable rabbi was, in fact, treating with the enemy. The passage in the Midrash relates, "Bar-Kosiba flew into a rage, kicked him with his foot and killed him."

The legend relates that a heavenly voice at once proclaimed a passage from the Book of Zechariah, prophesying his doom. Religious tradition attributes the fall of Betar to this crime.

The ambivalence on the part of religious Jews toward Bar-Kokhba is best illustrated by the statement of the twelfth-century Jewish scholar Moses Ben-Maimon. Known to the Jews as the Rambam, and to the world as Maimonides, the pre-eminent Jewish scholar of the Middle Ages said: "Rabbi Akiva, the greatest of the sages of the Mishna, was a supporter of King Ben-Kosiba, saying he was the King-Messiah. He was the King-Messiah, until he was killed for the sins which he had committed."

WITH THE establishment of the State of Israel in 1948, Bar-Kokhba was revived as a patriotic hero, and the legend was further reinforced by the dramatic discoveries of Yadin's team in the Judean desert caves.

When Yadin announced the discovery of a document bearing the inscription "Shimon Bar-Kosiba, President over Israel," the national radio interrupted its scheduled programme to broadcast news of the discovery. The newspapers came out with banner headlines the next day.

"It was," enthused the soldier-archaeologist, "the retrieval of part of the nation's past heritage . . . the desert had given up factual links with the man who led the last attempt of his people to overthrow their Roman masters."

However, another Israeli general, Yehoshafat Harkabi, a former Chief of Military Intelligence, has recently criticized the glorification of Bar-Kokhba and the other rebels against Rome.

Harkabi argues that Bar-Kokhba — and the leaders of the 66–73 war — were wrong to wage a hopeless struggle against a far stronger enemy. Bar-Kokhba, he points out, led his people to a disastrous defeat. His uprising led to the expulsion of most of the Jews from their country.

Harkabi believes that, even if the zealots had been united in the first war against Rome, they would not have won. He particularly objects to the way that Bar-Kokhba and the zealots are depicted as patriotic heroes in the history books used in Israeli schools.

Judea, he says, was too important strategically, and the Roman army was too powerful, for any of the revolts to have had any chance of success. A clear-headed assessment would have shown the rebel leaders that they should not have embarked on the struggles.

His view has been disputed by a religious historian, Rabbi Yoel Bin-Nun, who maintains that the Roman Empire was breaking up in the period between 66 and 68 A.D., particularly in 68, the year when four emperors succeeded each other in short succession.

Bar-Kokhba, he admits, could not have won; but he could not have been expected to know that there would not be other conflicts within the Roman Empire during the years 132–135. Bin-Nun argues that the Maccabee uprising, which ultimately did succeed, was far more of a gamble than the later revolts.

Bar-Kokhba, then, is as controversial a figure in modern Israel as he was during the period that the Talmud was being written.

It is difficult to adopt a position concerning incompletely chronicled events, which took place so long ago. There is undoubtedly logic in General Harkabi's contention; but, although his struggle did end in total disaster, Bar-Kokhba left a legacy of resistance and refusal to surrender that went far beyond the call of bravery, becoming part of the imperishable heritage of the Jewish people and inspiring the modern revival of the Jewish nation.

7 🐦

The Years Between:
The Spiritual Heroes

🐦 I₍ₙ₎ THE centuries following the defeat of Bar-Kokhba, no military leaders emerged among the Jews comparable to those of the biblical and Second Temple periods. There were a number of Jewish fighters, and even commanders; but, without their own land to defend, the Jewish people did not produce leaders like King David or Judah the Maccabee.

Jewish military exploits, as opposed to sporadic resistance to oppression led by local communal leaders, would only be revived with the return to Zion. The intervening period was one of spiritual heroism, with the Jews struggling to maintain their identity against overwhelming odds.

IN 68 A.D., according to a legend, while the Roman siege of Jerusalem was at its height, a group of Jewish scholars received permission to take the body of their revered teacher, who had died during the siege, out of the city for burial. However, when the

Roman soldiers checked the coffin, they found that the elderly sage inside it was very much alive.

Emerging from the wooden box, Rabbi Johanan Ben-Zakkai confronted Vespasian, the Roman commander, hailed him as emperor of Rome and requested permission to found an academy of learning. Vespasian must have been surprised at the title conferred on him, for he was far from being in line for the Roman Empire's top job; but he told Ben-Zakkai that, if his prophecy came true, he would grant his request.

That year Rome was beset by continuous intrigue. The Emperor Nero was murdered and, after his death, three generals seized power in succession, only to be assassinated after a few months in office. Vespasian's legions saw no reason why their commander was less qualified than the others and proclaimed him emperor. In 69, he was confirmed by the Senate.

Assuming that the legend has a historical basis, it seems that, rather than possessing the gift of prophecy, the venerable rabbi had made an educated guess. Following the initial success of the Jewish revolt, Nero had sent his best soldier, Vespasian, to restore order. As Rome's most able general, he was a candidate for eventual succession.

He became emperor and kept his word. Johanan Ben-Zakkai founded his academy in the small town of Yavneh in the coastal plain; even before the age of the Jewish fighter had ended, the era of the Jewish scholar, as the guarantor of Jewish survival, had begun.

With the Temple destroyed, the synagogue (house of prayer) and the *beit midrash* (house of learning) became the central institutions of Jewish life. The rabbi (teacher) replaced the priest as the religious leader of the community.

The Sanhedrin (supreme religious council), which had formerly been a largely hereditary body dominated by the priests of the Temple, was reconstituted at Yavneh. Although headed by a hereditary president, or patriarch, erudition became the basis of selection for the revived body, rather than power, wealth and influence as previously.

The Bar-Kokhba revolt caused a temporary setback for the Sanhedrin, as Jews were banished from Judea and the practice of

Judaism was forbidden. Judea was renamed Syria Palestinea, eventually Palestine. However, Hadrian's successor as emperor, Antonius Pius, repealed many of the anti-Jewish laws, and the Sanhedrin was re-established at Usha in western Galilee.

There, during the presidency of Judah (170–217 A.D.), the Mishna, the oral tradition of laws and legends, which explained and amplified the Torah, was codified and written down. It was Rabbi Akiva who had started to bring some system into the oral tradition, but his work was interrupted by the rebellion. Now the work of 148 scholars and rabbis was sorted into six sections and written down.

Conditions in Galilee were far from stable and the seat of the patriarchate moved more than once, being permanently established in Tiberias, which was, however, destroyed in 351 A.D. As Christianity became the established religion of the Roman Empire, Jewish life in Galilee deteriorated and the last patriarch finally died without a successor in 425.

However, the Jewish community which remained in Mesopotamia when the Jews returned to Judea from Babylon in 538 B.C. had flourished. During the six centuries of the Second Temple in Jerusalem, the Jews of the *Golah* (Diaspora) in Mesopotamia had continued their links with Jerusalem and the Temple.

Jewish religious development did not end with the Mishna. Just as the Mishna amplified and explained the laws of the Torah, the rabbis and scholars continued to comment on the Mishna.

These commentaries were collectively called the Gemara, and the combined Mishna and Gemara became known as the Talmud. Work on the Talmud, which was in Aramaic as well as in Hebrew, continued both in Galilee (the Jerusalem Talmud) and in Mesopotamia (the Babylonian Talmud). It was the latter which was to become the better-known work.

The head of the Mesopotamian community, also recognized as an official representative of the Jews, was known as the exilarch. Whereas the Judean presidency died out in the fifth century, the Mesopotamian schools of Jewish scholarship continued into the eleventh century A.D.

Although both Galilean and Mesopotamian centres became less important as time went on, the Talmud, together with the Bible, created an environment for the Jewish people which replaced their lost territory. The Talmud was a world in which Jews could escape when the tribulations of that in which they lived became unbearable. It enabled them to maintain their separate identity over the centuries.

JEWS HAD meanwhile formed communities all over the Roman Empire and beyond. They lived in Egypt and Arabia, India, Mesopotamia and Greece, Italy, France, Spain and North Africa. Everywhere they continued to practise their religion, to study the Torah and Talmud, and to regard themselves as living in exile, maintaining their loyalty to their former homeland.

They prayed facing the site of their ancient Temple, celebrated the festivals according to the seasons and harvests of Judea, repeated the fervent wish, "Next year in Jerusalem," and continued to believe in a Messiah who would one day lead them back to the land of Israel.

Despite the dispersion, or diaspora, there were always some Jews in Galilee and Judea. Remains of synagogues have been found in the Jezreel valley, Jericho, Ashkelon and Gaza.

When the Roman Empire was replaced by that of Byzantium, the Jews faced forcible conversion, expulsion and massacre. For this reason, they welcomed the ninth-century Muslim conquests of Egypt, Syria, Mesopotamia and Persia.

At the end of the eleventh century the Christian world launched a series of Crusades to "win back the Holy Land from the infidel." Many Jewish communities were attacked and pillaged by the Crusaders on their way to Palestine. When the Christian armies reached their destination, Jews participated in the defence of Haifa, fighting bravely alongside their Muslim allies. During the Muslim period, there were flourishing Jewish communities in Galilee and Jerusalem and thousands of Jews met their deaths at the hands of the Crusaders.

Although regarded as second-class citizens, the Jews prospered under Muslim rule in Palestine and other countries. In Muslim Spain, in particular, the Jews experienced a "Golden Age," with Jewish doctors, writers, philosophers, traders and diplomats achieving prominence.

Maimonides, for example, was born in Spain, moving later to Morocco and Egypt, where he became the personal physician of the caliph. Although the Jews for the most part fared better under Muslim rule than they did in Christian countries, they were not immune from persecution under Islam.

Morocco and Tunisia, two formerly tolerant Muslim communities, were the scene of Jewish massacres in the thirteenth century; but it was during the fourteenth century, in Christian Europe, that the Jews suffered most. All over Europe Jews were blamed for the Black Death and thousands were massacred.

Increasing numbers of Jews fled eastwards, where they established communities in Poland and later in Russia. In some instances, the Jews tried to defend themselves, notably in Germany. Jewish self-defence groups fought bravely in Cologne, Mainz and Frankfurt; but, deprived of a territorial base, they lacked the national cohesion necessary for military action.

In the fourteenth century, Muslim Spain was reconquered by the Christians, leading to the worst persecutions so far. Thousands of Jews tried to save themselves by converting, becoming Marranos, or secret Jews, the only known case in Jewish history where large numbers abandoned their Judaism — at least publicly.

It did not help them. For a time the Marranos were persecuted under the infamous Inquisition even more than those who continued to profess Judaism openly. Eventually at the end of the fifteenth century, more than 150,000 Jews were expelled from Spain and Portugal, settling in North Africa, Holland, France, Italy and all parts of the Ottoman Empire, including Palestine.

Jewish communities were strengthened or re-established in Jerusalem, Hebron, Ramla and Gaza and in villages around Lake Kinneret. A new community was established at Safed in Galilee, which became a centre of Jewish learning, notably mysticism.

During the Middle Ages Jewish heroism had not died. The very fact of survival under conditions of dreadful persecution denotes spiritual courage on a vast scale, and there are numerous cases of individuals and communities who obstinately maintained their identity and beliefs despite the terrible things that were done to them.

Many rabbis were burned at the stake or tortured on the rack, dying with Hebrew prayers on their lips; others fought with foreign armies or in defence of their fellow Jews.

During the sixteenth century, Jews, who had generally been excluded from the main centres, were permitted to settle in Venice, but they were confined to a small neighbourhood of narrow streets known as the "ghetto." The ghetto became a widespread institution, and Jews all over Europe lived in ghettos, which kept them separate from the surrounding Christian communities.

THE DAWN of the modern era did not bring an end to anti-Jewish persecution, quite the reverse. Jews continued to suffer in both the Christian and Muslim worlds. Massacres of Jews in Europe dwarfed even those of the Middle Ages.

Between the seventeenth and eighteenth centuries, legislation in European countries had driven the Jews out of professions such as medicine, architecture, printing, writing, music, bookselling and wagon-making. By 1800, peddling and petty shopkeeping had become the main Jewish occupations.

The nineteenth century saw both emancipation for Jews and continued anti-Jewish prejudice. Even as Jews emerged from the ghettos, and occupations hitherto prohibited to them became open, there were anti-Jewish riots in Germany, because Jews were blamed for the economic hardships which followed the Napoleonic wars.

Many Jews saw a solution in conversion; but others, taking the cue from the revival of nationalism all over Europe, began to think of rebuilding a Jewish nation. There had always been small numbers of Jews returning to the land of Israel, but a mass return was supposed to await the coming of the Messiah. Now there was talk of a revival of the ancient homeland even in advance of the Messiah. One of the first to propose such a course of action was Rabbi Hirsh Kallisher, who travelled all over Europe seeking backing for his idea of a Jewish return to Jerusalem.

Support came from an unlikely quarter. Moses Hess, a colleague of Karl Marx and Friedrich Engels who had helped them write the *Communist Manifesto,* published *Rome and Jerusalem* in 1862, proposing the establishment of a new socialist Jewish society in the

Captain Alfred Dreyfus is stripped of his honours and rank and sent to Devil's Island on trumped-up charges of treason, Paris, January 4, 1895. Lithograph by Leon Fauret. (*National Library, Jerusalem*)

land of Israel. In 1870, a Jewish agricultural school called Mikve Yisrael was founded in the coastal plain, largely by the efforts of Karl Netter, a French Jew.

However, although the idea of a return of the Jews to Zion — Zionism — began in Western Europe, it was among the masses of Jews in Eastern Europe that it began to be seen as a political reality. In Russia, particularly, where Jews were still excluded from most of the occupations, confined to a small area known as the Pale of Settlement and increasingly the victims of pogroms (anti-Jewish riots), it found a growing number of adherents.

Committees of the Lovers of Zion were formed in Odessa and Warsaw, and their members immigrated to Palestine, still a part of the Ottoman Empire, to establish farming villages.

Between 1881 and 1914, prompted at least partly by the pogroms, more than two million Jews left Eastern Europe for

Theodor Herzl, 1860–1904, founder and visionary of modern political Zionism. Portrait by unknown artist. (*WZPS*)

Victims of a pogrom in Ekaterinoslav (today's Dnepropetrovsk), October 1905, in which sixty-seven Jews were killed. (*National Library, Jerusalem*)

America; half a million settled in Western Europe; 80,000 went to Palestine.

In 1896, Theodor Herzl, an assimilated Viennese journalist, published *The Jewish State,* which set out a detailed plan for the transfer of masses of Jews to Palestine. Herzl had been shocked by the anti-Semitism released by the trial for treason of Alfred Dreyfus, a Jewish officer in the French army.

Dreyfus was ultimately rehabilitated thanks to the efforts of writer Emile Zola among others. Zola's magnificent *J'accuse* remains a flaming denunciation of anti-Semitism which will last for ever; but the extent of anti-Jewish prejudice — even in an advanced society such as France — revealed by the trial left an indelible impression on Herzl, who wrote in the closing lines of his pamphlet: "Therefore I believe that a generation of wondrous Jews will grow forth from the earth. The Maccabees will rise again."

A year later, the first Zionist Congress, with over 200 delegates from all over the Jewish world, including Palestine, opened at Basel in Switzerland. On his return to Vienna Herzl confided to his diary: "At Basel I founded the Jewish State. If I said this out loud today, I would be answered by universal laughter. Perhaps in five years, certainly in fifty, everyone will know it."

Fifty-one years later, on May 14, 1948, the State of Israel was proclaimed by David Ben-Gurion in Tel Aviv. It was defended from its enemies by the Israel Defence Forces, the first Jewish national army since that of Bar-Kokhba; but, from the outset, the Jews of Palestine had been forced to revive their military traditions. A free people on its ancient soil, the Jewish people had resolved to defend its freedom.

Even before they actually arrived in the land, Jews fired with the Zionist ideal had dared to take up arms against their enemies. In 1903, when the Russian authorities fomented action against the Jews of Kishinev, causing the worst pogrom of that period, the Zionists of Gomel, a small town in the Ukraine, organized themselves for defence. Disguised as Russian peasants, they collected intelligence as to the intentions of the rioters. Collecting a small sum of money, they purchased weapons.

When the anti-Jewish riots started in Gomel, the response of the Jews was not the traditional one of barricading themselves in their houses and praying. The young Zionists of Gomel set up road-blocks, behind which they defended themselves, easily routing the drunken hooligans who came to loot their homes and shops.

When Czarist troops intervened on the side of the rioters, the young Zionists returned their fire in a battle that raged for three days. The following year a group of them set sail for Palestine. The Jews had served notice that passive resistance was a thing of the past.

Henceforth, they would not be content merely with maintaining their beliefs and identity in the face of persecution. If attacked, they would fight back — and fight back with increasing effectiveness. The Maccabees had indeed risen again.

8 ⌇

Joseph Trumpeldor:
To Fight as a Jew

⌇ THE DEBATE raged fiercely in the crowded Egyptian barrack in Alexandria early in 1915, where more than a thousand Jews had established an autonomous community after voluntarily exiling themselves from the Turkish province of Palestine. Their proposal to set up a Jewish Legion to participate in the conquest of Palestine from the Ottoman authorities had been rejected.

The British military command had stated categorically that there were no current plans to invade Palestine. Instead, the establishment of a mule transport corps for action "somewhere on the Turkish front" had been proposed to the Jewish volunteers.

Vladimir Jabotinsky, a Russian-Jewish journalist, fulminated eloquently against the British proposal to turn his magnificent idea of a Jewish fighting force into a group of "donkey soldiers."

His colleague, Joseph Trumpeldor, dissented. Less articulate than Jabotinsky, he nevertheless had the advantage of being an

Joseph Trumpeldor (1880–1920) in the uniform of a captain in the British army. His reputed last words were, "It is good to die for our country." (*Zionist Archives*)

experienced combat soldier, having served in the Russian army. The vital thing, he argued, was for Jews to fight as Jews.

Jabotinsky, who was later to become an important, if controversial, leader of the Zionist movement, was reporting for a Russian paper about the effects of the war in Europe. He had lived in Constantinople for several years, and, when he heard that Turkey had joined the war on the side of Germany, he became convinced that this represented an important opportunity for Zionism.

Whatever happened in the war, he reasoned, Turkey, the sick man of Europe, would be the loser. If the Jews fought on the British side, the cause of a Jewish return to Palestine would be dramatically enhanced; but the British proposal was not to his liking. It was an unworthy entrance for the Jews into modern military history.

Not so, countered Trumpeldor. Pointing out that transport was a vital component of modern warfare, he insisted that service in a mule corps was no dishonour. Possibly Trumpeldor's uniform, medals and, above all, his artificial left arm — he had lost his arm

Vladimir (Ze'ev) Jabotinsky (1880–1940), Zionist philosopher, writer and ora-
tor. Founder of the Revisionist Movement and the Betar youth movement. Together with Trumpeldor, he founded the Jewish Legion of the British army: the
photograph shows him in the uniform of the Legion. (*Jabotinsky Archives*)

in military action — prevailed over Jabotinsky's superior oratory.

On April 25, 1915, the Zion Mule Corps, 650 muleteers and their 750 mules, the first official Jewish army unit in almost two millennia, using Hebrew military terms and proudly bearing a blue-and-white Zionist flag, watched the landing parties fighting to secure a beachhead at Gallipoli.

During disembarkation, the muleteers formed a human chain to carry water-cans to the shore, and, as soon as enough mules were ashore, they began to carry supplies to the front. Along unknown trails, in driving rain and bitter cold, they delivered three convoys of much-needed supplies on the first night.

On the following days, they established their camp. At night, under withering fire, they took supplies to outlying brigades across the rough ground, through the network of trenches, along cliffs and ravines. Many of the Jewish muleteers showed outstanding bravery in getting their panicking animals through to the lines.

Trumpeldor, with the rank of captain, was second-in-command under Colonel John Patterson, an Irish professional soldier, who showed considerable understanding of Jewish aspirations. Patterson was later to write in his memoirs that Trumpeldor "actually revelled in heavy fire, and the hotter it became, the more he liked it."

Trumpeldor confided to his diary that he was trying to reassure his men, who had never been under fire before, that they should be prepared to carry on, despite the bombardment. "How will our boys do their jobs unless they see it's possible to laugh at these dangers and carry on as usual?"

Gallipoli was a disaster for the British army, taking nine months and costing over 200,000 casualties before it was over. The stalemate situation was not good for morale. With his previous combat experience, Trumpeldor attended to the smallest details, ordering the men to shave every other day and to maintain a smart appearance. He also reproached the officers for gambling, which he thought was inappropriate for Jewish soldiers.

Above all, he was concerned that "whatever happens we have to cherish the good name of our people, and behave in such a way that nobody can reproach the Jews."

In the winter, life became increasingly difficult, particularly for the Palestinians, many of whom had never seen snow before; but they continued to feed and water their mules, until they were called upon to assist in the evacuation. By this time, Trumpeldor was their commander, as Patterson had become incapacitated by illness.

Sir Ian Hamilton, the British commander at Gallipoli, praised the members of the corps for "showing a more difficult type of bravery than the men in the front line who had the excitement of combat to keep them going."

The Zion Mule Corps suffered eight killed and fifty-five wounded at Gallipoli. Many of its members were mentioned in dispatches, and several received high awards for bravery.

After the evacuation, the corps was disbanded, despite Trumpeldor's efforts to keep it going. One hundred and twenty members re-enlisted in the British army and eventually joined the Jewish Legion, subsequently formed in London under Patterson.

BORN IN 1880 in the Caucasus, Joseph Trumpeldor is thought to have been the only Jewish officer ever to serve in the Czarist Russian army. His father, Vladimir, also served with distinction in the Russian army, completing twenty-five years' service, but remaining loyal to his Judaism despite the pressures on him to convert.

The Trumpeldor household was not religious or even traditional. As a young man, Joseph was idealistic, becoming a vegetarian and a believer in the ideas of Leo Tolstoy. He used to set himself tests, such as sleeping on the floor, to toughen himself.

While studying dentistry, Trumpeldor became fascinated with a local group which was trying to put Tolstoyan principles into practice by forming an agricultural collective. Early on, he came to believe in the idea of agricultural communes in Palestine; but in 1902, aged twenty-two, he was drafted into the Russian army.

In 1904, while carrying out a dangerous volunteer mission in the Russian-Japanese war, he was seriously wounded and had his left arm amputated. Although he was entitled to be invalided out, Trumpeldor requested to be returned to the front. Cited in a special Order of the Day, he was promoted to noncommissioned officer.

He was taken prisoner in 1905, in the capture of Port Arthur. In prison, he attended to the welfare of his fellow soldiers, forming the Jewish soldiers into a group for settlement in Palestine. Returning to Russia in 1906, he was promoted to the rank of officer and awarded the Order of St. George for bravery.

Legal studies in St. Petersburg followed, and in 1911 he formed another pioneer group for settlement in Palestine. Arriving there himself in 1912, he worked at the settlements of Migdal and Degania on Lake Kinneret and helped to defend the Lower Galilee settlements against Arab marauders.

Tall, strong and distinguished-looking, he had the reputation of being able to accomplish more with one hand than most others could with two. Although he frequently emphasized the importance of defensive measures for the Jews in Palestine, he was known also as a lover of peace.

At Degania, he made it very clear that he did not need any special assistance as a one-armed man, reacting with anger when a fellow member tried to help him tie his bootlaces and even when someone placed the salt conveniently for him at a meal.

PALESTINE IN those days was a backward, badly administered province of the Turkish Ottoman Empire, which had already experienced three decades of modern Jewish settlement. The first settlers had come from Russia and Romania fired with the ideal of re-establishing the Jewish people in the land of Israel. They founded the early settlements of Petah-Tikvah and Rishon Lezion in the coastal plain, and Zichron Ya'acov, Rosh Pina and Yesod Hama'alah in Galilee. They were joined by young Jews from Jerusalem, the sons of Torah and Talmud scholars, who also wished to see a Jewish renaissance on the land.

Decimated by disease and hardship, the men and women of the First Aliya (first wave of Jewish immigration) fought a heroic battle to farm the land and build their villages. One of the early pioneers, Chaim Chissin, described the hardship of those early years:

> I did not have the faintest idea of what it was all about. Still I raised my hoe and started bringing it down on the earth. In a little while, blisters developed. My hands started bleeding and the pain was so excruciating that I had to lay down the hoe. But I immediately felt

ashamed of myself. "Is this how you mean to show that the Jews are capable of manual labour?" I asked myself. "Are you really able to come through this test?" I took new heart and picked up the hoe again, and despite the stinging pain I hoed for two solid hours, though it nearly killed me.

Despite the efforts of Chissin and others, the early villages were on the point of collapse, when they were rescued by the French Jewish philanthropist, Baron Edmond de Rothschild. Deeply concerned about the pogroms in Russia and aware of the anti-Semitism in his own country, "the Baron," as he came to be known, determined to support the settlers.

"I did not come to you because of your poverty and suffering," he told the settlers of Rishon Lezion in 1889. "I did it because I saw in you the realizers of the renaissance of Israel and of that idea so dear to us all, the sacred goal of the return to Israel in its ancient homeland."

Nevertheless, Rothschild, a banker, wanted to put the villages on a sound financial basis. To this end, he encouraged viticulture and the manufacture of wine. With his financing, and the assistance of his administrators, the villagers prospered; but they soon became gentlemen farmers, employing Arabs to work for them and Circassians (Muslims from the Caucasus) and Bedouin to guard their settlements.

This was anathema to the immigrants of the Second Aliya, who began to arrive around the turn of the century. Affected by the revolutionary atmosphere in Russia, these pioneers were socialists, determined to "conquer labour" as well as settle on the land. If the return to their ancestral homeland was to succeed, they felt, the Jews had to accomplish a social revolution as well as a national one.

Nowhere was this more vital than in the field of defence. Jewish villages, said the men and women of the Second Aliya, must be defended by Jews — not by Circassians and Bedouin, however competent.

A pioneer of this period called Israel Shohat was impressed, in his travels around the country, by the small community of Circassians, who had arrived in Palestine a few decades earlier. Number-

A group of immigrants on their way to Palestine during the Second Aliya (immigration), 1904–1914. (*Museum of the Diaspora*)

ing only a few hundred individuals, they had nevertheless established villages and were respected by the local population. Brave and independent, they were much sought after as guards. Shohat resolved to set up a Jewish defence group, modelled on them.

It was, in fact, a group from the town of Gomel, who had participated in the defence of their town against the rioters and Czarist troops, who formed the nucleus of an organization called Bar-Giora, a self-defence force named after one of the heroes of the war against Rome. The wheel had come a full circle. Ten young men swore allegiance to the new group in 1907 in a candle-lit room of an old house in Jaffa.

Finding little response to their idea of Jewish guards in the coastal plain, they went to Galilee and settled in Sejera at the foot of Mount Tabor, where Deborah and Barak had so soundly beaten the Canaanites. There they formed a collective, with Jews working the land and Jews standing guard.

Passover 1908 saw the convention of the Labour Party at Sejera. Among those present was David Ben-Gurion. In that year, Bar-Giora also secured a contract to defend the neighbouring village of Mes'cha (today's Kfar Tabor). The contract stipulated that they would continue to defend the village as long as only Jewish labour was employed there. The twin values of self-labour and self-defence were maintained.

The following year, Bar-Giora was merged into a larger Jewish defence group called Hashomer, the Watchman. The members believed in the principles of personal responsibility, vigilance, readiness for sacrifice and physical labour.

New members had to be on probation for a year, during which time they were expected to prove themselves. Often the year was extended for a second year, and many aspirants were rejected as unsuitable. It was a paradox: a group professing a belief in socialism and equality had created an elite.

Hashomer was also dedicated to developing honourable and friendly relations with the local Arabs. They set up their own Bedouin-style guest tents, where passing Arabs would stop for coffee and conversation about horses and weapons. Gradually, they began to win the respect of both the Jewish and Arab population.

Armed, mounted, wearing a combination of Circassian, Bedouin and Russian clothes, the members of the new group presented a romantic aura. Many of them were married, and their wives worked with them in the fields and guarded with them at night. Members of Hashomer were among those who founded Degania, the first kibbutz, a commune run on the basis of complete equality, on the shores of Lake Kinneret.

Seeing the need to deal effectively with the Ottoman authorities, Hashomer sent members to study law in Constantinople, among them Ben-Gurion and his friend Yitzhak Ben-Zvi, who would become the second president of Israel.

Since the time of Moses — if not before — the Jews had proved themselves to be fractious and argumentative, and the early years of this century in Palestine were no different. Among the many divisions, the one between the early settlers and the Second Aliya was particularly evident.

The Hashomer ("the Watchman") Jewish defence organization in Palestine at the beginning of the century. Page from a modern Passover Haggadah designed and illustrated by David Harel.

The first settlers hired Arabs, who were contented with lower wages than the Jewish pioneers, to work on their farms, and mostly preferred to be guarded by Bedouins or Circassians, rather than by the men of Hashomer. They had little understanding or sympathy for the dreams of the newcomers, which they regarded as impractical.

Trumpeldor was by both age and temperament a man of the Second Aliya. Working in the fields of Degania, or helping to organize the defence of the Jewish villages, he was clearly in sympathy with the ideals of Hashomer, although there is no evidence that he was a member; but, with the outbreak of the First World War, he parted company from them.

Most of the Yishuv, the Jewish community in Palestine, felt that they should become Ottoman citizens in order to prevent their expulsion by the Turks as enemy aliens. In this, old-timers and newcomers were in agreement. While preparing to defend Jewish settlements against the increasingly restless Arabs, the members of Hashomer also sought to reassure the Turkish authorities of their loyalty.

Trumpeldor could not see his way to becoming an Ottoman citizen and went with some thousand other Palestinians to Egypt, where he joined Jabotinsky in lobbying for a Jewish fighting force. It is likely that, having observed the corruption of Ottoman rule in Palestine, he concluded that the Turks would be defeated; but there is no doubt that he also felt a certain loyalty to the Russian uniform he had worn and the Russian medals he had been awarded.

FOLLOWING THE disbanding of the Zion Mule Corps, Trumpeldor was active in fighting for the formation of a Jewish regiment. He again joined forces with Jabotinsky, who had enlisted in the British army as a private. The two of them were received by Lord Derby, the Secretary for War, and it was agreed that Jewish units would be formed.

Most of the recruits were found among Jewish immigrants to Britain, encouraged by the lobbying of Jabotinsky. The unit of "Jewish tailors," which consisted of a number of battalions of the Royal Fusiliers under Patterson, was eventually to become the Jewish Legion.

Subsequently it was joined by Jews from America, Canada and Palestine in Egypt and crossed the Sinai desert to join General Allenby's campaign for the conquest of Palestine. Stationed in the Jordan valley, the Legion was placed in an important strategic position, with the object of blocking a Turkish thrust across the river; but it was not called upon to fight, as the Turks did not attack.

Trumpeldor did not serve with the Legion. He had become impatient with the slow formation of the force while still in London, and he left for revolutionary Russia, where he hoped to recruit a large Jewish army, which would break through the Caucasus into Palestine.

In Russia, he formed a federation of Jewish soldiers; he was also given permission by the revolutionary authorities to form a Jewish regiment which would defend the Jews against their enemies, but this was cancelled after the 1918 peace accord. The regiment was disbanded, the self-defence organization outlawed and Trumpeldor was arrested.

Before long, he was released and he immediately founded Hechalutz (the Pioneer), a movement of young Jews who aimed to settle in Palestine. Elected chairman of the new organization in 1919, he at once started establishing settlement groups and giving them military training.

Arriving in Constantinople with a group of pioneers, he established an information office and a pioneer training farm, before going on to Palestine. On his arrival he found that the Labour movement had split into two main factions, and he at once set about urging them to unite.

The Palestine to which Trumpeldor came in 1920 was very different from the country that he had left in 1914. The Ottomans had been driven out and the British had been granted a mandate by the League of Nations to administer the land. Furthermore, the British government had earlier issued the famous Balfour Declaration, "viewing with favour the establishment in Palestine of a National Home for the Jewish people."

The French had been given the League's mandate for Syria, including today's Lebanon; but there was some controversy about where the border between the two territories ran. The very north, or "Finger of Galilee," where four Jewish villages had been established, was a sort of no-man's-land between British- and French-administered territory.

The local Muslim Arabs were engaged in trying to expel the French and their Christian Arab allies from the area, and the Jews really did not want to be involved in the quarrel. Unfortunately, they were not able to keep out of it.

After some fighting, the French evacuated their forces northwards, and Arab irregulars laid siege to the Jewish villages, whose inhabitants they suspected of collaborating with the French. Two of them, Hamra and Metullah, were evacuated; but Tel Hai and Kfar Giladi held out. Only shortly after his arrival in the country, Trumpeldor hastened to the area and immediately surveyed the whole terrain on foot.

He took over the defence of the two villages, taking up residence at Tel Hai, which was the farther north, and thus the front line. His military duties did not prevent his going out daily to plough the fields. He also sent repeated messages to the Jewish leaders in Tel Aviv demanding reinforcements.

In Tel Aviv there was no unanimity in favour of helping the northern settlements. Even Trumpeldor's old colleague Jabotinsky, who had become increasingly militant in his Zionism, doubted whether the Jews had sufficient resources of manpower and weapons to hold on to the villages.

Trumpeldor had no doubts: in his view, a village farmed by Jews must never be abandoned. There was some debate at Tel Hai as to whether they should fight only irregular Arab forces, or whether they should also be prepared to resist a regular army; but the issue became increasingly irrelevant as all types of attacks multiplied.

A measure of the strength of the Arab forces faced by the two settlements can be gauged by the fact that the French army, which was equipped with artillery and machine-guns, had been driven out by the local Arab irregulars.

The Jews had no artillery. At Kfar Giladi there were twenty-five men and women with eighteen rifles between them; at Tel Hai there were eighteen people with sixteen rifles. They had about 100 rounds of ammunition per rifle.

In Tel Aviv, the argument continued and Trumpeldor wrote in his diary: "A new generation of the sons of the land of Israel is standing on the frontier, ready to sacrifice their lives . . . and inside the country they are endlessly debating. Will help arrive too late?''

Tel Hai is built of black basalt rock around a courtyard, rather in the style of a fort of the American West. The mountains of Upper Galilee tower menacingly above it. Today you may sit in the claustrophobic yard and imagine the attackers firing down at you. The building has been converted into a museum, with weapons and farm implements of the period of its defence.

Trumpeldor had endeavoured to maintain good relations with the Arabs of the surrounding area, so when the son of the local sheikh rode up to the gate of Tel Hai and demanded to see for himself that there were no French troops hiding in the compound, he saw no reason to refuse.

At the same time, the local villagers massed in the hills outside the settlement. At this point accounts are somewhat confused. The sheikh's son went up the staircase to the upper floor and apparently threw a grenade into the ammunition store, which was being guarded by four settlers.

The villagers launched a simultaneous attack from the outside, while the sheikh's son was still in the building. Trumpeldor ran into the yard to assist the defenders and was shot in the stomach. He managed to crawl to the kitchen, where he calmly instructed his comrades to wash their hands carefully, put back his intestines, which were hanging out, and bind his wounds.

Then, demonstrating the same coolness he had shown in previous military engagements, he continued to direct the defence of Tel Hai until reinforcements arrived from Kfar Giladi. Seven defenders had lost their lives and the remainder were left without ammunition, so there was no alternative but to evacuate Tel Hai.

Trumpeldor died on a stretcher on the way to Kfar Giladi. "These are my last moments," he said. "Tell them to hold out to the last for the honour of the Jewish people." Just before he died, he spoke the words carved on his memorial: "It is good to die for our country." That at least is the legend. Another version says that he died with an earthy Russian curse on his lips. Quite possibly both versions are true.

The settlements were, in fact, evacuated for a few months; but, by his heroic defence of Tel Hai, Trumpeldor had staked out the Jewish claim to the northern Galilee and they were resettled by the winter of 1920. The example of Tel Hai lived on. It was in the minds of the defenders of Degania, Mishmar Ha'emek and Negba in Israel's War of Independence in 1948.

It has already been noted that the great leaders of the Jewish people — Joshua, King David, Judah the Maccabee — were those who unified them. Trumpeldor was just such a unifying figure, although he did not live to carry out his purpose.

Even after his death, though, his influence lived on in promoting the ideal of unity. He had called for a single Labour movement, and the Histadrut Confederation of Labour was formed shortly after his death. He had worked for a unified defence force, and the various groups were unified in the Haganah.

Both left-wing and right-wing Zionists formed organizations named after him. Gedud Ha'avoda, the Labour Battalion, a mobile commune which carried out work projects all over Palestine, bore his name, as did Kibbutz Tel Yosef.

At the same time, Jabotinsky named his right-wing youth movement Betar (Brit Joseph Trumpeldor) after his old friend. Left and right unite in making an annual pilgrimage to Trumpeldor's Lion, the statue of a lion erected at Tel Hai in his memory.

To the right, Trumpeldor is a proud nationalist who fought for Jewish nationhood and refused to abandon territory. To the left, he is these things, but also a socialist and labourer, a believer in the communal way of life. Israelis differ vociferously over the greatness of their national leaders, but all are united about Joseph Trumpeldor.

To all Jews he is a hero, a man of integrity, honesty, modesty, bravery and honour. From Port Arthur, via Gallipoli to Tel Hai, he fought proudly as a Jew, entitled in every way to take his place alongside the heroes of old.

9 ⟦⟧

The Nili Spies:
Going It Alone

⟦⟧ O N NOVEMBER 29, 1967, some
five months after Israel's spectacular victory in the Six Day War, a
funeral took place at the military cemetery on Mount Herzl, Jerusalem, in the presence of many of the nation's leaders. Eulogies
were delivered by the Speaker of the Knesset, Israel's parliament,
and by the chief chaplain of the Israel Defence Forces.

The remains, which were being reinterred with full military
honours, were not of a soldier killed in the recent war, but of a man
who had met his death in the sands of the Sinai desert half a
century earlier. His bones had been discovered under a palm tree,
called by local Arabs "the Jew's tree," near Rafah after Israel
captured the area.

When Avshalom Feinberg was killed by a Bedouin gang in
1917, he was not generally recognized as a national hero. On the
contrary, he and his comrades of the Nili organization, who carried out intelligence work in Palestine for the British army, were

widely reviled in the local Jewish community for their "irrespon-sibility," which, it was said, endangered the security of the Yishuv.

In his address at the Mount Herzl ceremony, Knesset Speaker Kaddish Luz, a man of the Labour movement, whose members had been strongly opposed to Nili, spoke of "one of the tragic misun-derstandings with which Jewish history is so rich." He continued: "As a *sabra* [locally born Jew], Feinberg gave expression to his nationalist aspirations with every breath he drew; at twelve he had already founded a youth movement, the goal of which was a Jewish state." Lauding the members of Nili, Luz asserted: "Our presence here in united Jerusalem is in some measure thanks to their sacrifice."

An ancient wound had been partly healed; but a further twelve years were to pass before the remains of Feinberg's Nili comrade, Yosef Lishansky, hanged by the Ottoman authorities in Damascus in 1917, were reinterred beside him on Mount Herzl. Nili had finally been rehabilitated, its members recognized as heroes of the Jewish people.

All the personalities chosen so far have been unifying national figures. Indeed, emphasis has been laid on their achievements in uniting the fractious Jewish people with a common purpose. In choosing the Nili spies, a group which struck out on its own and caused bitter dissent, tribute is being paid both to their bravery and their judgement.

Their daring was never really in doubt, but for many years only a minority praised their actions. Today it is possible to state cate-gorically that Feinberg, Lishansky, Aaron and Sarah Aaronson and the other Nili members were right in serving British interests against the Ottomans.

The British won the war, conquered Palestine, issued the Bal-four Declaration and were given the mandate by the League of Nations to implement it. Although a bitter confrontation was eventually to develop between the Yishuv and the British manda-tory authorities, it was the mandate which led to the establish-ment of the State of Israel.

The moral courage of the Nili spies, in sticking to their mission in the face of the disapproval—even condemnation—of their contemporaries, is no less striking than their physical bravery.

THE STORY of Nili goes back to the days of the First World War, when the Turks who ruled Palestine joined the war on the side of the Germans against the British, French and Russians.

Early in 1915, around the same time that Trumpeldor and Jabotinsky were in Egypt, lobbying for the establishment of a Jewish unit in the British army, Sarah Aaronson was on her way home from Constantinople to Palestine.

The daughter of prosperous farmers from Zichron Ya'acov, pioneers of the First Aliya, she had married and gone to live in Constantinople; but the marriage had not been a happy one.

Sarah was essentially a village girl. An accomplished horsewoman, who was accustomed to hike in the hills around her village, and ride her horse down to the coastal plain and along the sands by the sea, she was suffocated by the formality of life in the Jewish community of Constantinople, with its calling cards and tea parties.

When Turkey joined the war and moved troops into Palestine, Sarah felt compelled to return home to her family. She received letters from Zichron Ya'acov, which painted a worrying picture. The Ottoman authorities in Palestine, after first agreeing to the formation of a Jewish militia, changed their minds and began confiscating the few arms that the Jewish villagers held for their self-defence.

The Hashomer self-defence organization, which had proposed the idea of a Jewish militia, tried to keep as many weapons as it could. Members of Hashomer confiscated weapons from the villagers before the Turks got them, hiding them in secret stores. As a consequence, the villagers were often forced to buy arms from local Arabs to give to the Ottoman officials who came to take them.

Any manifestation of Zionism, such as flying the Zionist flag, was banned. Even the Hebrew street signs in Tel Aviv, the Jewish suburb of Jaffa, were taken down. Numbers of Jews were arrested, accused of contacts with the British.

During her long and arduous journey back to Zichron Ya'acov, Sarah personally witnessed horrible massacres of the Armenian Christians by the Turks in Anatolia.

On her return home she told her brother, Aaron, of the expulsions from the villages, the burning churches, the mass graves, the camps surrounded with barbed wire. If the Turks could behave like that towards the Armenians, she said, was the Yishuv safe? Couldn't the same fate await the Jewish villages in Palestine?

One can easily imagine the incredulity with which Sarah's story was received. In the Aaronsons' spacious rose-coloured villa on the hill of Zichron Ya'acov, sitting in her brother's study (which can still be viewed today) with its antique desk, Arab rugs and oriental cushions, Sarah herself must have wondered whether she had been dreaming.

However, her vivid account finally convinced Aaron to go ahead with a plan, which he had been discussing with his friend Avshalom Feinberg: the establishment of an information network which would make contact with the British in Egypt. It was a risky enterprise, which might invite terrible retaliation against the Jews of Palestine; but, after hearing about the Armenians, the necessity of assisting the British seemed undeniable.

Aaronson and Feinberg were a study in contrasts. Aaronson, brought to Palestine by his parents at the age of six, had a love of nature, which prompted him to explore the hills around his home. As his knowledge of botany and zoology developed, he had become a brilliant scientist. Sent by Baron de Rothschild's officials to study in France, he had briefly worked for Rothschild at the northern settlement of Metullah on his return to Palestine. Subsequently he explored the entire country, mapping its botanical features, often crossing the Jordan, and becoming a leading expert on the local flora and fauna.

On a field trip in 1906, he had discovered on Mount Hermon single-grained wheat, "the mother of wheat," or the earliest known prototype of bread-producing grain, a find of importance both to agronomists and to students of the history of civilization.

The discovery made him world-famous, and, on a trip to America, he secured Jewish financial backing for an agricultural research station, which he established at Athlit, on the coast below Zichron Ya'acov, near the ruin of a Crusader fortress. There, in the salt marshes of the area, he grew produce where none had grown before, and conducted his agricultural experiments, which became famous in Europe and America. The double line of date palms, which he planted, can be seen there to this day. Athlit is a flourishing farming village, but only a shell remains of the pioneer research station.

Aaronson's brilliance as a scientist did not detract from his devotion to the Zionist cause. Colonel Richard Meinertzhagen, the British military intelligence officer who became a strong supporter of the Zionist movement, recalled that he had been inclined to anti-Semitism before he met Aaronson, "a Palestinian Jew, a man of great courage and superior intelligence, deeply devoted to Palestine." Meinertzhagen said that "many conversations with Aaronson" had made him an ardent Zionist.

Avshalom Feinberg had also spent some years in France, but in the poetic ambience of the left bank in Paris. He wrote poetry in Hebrew and French. His father and uncle had been founders of Rishon Lezion.

Passionate and idealistic, Feinberg once stopped the performance of a play depicting the pogroms in Russia, because he could not bear to see Jews cowering in the face of their tormentors. Observing the movements of national revival in Europe, he wrote to his family from Paris: "Why should the Greeks and the Bulgarians have a state, and we who have given so much have none?"

On his return from France, he worked as an assistant to Aaronson in Athlit. When the war started, he made a number of suggestions for Jewish action against the Ottoman authorities. "Either we are facing our end or our rebirth," he said. "If our end, let us die like heroes. If our rebirth, then we don't have to be Turkish politicians."

Rejecting Feinberg's wilder ideas, such as a Jewish military uprising against the Ottomans, the practical Aaronson agreed to the idea of a pro-British spy ring. The secret Nili organization was established, with a handful of members. The name—and password—came from the biblical quotation, *"Netzah yisrael lo yishaker,"* "The Strength of Israel will not lie" (I Samuel 15:29), meaning roughly, "God won't let us down."

Feinberg wrote: "Even if we are caught and hanged as spies, we must do it, so that we will have the right to tell the world not only about our agricultural settlements, but that our blood has been spilled for our country."

Aaron, Sarah and Alex Aaronson and Avshalom Feinberg (clockwise from top left). The Nili spy ring was set up in 1916 to help provide the British with information about Turkish military plans, battle strength and troop movements. (*Zionist Archives*)

Nili was entirely a movement of the children of the First Aliya, mostly residents of Zichron Ya'acov, Rishon Lezion and Hadera. They worked on their own, with little support or understanding from the rest of the Yishuv.

The parents of its members, long used to coexisting with the Ottoman authorities, placating them and bribing them where necessary, could not have been expected to support the idea.

However, the more militant Hashomer members, despite their precautionary measures, were also concerned to co-operate with the authorities. While secretly planning to defend Jewish villages in the event of attacks by local Arabs with the weapons hidden in their stores, they sought to reassure the Turks of their loyalty.

The Aaronson group tried to achieve co-operation with Hashomer, but met with suspicion and distrust. Hashomer had a long-standing personal grudge against Aaronson, who employed Arabs at his research station and haughtily rejected their demands that he give preference to Jewish labour. The crisis in which the Yishuv found itself was not sufficient to break down the divisions between the early pioneer families and the later immigrants.

Even before Nili started its operations, Feinberg was imprisoned and tortured by the Ottoman authorities, wrongly (at that time) accused of contact with the British. At the same time a plague of locusts arrived, devastating crops in Palestine and the surrounding area.

Worried about feeding their troops stationed in Syria and Palestine, the Turks turned to Aaronson, the country's leading agronomist, and asked him to take charge of the locust control campaign. First, he managed to secure the release of his assistant, Feinberg, to help in the operation.

Aaronson was indeed concerned to fight the locusts. The Yishuv was already short of food because of the demands of the Ottoman occupation army; the locusts threatened utter starvation. But he also resolved to utilize his new position to further the operations of Nili. His assistants were given permission to go wherever they pleased to destroy locusts; they were also uniquely well-placed to collect information about Turkish army camps and troop deployments.

Aaronson's men went everywhere, following both the locust

swarms and the rumours of sightings, which gave them enormous flexibility. Digging up the eggs, destroying some crops by fire to save others, they worked their way around the country, at the same time taking note of Turkish military positions and troop movements.

The initial problem was how to make contact with the British and transfer the information. Aaronson's younger brother, Alexander, tried to contact British Military Intelligence in Cairo, but he was not taken seriously; he went on to the United States, where he was active in anti-German and anti-Turkish propaganda campaigns.

Feinberg was the next one to try. He met with a British intelligence officer in Port Said, who promised to maintain contact, but the months passed and Nili still had no way of sending the information it was gathering.

The locusts ravaged much of the country, but Aaronson and his team had some success in limiting the damage. When the plague was over, he persuaded the Turks to let him go to Berlin to participate in research with German scientists. From there, Aaronson crossed over to neutral Denmark, where he made contact with British agents.

The problem was how to get him to London, without endangering his colleagues back in Palestine. Finally a plan was worked out, whereby he embarked for the United States, and the boat was intercepted by the Royal Navy on the high seas. Aaronson was arrested and taken to Britain. If the news got back to Palestine, there would seem nothing treacherous in his being detained by the British.

In due course Aaronson convinced the British of the worth of Nili and was sent to Cairo; but all this took many months, and in Palestine members of Nili, who had heard nothing of Aaronson's fate, were getting desperate. They had been joined by Yosef Lishansky.

Lishansky, born in the Ukraine and brought to Palestine as an infant, had set up his own group for guarding some of the southern Jewish villages, after failing to gain admittance to Hashomer. He had a reputation for wildness and irresponsibility.

In January 1917, Feinberg and Lishansky determined to cross

Sinai to make contact with British troops. In an armed clash with a Bedouin tribe near Rafah, Feinberg was killed and Lishansky wounded.

It is a measure of the suspicion with which the Yishuv regarded Nili that for years it was said that Lishansky killed Feinberg because both of them were in love with Sarah Aaronson. Surviving photographs indicate that Sarah was an extremely attractive woman and her name was romantically linked with Feinberg's, although Feinberg was engaged to her younger sister Rivka, who had been sent out of danger to the United States.

The story that Lishansky had murdered his comrade was only finally laid to rest with the discovery of Feinberg's remains near Rafah after the Six Day War.

The wounded Lishansky reached the British lines and was taken to Cairo, where he met the recently arrived Aaronson. The British, at last convinced of Nili's importance, sent the two men back to Palestine aboard a supply ship, the *Monegan*. The ship did not land and Aaronson remained on board; but Lishansky swam ashore alone to the Crusader ruins at Athlit, near the experimental farm.

For the next eight months, from February to September 1917, while Aaronson remained in Cairo working for British intelligence, the *Monegan* sailed regularly to a point off the coast near Athlit, putting ashore an agent, who collected the reports gathered by Nili.

When she saw smoke on the horizon, Sarah would hang out a sheet to indicate that the coast was clear and, the same night, would ride her horse down to the Crusader ruins with her satchel of reports, which she had been keeping behind a secret panel in the wall of her home.

She would hand over the documents and, at the same time, receive desperately needed money, which had been sent for the starving Jews of Palestine from the United States. Only prewar gold coins were used in the consignments, because at least some of the money would reach Turkish hands in the form of bribes, and it was vital that the increasingly paranoid Turks should not suspect the source of the gold.

The Yishuv, despite its suspicion of Nili, was glad to accept the money. Food had become scarce, both because of the locusts and the demands of the Turkish occupying forces, and the Turks were treating the Jewish residents of Palestine with increasing severity. The Jews of Jaffa and Tel Aviv were expelled from their homes and had to seek refuge in the settlements farther north.

The presence of German submarines off the Palestinian coast made the trips of the British boat too risky, and on one of its last visits the *Monegan* brought a number of carrier pigeons, which were now used to send coded messages to Egypt.

In September, a pigeon came down in a Turkish army camp. The Nili code, which involved Hebrew, Aramaic, French and English, was complicated and took the Turkish army experts a week to crack it. But then the authorities had proof that a pro-British intelligence group was operating in the Yishuv, something they had long suspected.

Many Jews were rounded up, imprisoned and tortured, including members of Hashomer. In October, Turkish troops surrounded Zichron Ya'acov and arrested Sarah Aaronson and her father. For several days they were horribly tortured, but Sarah refused to betray her comrades.

Beaten on the soles of her feet — the infamous *bastinado* — Sarah still refused to talk. Finally she was lashed to the gate-post of her house and whipped mercilessly, but still she resisted. After four days, it was resolved to take Sarah to Nazareth, where more refined torture equipment could be brought into play.

Persuading her captors that her bloodstained dress would create a bad impression, Sarah obtained permission to change her clothes. In her bathroom, she took the pistol, concealed there against just such an emergency, and shot herself.

Her colleague, Lishansky, escaped, and the authorities threatened to destroy Zichron Ya'acov and other villages unless he surrendered. More villagers were rounded up, tortured and threatened with execution.

In the Yishuv, the debate raged. British support for Zionism had become clear, the Balfour Declaration was shortly to be issued and the British army was poised to invade Palestine. The logic of Nili's pro-British stance had become evident. Furthermore, there was admiration for the courageous way in which Sarah had met her death. But many pointed out that Nili had acted on its own, without authorization from any official Yishuv body. By its actions, the spy ring had endangered the very existence of the Jewish community in Palestine.

After a bitter discussion, the members of Hashomer, who had been hiding Lishansky, resolved that he must not be permitted to be taken alive. Another Nili member, Naama Belkind, had been captured by the Turks and it was said that he had talked to his interrogators. It was widely believed that many of the arrests of Hashomer members and others were the result of Belkind's confession.

Desperately fleeing from village to village, Lishansky was hunted by his own countrymen. Eventually he was wounded by a Hashomer force, but he managed to escape, only to be captured by some Arab villagers and handed over to the Turks.

Some said that he took revenge on his former comrades in Hashomer by giving their names to his interrogators; others reject this as an unworthy calumny. In December, only weeks before the British conquest of Jerusalem, Lishansky and Belkind were hanged in Damascus.

General Edmund Allenby, who led the British invasion of Palestine, did not attack, as expected, through Gaza. Ordering the bombardment of Gaza by Royal Navy ships, he launched his main attack against Beersheba. Accompanying the British troops, Aaronson utilized his knowledge of the desert to secure them water sources to the west of the town.

Following the capture of Beersheba, Allenby turned his forces against Gaza, only then pushing on to Jerusalem, which he had promised to British Prime Minister David Lloyd George "as a Christmas present." By then, the Balfour Declaration had been issued.

After the war, Aaronson tried to convert Nili into a political movement representing the sons of the old villages; but, before he could get organized, he was called to Paris by Chaim Weizmann, the leader of the World Zionist Movement, to work at the Versailles peace conference.

Weizmann had met Aaronson in London, where he had expressed reserved support for Nili. The Zionist leader had been impressed by the young agronomist's intimate knowledge of the natural resources and potential of Palestine, and thought that his presence in Versailles would be invaluable.

By a sad stroke of fate, the plane carrying Aaronson across the Channel disappeared in fog and was never seen again. In the superheated atmosphere of the time, when Lishansky had been suspected of killing Feinberg, the death of Aaronson, the oldest member of Nili at the age of forty-three, was also regarded by some as part of a conspiracy.

There remains one intriguing footnote to the tragic story of the Nili spies. T. E. Lawrence, Lawrence of Arabia, whose work among the Arabs paralleled that of Nili among the Jews, wrote an epic account of the Arab revolt entitled *The Seven Pillars of Wisdom*. It carries the following dedication:

> To S.A.
> I loved you, so I drew these tides of men into my hands
>   and wrote my will across the sky in stars
> To earn you, Freedom, the seven pillared worthy house
>   that your eyes might be shining for me
> When we came.

There is conflicting evidence as to whether Lawrence of Arabia, the magnetic leader of the desert nomads, and Sarah Aaronson, the heroic martyr of Jewish nationalism, actually met; but nobody has ever positively identified "S.A."

The entire Nili story has been wracked by controversy. Many of its opponents maintain that the organization operated in an amateurish fashion and did not achieve anything of value; but General MacDonough, the British Chief of Military Intelligence, has been quoted as saying:

> General Allenby knew with certainty from his intelligence in Palestine all the movements of the enemy. All the cards of the enemy were revealed to him, and so he could play his hand with complete confidence. Under these circumstances, victory was certain before he began.

10 ⟋⟍

The Ghetto Fighters:
Beyond Bravery

⟋⟍ ON JANUARY 18, 1943, after a
pause of almost four months, the Germans resumed deportations
from the Warsaw Ghetto. Only some 40,000 Jews remained of the
more than 400,000 who had been concentrated there; the others
had been taken to the death camp at Treblinka, where almost all of
them were gassed.

The special SS task-force entered the Ghetto, as it had so many
times before, proceeding from house to house, killing people at
random, including children and the elderly, throwing their victims out of the windows. The Jewish hospital was emptied. Pa-
tients who could still walk were dragged to the central square of
the Ghetto for deportation; those who could not were killed on the
spot. Rifle and machine-gun fire mingled with the cries of the
victims. Several hundred Jews were killed and some 5,000 were
rounded up.

Suddenly a small group of eleven Jews, armed with pistols and
grenades, attacked a force of German guards and SS men, killing

several of them and forcing the others to retreat. Nine of the Jewish fighters lost their lives in the exchange of fire. The two survivors then joined their comrades in a small house where a barricade had been set up.

From behind the barricade, they resisted a German unit which tried to fight its way into the house. Despite the superiority of their weapons, the German soldiers were unable to advance, so they set the house on fire. The Jews continued fighting until they had used up their last bullet. A young man called Mordechai Anielewicz, the leader of the initial attack, was the only survivor. He fought on with a rifle that he had seized from a German soldier, before making his escape.

The German troops, who had marched confidently into the Ghetto to conduct the evacuation, had been forced to run for cover and resume their advance with caution, clinging to the walls, crawling on the ground. Finally they were compelled to retreat.

On the following days the Germans renewed their attacks, firing into windows and hurling grenades, killing hundreds of people; but some forty Jewish fighters, with ten pistols between them, continued to resist, moving from house to house, often via the rooftops.

On January 21, the Germans withdrew from the Ghetto: incredibly the Jews had won a temporary respite from the deportations. The German troops had been astounded to meet resistance. "The Jews are shooting," cried an SS officer in amazement. "They have guns!" Eighteen years later at the trial in Jerusalem of Nazi war criminal Adolf Eichmann, a leader of the underground, Yitzhak Zuckerman, testified: "We gained faith that we can fight; we know how to fight."

DESPITE THE surprise of the Germans — and, indeed, of the Jews themselves — the defiance in Warsaw in January 1943 was by no means the first Jewish act of armed resistance to the Nazi plan to exterminate the Jews of Europe, the so-called Final Solution.

At the very same time that the Jewish fighters were driving the German forces out of the Warsaw Ghetto, Jews in the town of Czestochowa, to the southwest, killed twenty-five German soldiers; 250 Jews were killed in reprisal.

Adolf Eichmann, the Nazi official responsible for the implementation of the *Endlösung* — the "Final Solution" to the Jewish problem — on trial. Caught in Argentina by Israel's Secret Service in 1960, he was tried, found guilty of genocide and hanged in 1962 — the only death sentence carried out in the State of Israel. (*Israel Government Press Office*)

Among the many acts of defiance before January 1943 were the resistance of Jews in the Minsk Ghetto in March 1942, as a result of which 5,000 were murdered; the formation of a Jewish partisan group in Ija, Poland, of which 900 Jews were killed; the knifing of a Ukrainian guard at Treblinka in August 1942, which led to the machine-gunning of an entire trainload of Jewish deportees in retaliation; and numerous break-outs and mass escapes from ghettos and concentration camps all over Europe.

In July 1942, there were uprisings in four Polish ghettos, notably Nieswiez, where a large group of Jews barricaded themselves in their synagogue, refusing to permit German troops to round up Jews for deportation. Two Jewish girls, employed in a weapons repair shop, had managed to smuggle the parts of a machine-gun and several other guns to the resisters, and to help them to reassemble them.

When the Germans opened fire on the synagogue, the fire was returned. The German soldiers burst into the building, and the Jews opposed their automatic weapons with knives, iron bars and stones, as well as their few guns. Old men armed with bars attacked German soldiers armed with submachine-guns, in vicious hand-to-hand fighting. After putting up a prolonged resistance, the Jews set their houses alight, upon which hundreds of local peasants swarmed into the Ghetto in an orgy of looting.

Lachwa in southwestern Byelorussia was the scene of an even more remarkable uprising in August 1942, without modern weapons of any description. The Jews who were about to be shot beside a large ditch, specially dug for them to fall into, attacked the well-armed soldiers with axes, hammers and clubs. Others set the Ghetto on fire. Of the town's 2,000 Jews, 600 reached the nearby forest; but most of them were hunted down. Only 120 survived to join the local partisans.

Amazingly though, several hundred Jewish fighters managed to escape from the other ghettos and join the anti-German partisans in the forests. Jews were prominent in the partisan movements of all the countries occupied by the Nazis.

AS SOON AS Adolf Hitler became Chancellor of Germany in 1933, he moved swiftly to carry out the anti-Jewish policies that he had outlined in his book, *Mein Kampf,* twenty years before.

Implementing his plan in stages, he passed a series of laws, prohibiting Jews from practising the professions, depriving them of the rights of citizenship and effectively putting them outside the framework of German society.

The Dachau concentration camp was established for Communists, socialists, trade unionists and other opponents of the Nazis. Many of Hitler's political opponents were, indeed, Jews; but before long they were joined in Dachau by Jews who had been sent there solely because of their Jewishness.

At the same time groups of Nazi party stormtroopers attacked

Jews on the streets, in their shops and synagogues. Schoolchildren were taught that Jews were their enemies, patriotic songs spread hatred of the Jews and anti-Jewish violence and discrimination was so serious and widespread that by 1938 some forty percent of Germany's half million Jews had left the country.

Jews were also suffering at the hands of right-wing regimes in Poland, Hungary and Romania, which drew strength from the Nazi example in Germany. When Hitler entered Vienna in March 1938, anti-Jewish measures were implemented there too. Jews were thrown out of their apartments, attacked, beaten and deported to concentration camps.

As time passed, Jews who wished to leave Germany and Austria had nowhere to go, for even countries which had previously admitted them were setting limits on the number of immigrants they were prepared to accept.

A special international conference was convened at Evian in France in July 1938 to discuss the plight of the Jewish refugees. Representatives of more than thirty countries, including Britain, France and the United States, deplored the situation, but not one of them agreed to increase their national immigrant quotas. A number of countries even tightened their regulations.

Anti-Jewish legislation was extended; more concentration camps were established; synagogues were destroyed. When the Sudetenland region was transferred from Czechoslovakia to Germany, the area's Jews were expelled to Czechoslovakia, which refused to admit them. Many Jews were stranded for a time on an island in the middle of the Danube.

In October 1938, the Polish government revoked the citizenship of all Polish citizens who had lived abroad for five years or more, transforming 15,000 Polish Jews living in Germany into stateless residents. The Germans promptly organized special transports of Jews by train to the Polish frontier, where they were turned off the train and forced at gunpoint to walk into Poland. After examining the special papers which they had been given, showing they were Polish citizens, the Polish frontier guards let them into the country, where they found shelter with fellow Jews.

In Paris, a Polish Jew, Herzl Grynszpan, hearing about the

Kristallnacht, November 9, 1938. The crash of shattered glass of Jewish businesses and homes throughout Germany signalled the beginning of the end of European Jewry in the Holocaust of the Second World War. The synagogue of Börneplatz, Frankfurt, in flames. (*Museum of the Diaspora*)

suffering of his family at the hands of the Nazis, assassinated a German diplomat in November 1938. This was the signal for even greater anti-Jewish excesses, as synagogues, homes and shops were burnt and smashed all over Germany on the infamous *Kristallnacht,* "Night of Broken Glass." Many Jews were arrested and detained in the Dachau and Buchenwald concentration camps.

Horrible though it was, *Kristallnacht* was only the beginning. The campaign against the Jews was stepped up. It was to reach a climax in August 1942, when over 400,000 European Jews were murdered by the Nazis and their collaborators in a single month. Earlier, in 1941, there had been killings on almost the same scale, when the German army invaded Russia, systematically exterminating Jews wherever they found them.

By the end of the Second World War, an estimated six million Jews, a quarter of them children, had been murdered by the Nazis in what came to be known as "the Holocaust."

The destruction of a people. A Hungarian Jew sitting among the remnants of his possessions before deportation to Auschwitz, and Chana Lehrer, a young girl from Munich (*Yad Vashem*).

A small boy in Slonim, Poland (from Roman Vishniak's *A Vanished World*).

ON SEPTEMBER 1, 1939, the German army invaded Poland, bringing nearly two million more Jews under Nazi rule. While military
operations were still going on, the advancing Germans rounded
up hundreds of Jews, including children, and shot them on the
spot, or after mock trials. Synagogues were set on fire and Jews
who tried to save their Torah scrolls were shot or thrown into the
flames. Religious Jews had their beards shaved and were forced to
dance around bonfires of religious books.

New concentration camps were established on Polish soil and
thousands of Jews were imprisoned in them. At the same time,
walled-off ghettos were established in the major towns, the largest
being Warsaw. The Nazis always took special care with dates: the
Warsaw Ghetto was established by an edict on Rosh Hashanah, the
Jewish New Year, 1940.

There, in the neighbourhoods where 240,000 of the city's
360,000 Jews lived, a special Jewish location was created. The
Christians living in the area were forced to move out, and thousands more Jews were moved in, confined by walls and barbed
wire. By 1942, 430,000 Jews were living in the Warsaw Ghetto in
appallingly overcrowded conditions.

Administering the affairs of the Ghetto under Nazi supervision
was the Judenrat, the Jewish Council, the members of which were
faced with an impossible task. The natural tendency of most Jews
was to avoid collaboration with their oppressors; but, if they refused to co-operate, they and their families were liable to savage
reprisals. At the same time, many leaders of the Jewish community persuaded themselves that, if they served on the Council, they
might be able to ease the lot of their families and friends, and of the
Jews in general.

If the Jews of Warsaw felt ambivalent towards the members of
the Judenrat, they openly despised the Jewish police, recruited by
the Germans to keep order in the Ghetto. These people were certainly collaborators; but they also faced a dilemma, forced to
choose between their families and their neighbours.

German forces would patrol the Ghetto shooting people indis-
criminately. The population was systematically starved: Jews in
the Ghetto were permitted 194 calories per day, the Poles were
allowed 634, while the German occupation troops received 2,310

The Warsaw Ghetto, 1942. Photographer unknown.

calories per day. Some 40,000 Jews are estimated to have died from malnutrition.

Doctors were refused drugs, epidemics raged and heating was almost nonexistent. In such conditions, a black market flourished. Although smuggling was a capital offence, the food, fuel and other necessities smuggled in from outside the Ghetto ensured physical survival for many.

The attitude towards the smugglers was ambivalent: on the one hand, they were profiting from other people's misery and hardship; on the other, they were saving thousands of lives. Emmanuel Ringelblum, archivist of the Warsaw Ghetto, who saved records and documents throughout the entire period and kept a journal, *Notes from the Warsaw Ghetto*, suggested that a statue be erected to "the Smuggler." If his intention was ironic, it must have been only partly so. Later, smugglers were to play a vital role in supplying the Jews of the Ghetto with weapons, and the underground set up its own smuggling network.

Slave-labour factories were established in the Ghetto, where men were forced to make uniforms for the German army and other products. Often the minuscule wages earned at the factories were a family's only means of support, but Ringelblum recorded acts of sabotage even in the early years.

The Jewish tailors sent off a consignment of uniforms "with trousers sewn together, buttons on backwards, pockets upside down, sleeves reversed [the left sleeve where the right should be]." He continued: "The transport was returned from Berlin, and now the production department is all agog. There are threats of drastic punishment."

Despite the terrible conditions of death and malnutrition, dirt and disease, fear and corruption, a vibrant social and cultural life flourished in the Warsaw Ghetto. Four theatres performed in Hebrew, Polish and Yiddish; concerts were given; lectures were well-attended; schools and Hebrew classes were organized; newspapers were published.

Jewish welfare organizations operated: each block of houses

Jewish women are led through the streets of Budapest on their way to deportation, 1944. (*Beit Lohamei Haghetta'ot*)

Janusz Korczak and the Children, sculpture by Baruch Sakcier, a new immigrant to Israel from the Soviet Union, at Yad Vashem. (*Yad Vashem*)

had a charitable organization, with a soup kitchen dispensing to the needy. Until the United States declared war on Germany (after Pearl Harbor at the end of 1941), American Jews managed to send some money to Warsaw to relieve the hardship. A hospital tried to cope with disease; orphanages were established for the many children who had lost their parents.

On July 18, 1942, the children of the orphanage of Janusz Korczak, the world-famous educator, gave a performance of *The Dying Prince,* written by Korczak himself. That same day, Adam Czerniakow, chairman of the Jewish Council, announced that he had received assurances from the German authorities that there was no intention of moving the inhabitants of the Ghetto, who would be permitted to remain in Warsaw.

Four days later, the deportations began. Armed Ukrainian and Latvian guards surrounded the Ghetto walls, and other forces moved in. Adolf Berman, who was responsible for some of the orphanages, testified at the Eichmann trial:

> On that very first day, the victims were the Jewish children, and I shall never forget the harrowing scenes and blood-curdling incidents when the SS men most cruelly attacked children — children roaming in the streets; took them by force to carts, and I remember fully, those children were defending themselves. Even today the cries and shrieking of those children are clear in my mind.

The Jewish Council was assured that only unemployed Jews would be sent for "resettlement in the east" (as it was euphemistically called), initially convincing Czerniakow that only a maximum of 20,000 Jews would be deported. But, when the Germans demanded 6,000 Jews per day, and further said in reply to his question that the "resettlement" would continue seven days a week, Czerniakow realized what was really happening. On July 23, unwilling to co-operate in sending Jews to their deaths, but unable to refuse, he committed suicide.

Chaim Kaplan, a school principal, whose diary of life in the Ghetto has been published under the title, *Scroll of Agony,* wrote this account of the deportations:

From a display in the Chamber of the Holocaust, Mount Zion, Jerusalem. *Left:* a jar of Zyklon B, the poison gas used in the camps; *right:* soap rendered from human bodies. Underneath the cabinet are urns containing ashes from the camps. (*WZPS*)

The Ghetto has turned into an inferno. Men have become beasts. Everyone is but a step away from deportation; people are being hunted down in the streets like animals of the forest. It is the Jewish police who are cruellest towards the condemned. . . .

Whenever a house is blockaded a panic arises that is beyond the imagination. Residents who have neither documents nor money hide in nooks and crannies, in the cellars and in the attics.

The children in particular rend the heavens with their cries. The old people and the middle-aged deportees accept the judgement in silent submission and stand with their small parcels under their arms. But there is no limit to the sorrow and tears of the young women.

Janusz Korczak was one of several school and orphanage principals who could have escaped deportation, but refused to abandon their children and voluntarily accompanied them to the concentration camp.

The deportations continued until September 12, 1942, during which time some 300,000 Jews were taken to Treblinka and gassed. As the daily round-ups continued, Ringelblum kept records of what was going on, recounting many acts of resistance. When one Jew sprung at a German guard and half-strangled him, the man immediately shot him and thirteen others. Two Jewish porters, about to be shot, sprung at their killers, and 110 Jews were shot in reprisal. Whole groups of youngsters resisted arrest, fighting the soldiers with their bare hands.

Despite their isolation in ghettos, the Jews all over Poland knew what was happening to each other. Contact between the various ghettos was maintained by couriers, who risked their lives by travelling all over Poland with forged "Aryan" papers.

Ringelblum writes of two girls, Chaike and Frumke:

They are in mortal danger every day. They rely entirely on their "Aryan" faces and on the peasant kerchiefs that cover their heads. Without a murmur, without a second's hesitation, they accept and carry out the most dangerous missions. Is someone needed to travel to Vilna, Bialystok, Lvov, Kowel, Lublin, Czestochowa or Radom to smuggle in contraband such as illegal publications, goods, money?

The girls volunteer as if it is the most natural thing in the world. Are there comrades who have to be rescued from Vilna, Lublin or some other city? They undertake the mission. Nothing stands in their way, nothing deters them.

Frumke Plotnika was eventually hunted down to a cellar in Bedzin in August 1943; she died resisting, with her pistol in her hand. Chaike Grossman survived to fight in the Bialystok Ghetto and to join a kibbutz in Israel, where she became a member of the Knesset and one of the country's most respected citizens.

In August 1942, when the deportations had reached their height, Ringelblum buried his archives in tin boxes and sealed milk cans. The archivist and his friends (including Chaim Kaplan) were not sure that there would be any survivors from the Warsaw Ghetto, so they determined to do whatever they could to preserve a record of what had happened. In the event, their writings, reinforced by the accounts of the survivors, have been an invaluable source about these terrible events.

IN THE winter of 1941, Zionist groups in Warsaw had started organizing an underground, with the purpose of armed resistance. Most of the Jewish movements and organizations in the Ghetto were eventually involved in the underground; but the initiators were the pioneering Zionist youth movements, whose members had been training for a life of agricultural settlement in Palestine.

The young pioneers, who had already resolved on emigration, saw things more simply and directly than their elders. Dedicated to the principle of acting on their convictions, it was natural for them to begin planning a resistance movement.

Spearheading the drive was the left-wing socialist Zionist Hashomer Hatza'ir, led by a young man called Mordechai Anielewicz, who headed the attack on the German forces in January 1943. Among Ringelblum's many documents and diaries are some thumbnail sketches of leading personalities in the Ghetto. His memoir of Anielewicz, "Comrade Mordechai," gives us some information about the remarkable young man who became leader of the Warsaw Ghetto revolt.

The archivist describes him as a "young fellow, about twenty-five, of medium height, with a narrow, pale, pointed face and a pleasant appearance." He used to borrow books from Ringelblum — in particular books about Jewish history and economics.

Soon after the outbreak of war, Hashomer Hatza'ir started to organize educational and cultural activities for young people, providing both general and Jewish education. The leaders of the movement risked their lives, using forged documents, to visit areas outside Warsaw where Jews lived, distribute educational material and keep the groups going. Senior leaders from all over Poland attended the movement's seminars in Warsaw, sometimes walking several days to get there.

"I lectured several times at the Hashomer seminars," wrote Ringelblum. "When I peered into the glowing faces of the eager youth, I forgot that there was a war on in the world."

Once their singing and folk dancing attracted the attention of a German guard, who came to find out what was going on. He continued chatting to the youngsters until dawn.

The youth movement ran a "kibbutz" in Warsaw, with a communal kitchen for the members, who worked at a variety of jobs inside and outside the Ghetto, contributing their earnings to the common pool.

In the winter of 1941 – 42, Anielewicz organized a mass meeting of youth movement members which was addressed by Ringelblum on the "History of the Jewish Resistance Movement." In an interval between the lectures, Anielewicz took the lecturer into a private room and showed him two revolvers for training their members in the use of weapons. "That was the first step taken by Hashomer," recorded Ringelblum, "even before the creation of the Fighters' Organization."

Anielewicz quickly became commander of the Jewish Fighters' Organization, which mobilized fourteen Zionist and eight non-Zionist units. Ringelblum recalled that he was utterly single-minded about it, interrupting all his educational and cultural activities. According to the archivist, Anielewicz regretted the years he had "wasted" on educational work. He felt that, from the first days, he should have been training his members for fighting and "revenge against the greatest enemy of the Jews, of all mankind, and of all time."

Movingly Ringelblum recorded the paradox whereby,

> the older generation, with half a lifetime behind it, spoke, thought and concerned itself about surviving the war, dreamed about life. The youth — the best, the finest that the Jewish people possessed — spoke and thought only about an honourable death. They did not think about surviving the war. They did not procure Aryan papers for themselves. They had no dwellings on the other side. Their only concern was to discover the most dignified and honourable death, befitting an ancient people with a history stretching back over several thousand years.

When it was decided to try to resettle much of the communal leadership over on the Aryan side, Ringelblum wrote that Anielewicz remained very cool to the idea (although other accounts suggest that he encouraged noncombatants to escape). He preferred to use the limited money available for purchasing arms and equipment for the resistance.

He was, wrote the archivist, fiercely loyal to his youth movement friends. "For a fellow member he was ready to leap into a fire." In January 1943, he led a mission to rescue a member imprisoned by factory guards, just a few hours before the advance of the German troops into the Ghetto.

Anielewicz threw himself into the defence activity with all his zeal, reported Ringelblum. "He was not one of those leaders who sent others into the line of fire and themselves remained at a distance. In January 1943, he participated actively in the fighting. His revolver claimed German victims."

After the Germans were repulsed in January and again in February, Heinrich Himmler personally ordered the destruction of the Warsaw Ghetto. General Jurgen Stroop, who had gained experience fighting partisans in the Ukraine and the Balkans, was appointed to command the operation.

Meanwhile, the Jewish fighters continued to smuggle arms into the Ghetto via the sewers, burial parties which went out of the area and all other means possible.

Once again, the Nazi timing was remarkable: the operation to wipe out the Ghetto was set for April 19, 1943, the eve of Passover, the Jewish Festival of Freedom, which commemorates the exodus from Egypt. Alerted to the situation, the Ghetto underground met the previous evening under the chairmanship of Anielewicz. At the end of the meeting weapons, ammunition and food were distributed.

The entrances to the houses were barricaded with furniture, sandbags and pillows were placed in the windows, blue-and-white Zionist flags were hung out of buildings, and the all-night vigil began.

THE GERMANS had mobilized over 2,000 of their crack SS troops, supported by artillery, sappers, police and Polish, Latvian and Ukrainian auxiliaries for the operation. Opposing them were 600 organized Jewish underground fighters of both sexes. Several hundred other Jews — the so-called wild groups — also participated in the armed struggle, and thousands resisted passively, refusing to give themselves up voluntarily, when the Germans came to round them up for deportation.

In armament, the discrepancy was even greater. The Germans had thirteen heavy machine-guns, sixty-nine light machine-guns, 135 submachine-guns, 1,258 rifles, howitzers and artillery; they were also able to deploy tanks, panzer vehicles (armoured personnel carriers) and — on two occasions at least — aircraft. Against this the Jews had acquired two submachine-guns, seventeen rifles, pistols, hand-grenades and fire-bombs consisting of petroleum-filled bottles. They had also laid some primitive, improvised mines.

The German plan was to liquidate the Ghetto in three days, and give a *Judenrein* (Jew-free) Warsaw to the Führer as a "birthday present" on April 20.

At six o'clock on the morning of April 19, the attack was launched. After their earlier experiences, the Germans sent in auxiliaries and Jewish police first. Jewish police who refused to participate were shot. The German units followed with trucks, panzer vehicles, heavy machine-guns, ambulances and a field kitchen.

As the troops advanced into the Ghetto, they were stopped at two locations by Jewish fighting units, hidden behind windows, balconies and attics, who directed a hail of bullets, fire-bombs and hand-grenades at them.

In the first engagement, the attacking troops fled in a panic, and, when they regrouped and advanced to retrieve their dead and wounded, they were again driven back by a fierce hail of missiles. Jewish fighters came out into the open to fire with their pistols. German reinforcements arrived and began shooting chaotically at the houses where the Jewish fighters were holed up, but they too were forced to withdraw.

In the second location, four resistance groups permitted the Jewish police to pass, only opening fire when the Germans and Ukrainians arrived. The troops fled, seeking shelter, and the Jews fired on their hiding-places. Germans and Ukrainians struggled with each other in their haste to gain cover, until SS officers, using whips, forced the Ukrainians back to their positions.

The Germans now brought in three tanks; but the lead tank was immediately hit by fire-bombs and put out of action. The other two withdrew. As the Germans retreated there was a burst of jubilation from the Jews. An eyewitness account related: ''Those faces, which only yesterday reflected terror and despair, now shone with an unusual joy difficult to describe. This was a joy free from all personal motives, a joy imbued with a pride that the Ghetto was fighting.''

At this point General Stroop took over personal command of the action, ordering his forces to advance cautiously, one building at a time. He also laid down an artillery barrage on the houses where the Jews were positioned.

The Jewish forces fought back; but pistols and bottles were no match for artillery, and they were forced to withdraw. Before they retreated, they set fire to a large warehouse to prevent anything of value falling into German hands.

In the afternoon, a large German force drove Jewish fighters from a block of buildings, but they managed to withdraw, via roofs and attics, and regroup. Unable to dislodge the Jewish fighters permanently, Stroop withdrew his forces at nightfall.

In his report to Himmler, Stroop admitted:

At our first penetration into the Ghetto, the Jews and Polish bandits succeeded, with arms in hand, in repulsing our attacking forces, including the tanks and panzers.

The tank was twice set on fire. This attack caused the withdrawal of the units. The losses during the first attack were twelve men.

In her testimony at the Eichmann trial, one of the fighters, Zivia Lubetkin, said:

The rejoicing among the Jewish fighters was great and, see the wonder and miracle, those German heroes retreated, afraid and terrorized by the home-made Jewish bombs and hand-grenades.

After an hour we saw the officer urging his soldiers to collect the dead and wounded. But they did not move, they did not collect their dead and wounded. We took their arms later. Thus on the first day, we the few with our poor arms drive the Germans from the Ghetto.

The Jewish forces, who only lost one man that first day, received twenty-two rifles from the Home Army, a Polish underground organization. Unfortunately the Home Army, riddled with anti-Jewish sentiment, did not always prove so helpful to the Jewish fighters.

That night the Jews of the Warsaw Ghetto celebrated the *Seder* (festive meal) commemorating the exodus from Egypt. Amid the destruction, families sat and read the *Haggadah,* which tells the story of the Children of Israel leaving slavery to achieve freedom.

ON THE second day, the Germans delivered an ultimatum to the Jewish fighters, demanding that they lay down their arms, or the Ghetto would be razed. When this was rejected by the Jewish underground, the Germans brought up truckloads of troops and police.

Once again these forces were attacked by the Jewish fighters with deadly effect, forcing the Germans to bring up tanks. One tank was again put out of action with a fire-bomb, but the others subjected the Jewish positions to a fierce bombardment. Having destroyed the houses, the German forces now charged into the ruins with machine-guns and grenades, meeting fierce resistance. After using up all their ammunition, some Jews were taken prisoner.

The same day, the Germans broke into a hospital, where they shot all the sick lying in the beds. They then went through the wards killing everyone they found, before setting the hospital on fire.

In one area, Stroop himself, heavily ringed by troops, personally conducted operations. After a large number of Germans were killed and wounded by an improvised mine, the Germans proposed a fifteen-minute ceasefire to enable them to collect their dead and wounded. The local Jewish leaders rejected the request with contempt, particularly as the SS were setting houses alight as the offer was being made.

Stroop was now moving cautiously. Under cover of heavy shellfire, his forces were attacking one house at a time, blowing up each position and setting it on fire. Many Jews jumped from the buildings onto mattresses that they threw into the streets below; but others managed to escape via the attics and rooftops. In many cases, evacuated positions were reoccupied after the Germans had gone past.

Leon Najberg, a fighter who survived the war, wrote in his diary:

> Each house in the Ghetto is a defensive fortress, each apartment is a citadel. Jewish defenders are showering missiles from windows . . . the defenders are passing through attics from one street to another, recapturing places threatened by the German bandits. The murderers have introduced flame-throwers, setting houses on fire.

In another part of the Ghetto two German factory managers had suggested that the soldiers keep away, as they were sure that their Jews would agree to be deported voluntarily. They miscalculated: not only did the Jews refuse, but when a German force did finally come to the factories, they attacked it.

The same day, the left-wing Polish underground movement, the People's Guard, launched an attack on one of the German artillery positions, killing the crew and silencing the gun. Workers and students also attempted to blast a breach in the Ghetto wall so that

Jews could escape; but they failed to do so, although they killed two Germans and two Polish policemen.

ON THE third day, the Germans started to burn the Ghetto down systematically. Thousands of unarmed Jews were rounded up, after fleeing from the burning houses; but the underground fighters continued their resistance from a network of cellars and bunkers, often connected via the sewers.

The Jewish underground issued a defiant communiqué: "Realizing that in armed combat they will not crush the resistance of the Jewish fighters, the Germans decided to destroy them by fire." There followed a description of the hundreds of women and children being burned alive or suffocated by the smoke, people leaping from windows "like lighted torches."

The underground also managed to put up posters on the Aryan side, describing the battles and calling on the Poles to join in the struggle against "our common enemy." Except for the attack on the artillery position and the attempt to breach the Ghetto wall, the response was minimal.

The fires continued to rage on April 23, and Stroop wrote a report to his superiors, stating, "The action will be completed this very day." Sappers went through the streets, blowing up the houses one by one. Overhead, aircraft dropped incendiary bombs. The Jewish fighters responded by setting fire to the German factories and workshops in the ghetto.

Anielewicz wrote to his colleague Yitzhak Zuckerman, who was on the Aryan side:

> What we have lived through here is beyond description. All we know is that what has happened has surpassed our most daring expectations. . . . I have a feeling that great things are happening, that what we have undertaken is of tremendous significance.

He then went on to report on the change of tactics because of the fires. The fighting groups would stop seeking confrontations with the Germans, concentrating instead on reconnaissance, sabotage and the capture of weapons. Pistols were of no use, he informed his comrade; grenades, rifles, machine-guns and explosives were needed.

The young leader wrote:

> It is impossible to describe the conditions under which Jews in the Ghetto are living today. Only a few will survive. All others will perish sooner or later. Their fate is sealed. In practically all the bunkers where thousands of Jews are hiding it is impossible to light a candle for lack of air.

On the night of April 23 – 24, Anielewicz sent out his first new-style group, wearing captured German uniforms, their feet muffled with rags. The following day a group was sent to the Aryan side to try to arrange for an evacuation of the fighters, but it ran into a German patrol and all but one of the members were killed.

When the battle had been raging for a week, Anielewicz wrote: "We are nearing our last days, but so long as we have weapons in our hands we shall continue to fight and resist."

On the night of April 27 – 28, the leadership of the Jewish Fighters' Organization resolved to start evacuating members to join the partisans outside the Ghetto. A woman leader, Regina Fudin, assembled a group of forty armed members and led them through the sewers to the Aryan side, from where they were taken by truck to the forest of Lomianka, some five miles from Warsaw. A subsequent party emerged from the sewers straight into a German ambush. In the ensuing battle, all of them were killed.

Even the German action in flooding the sewers, which were a main channel of communication and where many Jews were holed up, was foiled when a group of fighters blew out the valves.

On April 30, the twelfth day of the battle, when it seemed sure that the Jews could not hold out any longer, new groups of fighters appeared in locations which had been peaceful and gave battle to the Germans. On the following day, the Jews celebrated May Day, gathering in their bunkers, listening to speakers and singing songs. At the same time, they stepped up the resistance, sending groups dressed in German uniforms to engage the enemy.

The baffled Stroop reported:

> Over and over again, battle groups, consisting of twenty to thirty or more Jewish fellows, eighteen to twenty-five years of age, accom-

panied by a corresponding number of women, kindled new resistance. These battle groups were under orders to put up armed resistance to the last, and if necessary to escape arrest by committing suicide.

He was particularly impressed by the women fighters, who fired their pistols with two hands and who concealed grenades in their clothes, suddenly throwing them at unsuspecting Germans.

ON MAY 8, the Germans finally reached the underground headquarters at 18 Mila Street and surrounded all five exits. Some 300 civilians who were living there surrendered; but the eighty fighters, led by Anielewicz, refused to give up even when the Germans bombarded the exits.

When the Germans pumped gas into the bunker, many Jews committed suicide; others came out fighting. Anielewicz was among those who met their deaths that day.

As German troops combed through the Ghetto, destroying all the buildings still standing and hunting survivors, the resistance went on. The organized underground was no more, but individuals and small groups of fighters continued to give battle to the Germans. Starving, in rags, almost without weapons, finding it increasingly difficult to breathe in the burning Ghetto, they nevertheless fought on.

On May 16, Stroop announced that, with the blowing up of the Warsaw Synagogue, "the Warsaw Ghetto is no more." But even then survivors lingered on, starving in bunkers. Leon Najberg was among those who survived, managing to cross to the Aryan side in September.

In October, the Germans brought in several hundred Jews from the Auschwitz concentration camp to clean up the Ghetto area. A survivor of this group recalled later that he and his colleagues discovered a bunker with the fresh remains of a meal and a book of Sholem Aleichem on the table, proving that some groups were still holding out.

In June 1944, a unit of armed Jews killed three German police in the ruins of the Ghetto. The police rounded up and shot twenty-five Jews. This was the last report of a Jewish fighting force, but individual Jews survived in their bunkers to join the Polish uprising in Warsaw in August 1944.

GHETTO ARCHIVIST Emmanuel Ringelblum was deported to the Trawinki camp, but was rescued by the underground and reunited with his family in a bunker on the Aryan side of Warsaw. He continued with his writing and storing documents. In March 1944, the bunker was discovered and the Ringelblum family was arrested with the others.

Taken to the ruins of the Warsaw Ghetto, tortured and forced to watch the execution of his wife and son, he refused to betray underground secrets or disclose the whereabouts of the archives. He was shot. One part of the Ringelblum archives was dug up after the war in 1946; a second collection was found in 1950. Chaim Kaplan's diary was only discovered a decade later.

THE WARSAW GHETTO battle inspired other Jewish acts of resistance all over Europe. A survivor of the Treblinka concentration camp, Stanislaw Kon, wrote:

> There arrived in Treblinka the last transports of Jews from the Warsaw Ghetto. Unlike the men, women and children of previous transports these were not broken and defeated. Instead of tears in their eyes, they brought grenades and other explosives in their pockets.

The revolt in Treblinka occurred in August 1943. The rebels managed to blow up the ammunition store and set most of the camp alight. Some of them fought with weapons they had acquired; but many fought with blunt instruments and their bare hands. Less than 200 of the 700 workers escaped, and only a dozen of those survived.

Later, in September, a group of thirteen Jews, who were put to dismantling the camp, killed one of their Ukrainian guards. Their leader, an eighteen-year-old, put on the dead guard's uniform and "marched" his comrades out of the camp to freedom.

No less remarkable was the fighting in the Bialystok Ghetto, which raged for four days in August 1943. There were only 40,000 Jews left in the Ghetto, when the Nazis arrived to conduct the final

Abba Kovner (1918–1988), a commander of the Vilna Ghetto, a resistance fighter and partisan in Lithuania. He became one of Israel's leading poets and originated the idea behind the Museum of the Diaspora, Tel Aviv. (*Museum of the Diaspora*)

deportations on August 16. They were swiftly driven into an area of narrow streets, lined with single-storey houses.

The 500 Jewish fighters planned to storm the Ghetto wall, hoping to facilitate the mass escape of several thousand; but this operation failed. Nevertheless, with pathetically few weapons, they held out until August 20, and the Germans had to call in tanks to complete the "evacuation."

In October 1943, a group of 600 prisoners at the Sobibor concentration camp made a rush for the weapons store, but were cut off by automatic fire. They then charged the main gate, hurling stones and seizing the rifles of the guards. Four hundred broke out of the camp, about half of whom were blown up in the surrounding mine field. Others were pursued and killed by German troops and local Polish forces. Some sixty survived to join the Russian partisans.

Jewish resistance groups existed in almost every ghetto and concentration camp. Thousands of Jews fought with the partisans in occupied Europe—many of them ghetto survivors who managed to find the resilience to continue the struggle against the Nazis even after they had already fought beyond the call of bravery.

One of them, Abba Kovner, a leader of the resistance in the Vilna Ghetto, later became an important partisan commander and participated in the liberation of Vilna. He subsequently came to Israel, where with other former fighters he founded Kibbutz Lohamei Hagetaot (The Ghetto Fighters Kibbutz) in western Galilee. He became one of the most important teachers of the history of the Holocaust, and its foremost poet.

THE GHETTO fighters have given a new meaning to words like bravery, courage, pride, dignity and honour. Historian Cecil Roth wrote of the Holocaust: "It is difficult for the mind to grasp, or the pen to convey, the magnitude of the catastrophe."

Echoing his words, it can indeed be said that it is difficult for the mind to grasp or the pen to convey the unbelievable spirit of the ghetto warriors, who transformed the word *ghetto* from a concept of shame and humiliation to a badge of glory and honour.

Certainly Jewish history knows nothing more heroic. No

fighters, anywhere, at any time, have surpassed their achievements. Starved, decimated, humiliated and degraded, yet somehow rising from the profoundest depths of despair, they lit a fire that will blaze in people's hearts as long as human beings exist on this earth.

11 ⌒

Hannah Szenes: Hidden Strength

⌒ S HE WAS by all accounts an un-usually intelligent girl, talented, attractive and warm-hearted; but nothing in her personality and upbringing gives a hint of the extraordinary qualities of courage and steadfastness she was later to demonstrate. Although she was not a national leader, Hannah Szenes, who, at the age of twenty-three, parachuted on a rescue mission behind Nazi lines in Europe, kept silent under torture, and was executed by firing squad in a Hungarian prison on November 7, 1944, fully deserves her place of honour in the annals of Jewish heroism.

Hannah grew up in a comfortable, middle-class, assimilated Jewish home in Budapest. Her father, Bela Szenes, a successful playwright and newspaper columnist, died of a heart attack when Hannah was not quite six years old. Nevertheless, her childhood seems to have been a happy one, judging from the diary which Hannah kept from the age of thirteen. Reading the diaries, we see her develop from a very normal, if bright, schoolgirl, into a formidably purposeful young woman.

"Blessed is the match consumed in kindling flame." Hannah Szenes and five other Jewish parachutists from Palestine were executed by the Germans in 1944 when they dropped into occupied Europe with the aim of organizing resistance and rescuing Jews. (*Zionist Archives*)

Her Jewishness is at first marginal. Aged fifteen, attending synagogue on Rosh Hashanah, the Jewish New Year, she affirmed her belief in God, continuing, "Actually I'm relatively clear on the subject of religion too, because the Jewish fits in best with my way of thinking."

In 1937, at the age of sixteen, she was furious at being disqualified from a position to which she had been elected in the school Literary Society because of her Jewishness:

> Had I not been elected I would not have said a word, but this way it was a decided insult. Now I don't want to take part in, or have anything to do with, the work of the society, and don't care about it any more.

But for the most part, the diary is filled with accounts of holidays in the mountains, dances, parties, tennis, theatre performances, books she was reading and declarations of love from various boys, which she did not take too seriously.

There is not much indication of the rise of Nazism or the approach of the Second World War. In July 1938, when she was seventeen, her brother George, one year older, left to study in France. She was upset at his leaving, for her mother's sake as much as for her own: "I know she is crushed, but sure this is best for George — as far as anyone can tell these days." The last phrase is the first real indication in the diary that the situation in Hungary was potentially menacing.

Her social life continued; her mother showed Hannah's poems to a literary journalist, who pronounced them "better than average," and told her that she might become a writer, but not necessarily a poet. By September, she was increasingly concerned with the imminent war, while affirming: "I still believe there will be peace, perhaps only because I just can't possibly imagine war."

And then, suddenly, in an entry dated October 27, 1938: "I don't know whether I've already mentioned that I've become a Zionist." She noted that for her this meant that "I now consciously and strongly feel I am a Jew and am proud of it. My primary aim is to go to Palestine and work for it."

Although she wrote that her Zionism developed over some three years, it must have crystallized for her that winter, because her diary dealt increasingly with the subject: "The thought that now occupies my every waking moment is Palestine. Everything in connection with it interests me, everything else is entirely secondary." She and her mother went to France to visit her brother George, and she discovered that he had also become "an ardent Zionist."

In July 1939, just after her eighteenth birthday, she was overwhelmed with joy at receiving an immigration certificate for Palestine. While understanding her mother's ambivalence, she was grateful for her understanding: "Not many mothers would behave as she does."

She arrived at Moshav Nahalal in the Jezreel valley, where she attended agricultural college, enjoying the work, loving the land, but missing her mother and brother. She was not unaware of what was going on in the world. In May 1940, she asked herself: "How can I have the patience to study and prepare for an exam while the greatest war in history is raging in Europe?"

Yet, two months later there was a lyrical description of a visit to Galilee, the River Jordan and Lake Kinneret. For two weeks she forgot about the war, she confessed. She was courted by Moshe (but would not let him kiss her), and read the Hebrew poems of Rachel and Marx's *Das Kapital*.

Alex, another young man, proposed marriage; but she gently turned him down, feeling that the simple, pleasant life she would live with him would not fulfil or satisfy her. She speculated on her future, anticipating kibbutz life "for a year or two," but believing that her talent for leadership would eventually propel her into education, or even politics.

"Sometimes I feel I am an emissary who has been entrusted with a mission," she wrote in April 1941. "I feel I have a duty towards others, as if I was obligated to them."

On the completion of her studies in Nahalal she decided, after a certain amount of hesitation, to join Kibbutz Sdot Yam, near Caesarea. A poem written at that time expressed her love for the land and her consciousness of the heritage of her people:

> Hush, cease all sound.
> Across the sea is the sand,
> The shore known and dear

The shore golden, dear,
Home, the homeland.

But reaching the city of ruins
Soft a few words we intone.
We return. We are here.
Soft answers the silence of stone,
We awaited you two thousand years.

During this period, her diary expressed doubts about settling down permanently with the group, and then, in January 1943, there was this remarkable entry: "I've had a shattering week. I was suddenly struck by the idea of going to Hungary. I feel I must be there in these days in order to help organize youth emigration, and also to get my mother out." She was fully aware of the "absurdity" of the idea, but less than two months later she talked to a man who was organizing a group to attempt the rescue of Jews from Europe.

The group was formed. Its members were inducted into the British army and trained. She was absolutely determined to go and was duly recruited. "I pray for only one thing," she wrote. "That the period of waiting will not be too long and that I can see action soon. As for the rest — I am afraid of nothing. I'm totally self-confident, ready for anything."

Her brother George arrived in Haifa on the day she was due to leave for Egypt to start her mission, and her departure was postponed for twenty-four hours to allow them to be together. Later she sent him several letters from Cairo, explaining about life in Palestine, reassuring him about her safety and expressing concern about their mother.

She also wrote to the secretary of her kibbutz:

I leave happily of my own free will, with full knowledge of the difficulties ahead. I consider my mission a privilege and at the same time a duty. Everywhere, and under all conditions, the thought that all of you are behind us will help.

In March 1944, hours before parachuting into Yugoslavia, she wrote to her kibbutz comrades: "On sea, land, in the air, in war and in peace, we are all advancing toward the same goal. Each of us will stand at his post. There is no difference between my task and that of another."

"We came unto the land whither thou sentest us and surely it floweth with milk and honey; and this is the fruit of it" (Numbers 13:27). The spies in Canaan: *The Promised Land* by Henrik van Cleeve, 1525–1589, oil on wood. *(Israel Museum)*

"Then spake Joshua to the Lord . . . Sun, stand thou still upon Gibeon; and thou, Moon, in the valley of Ajalon" (Joshua 10:12). The valley of Ajalon. *(Werner Braun)*

"And the Lord discomfited Sisera, and all his chariots, and all his host" (Judges 4:15). Deborah, the only female prophet, and Barak, her general, defeated Sisera's army on Mount Tabor. *(David Harris)*

Samson fighting the lion. Illustration from the *Machzor Lipsiae* Festival prayer book, South Germany, fourteenth century. *(Israel Museum)*

"And Samson went and caught three hundred foxes" (Judges 15:4): the desert fox *(Vulpes vulpes)*. *(Werner Braun)*

King David. Detail from a tapestry by Marc Chagall hanging in the foyer of the Knesset, Israel's parliament building, Jerusalem. *(David Harris)*

"David ran, and stood upon the Philistine, and took his sword . . . and cut off his head therewith" (I Samuel 17:51). David and Goliath from *Sefer Emet,* an illuminated manuscript, Italy, fifteenth century. *(Israel Museum)*

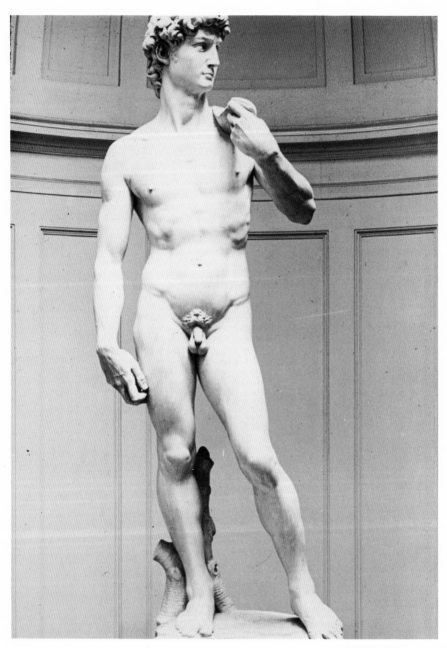

Michelangelo's *David,* Galleria dell'Accademia, Florence, completed in 1504. Perhaps the best-known figure in biblical iconography. *(The Bridgeman Art Library)*

The Cave of Letters, Nahal Hever in the Judean desert. Professor Yigael Yadin and his team of archaeologists unearth artifacts dating from the time of Bar-Kokhba, leader of the Jewish revolt against the Romans, 132–135 A.D. *(David Harris)*

The clifftop fortress of Masada, the palace built by King Herod, overlooking the Dead Sea. Nine hundred sixty Jews chose suicide rather than surrender to the Romans, in 73 A.D., three years after the fall of the Temple in Jerusalem. *(Werner Braun)*

Aerial view of Tel Hai. At this colony in northern Israel Joseph Trumpeldor met his death while fighting off Arab attackers in 1920. *(David Harris)*

"Leshana haba'a be'yerushalayim" — "Next Year in Jerusalem" — the millennia-old Jewish prayer. Illustration from the "Bird's Head" Passover Haggadah, Germany, *c.* 1300. *(Israel Museum)*

The "Roaring Lion" memorial to the defenders of Tel Hai. Avraham Melnikoff, granite, 1926. *(David Harris)*

The residence of the Aaronson family, Zichron Ya'acov. In this house Sarah Aaronson took her own life rather than reveal British military information to the Turks. *(David Harris)*

Memorial to Jewish resistance at Kibbutz Yad Mordechai. Mordechai Anielewicz, commander of the Warsaw Ghetto, with the kibbutz water tower, shattered during Israel's War of Independence, in the background. *(Werner Braun)*

The Hall of Remembrance at Yad Vashem, Jerusalem, Israel's central institution for research into the Holocaust and its commemoration. *(Werner Braun)*

Acre jail, the central British prison during the mandate. In this prison Dov Gruner was hanged and dozens of members of the IZL escaped in a spectacular prison break in 1947. *(David Harris)*

"Ammunition Hill," site of one of the bloodiest battles of the 1967 Six Day War, when the Jerusalem Brigade met the Arab Legion in hand-to-hand fighting. The reconstructed site is now a war memorial. *(Werner Braun)*

Military cemetery on Mount Herzl, Jerusalem. Many of Israel's war dead are buried on this quiet hillside, which is also the site of the tomb of Theodor Herzl, the seer of the Jewish state. *(Werner Braun)*

"They told us it was the eyes of the country." In these words, a young Israeli sergeant explained how he understood that the peak of Mount Hermon, straddling Israel and Syria, had to be recaptured in the Yom Kippur War of 1973. *(Werner Braun)*

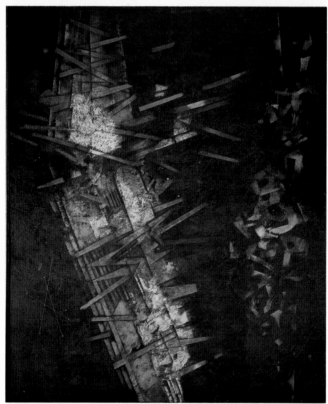

Entebbe, triptych by Mordechai Ardon. The left-hand canvas shows the hijacking; the middle, the release of the captives; and the right, Jacob's ladder as the spirit of redemption. *(David Harris)*

As THE fate of the Jews in countries occupied by the Nazis became known, the Jewish Agency, the embryo government of the Jewish community in Palestine, presented numerous plans to the British mandatory authorities for the despatch of Jewish volunteers to Europe. One plan called for dropping units into Poland to smuggle arms into the ghettos, another for supplying the ghettos with arms by submarine.

More than 30,000 Palestinian Jews were already enlisted in the British army; but when a group of Jewish women arrived from Poland in 1942, with more detailed news of the Holocaust, the Yishuv resolved to mount a rescue operation.

The Haganah, the Jewish self-defence organization, wanted to send volunteers to organize fighting units of young Jews — particularly young Zionists — who would conduct partisan resistance against the Germans. At the same time, noncombatants should somehow be smuggled out. These ideas were reinforced by reports of the heroic resistance in Warsaw and the other ghettos and camps.

After initially vetoing all the proposals, the British became convinced, by the summer of 1943, that they needed people to co-ordinate with the partisan movements in the Balkans and northern Italy. The Haganah proposed that hundreds of parachutists be dropped behind the lines, but the British whittled down the scale of the operation. The British authorities eventually agreed that thirty-two Palestinian volunteers could go, which meant that anything they managed to organize would only be on a small scale.

Furthermore, they insisted that the first task of the volunteers, who were formally British soldiers, was to assist Allied pilots who had been shot down to escape; the second was to help organize local resistance. Only after accomplishing these two missions were the Palestinian volunteers free to make contact with the Jewish communities, in order to attempt the rescue of some of the million Jews still thought to be alive in Hungary, Romania and Czechoslovakia.

The parachutists were trained by the British army in Cairo, and at the same time the Jewish Agency established a briefing centre in Haifa, where they interviewed new arrivals from Europe, building up a picture of contemporary life there, to ensure that the volunteers were well-informed.

"The Flag Revolt," Benghazi, North Africa, October 1943. Jewish-Palestinian soldiers in the British army demanded the right to fly their own flag beside that of Britain. (*Museum of the Diaspora*)

A group of parachutists from Palestine at an airfield in Slovakia before departing on a mission.

Apart from Hannah, there was one other woman in the group, Haviva Reik, who was parachuted into Czechoslovakia with two others. They established a transit camp for escaping Allied airmen and Russian prisoners, and helped set up a local Jewish underground force. All three were captured after a month and executed.

Another member of the group was Italian Enzo Sereni, the son of the personal physician of the King of Italy. After immigrating to Palestine, he had helped to found a kibbutz and was active in the Labour movement. Sociologist and philosopher, he was a man of great personal charm.

Before joining the parachutists, Sereni had already served with the Allies as a saboteur in Italy in the early stages of the war, and later produced an anti-Fascist newspaper in Egypt for Italian prisoners of war. Parachuting into northern Italy, he was captured by the SS and sent to the Dachau concentration camp, where he met his death.

Reuven Dafne, today the director of Yad Vashem, Israel's memorial to the Holocaust in Jerusalem, was one of the thirty-two. He has written extensively about the mission, and in one of his accounts he recalled the arguments between Hannah and Sereni, before the group's departure.

One of their disputes was about the existence of God. Although she had written earlier of her belief, Hannah had apparently become an agnostic by then, and she argued forcefully against the more mature and experienced Sereni, who was postulating the existence of God.

Listening to the discussion, Dafne was amazed at her self-assurance and afterwards remarked to Sereni that she would be a difficult colleague. "She certainly won't be easy to work with," agreed Sereni. "But believe me — and don't ever forget it — she's an unusual girl."

According to Dafne, Hannah was indeed difficult, but she was fearless, never considering the possibility of failure, or permitting her colleagues to become discouraged. Her inner conviction, recorded Dafne, reassured the others. He recalled her enthusiasm when they were informed that the mission was due to depart. "She sang the whole way back to the village where we were quartered, and made us sing along with her."

The picture that emerges both from the diaries and from Dafne's recollections is of an earnest, passionate, purposeful young woman, serious and almost grim. But Yoel Palgi, another member of the group, introduces us to a rather different Hannah Szenes, cheerful, laughing, almost frivolous.

Reassuring Palgi about parachuting, she said, "It's nothing. You go up in a plane, you jump, and you're right back on the ground." She then kept the party cheerful on the road to Egypt, joking with the British soldiers accompanying them, as well as with her colleagues.

When they returned from their mission, she told them, they would fly over Palestine in a big bomber, and each of them would parachute out over his or her settlement. Once in Sinai, she resolved that this was a good time for her to learn to drive, and, overriding the objections of her comrades, she took the wheel. After a few hundred yards of careful driving, she speeded up, gaining in confidence all the time, and drove most of the way to Egypt.

All the accounts of her colleagues stress that she was wilful and difficult to work with. However, on several occasions it was Hannah who prevented them from clashing with German patrols. "That is not what we came for," she lectured them. "We must save ourselves for our mission, not place our lives in jeopardy."

DAFNE, WHO parachuted into Yugoslavia with Hannah, later recalled the amazement of the British soldiers in the parachute store at discovering that one of the volunteers was a woman. "If I told it to my Jewish friends, they wouldn't believe me," said a Scottish sergeant.

In the plane, according to Dafne, Hannah's face was aglow, exuding happiness and excitement. "She winked at me and waved her hand encouragingly, and a delightful impish smile enveloped her features."

They spent three months together in Yugoslavia with the partisans, later meeting up with Yoel Palgi among others. The command structure of the volunteers seems to have been flexible — one account describes each of the thirty-two as "his own commanding officer" — but Hannah clearly occupied a special position in the group. When she encountered members of the partisan high command, she earned their respect.

"Hannah was unmistakably our leader," wrote Palgi. "She was the only woman who ever parachuted into Yugoslavia from a friendly country, and she knew how to talk to a general as well as to a private."

When some of the parachutists attended a partisan festival in a Yugoslav village, it was Hannah, neat in her British army uniform, her pistol strapped to her side, who spoke for them. Her greetings, translated by Dafne, were enthusiastically received by the crowd. Afterwards she joined the circles of folk-dancers, quickly picking up the rhythm and dancing for several hours.

Later, during a surprise encounter between a partisan unit and German soldiers, they were forced to flee for their lives. Hiding in the bushes, they saw the approach of a German unit. Dafne recalled that his finger tightened on the trigger, but Hannah firmly and quietly reminded him of the real purpose of their mission and persuaded him not to shoot.

Palgi found that Hannah Szenes in Yugoslavia was different from the girl he had come to know in Palestine: "She was cold, sharp, her reasoning now razor-edged." She suspected that the partisans were not really interested in helping them with their real mission — that of saving Jews.

While the parachutists were in Yugoslavia, the Germans occupied Hungary. Up to that time, only some eight percent of Hungary's million Jews had been deported or detained in work camps. The Germans had not formally occupied Hungary, and their regent, Miklós Horthy, had to some extent protected his country's Jews. They were certainly better off than their fellow Jews in the rest of Europe.

The German occupation was carried out, at least in part, because of the dissatisfaction of the Germans with the way Hungary was "solving its Jewish problem." Now, with the Germans directly in control and an extremist pro-Nazi government installed, the Jews of Hungary faced deadly peril.

Hannah was dreadfully upset by the news and became even more impatient to cross into her native Hungary. "We are the only ones who can possibly help," she insisted. "We don't have the right to think of our own safety; we don't have the right to hesitate."

Meeting with Jewish partisans, Hannah was deeply moved and prompted to write the poem *Blessed Is the Match,* which she gave to Dafne just before they parted on the Hungarian border in June 1944:

> Blessed is the match consumed in kindling flame.
> Blessed is the flame that burns in the secret fastness of the heart.
> Blessed is the heart with strength to stop its beating for honour's sake.
> Blessed is the match consumed in kindling flame.

Dafne saw Hannah for the last time when she crossed into Hungary. She was in high spirits, he recalled, bubbling with joy, joking and recalling funny incidents that had happened to them in Yugoslavia.

Shortly before crossing the border, Hannah finally confessed to Palgi her inner doubts. She realized, she told him, that she was not always sensible, but she could not wait on the sidelines while thousands were being slaughtered.

"Each of us is free to act as he thinks best," she said, "and I quite understand the way you feel about discipline. But for me this is not a question that can be decided by authority."

Soon after this, Hannah realized that she was not going to get any help from the partisans in entering Hungary, but was still determined to go. She met a group of three refugees: two Jews who were hoping to reach Palestine and a non-Jewish Frenchman. The three of them agreed to return with her to Hungary.

They crossed the border and reached a Hungarian village. Hannah and the Frenchman hid nearby, while the two others went forward to reconnoitre. Stopped by Hungarian police, one of the boys shot himself. The villagers then betrayed Hannah and her companion, who were immediately surrounded and captured.

Hannah managed to hide her radio transmitter before she was caught, but the police found a pair of earphones in the pocket of one of the boys. A search then turned up the transmitter.

During her first, brutal interrogation, Hannah, who refused to disclose anything under torture, fell into a trap. An interrogator told her that one of the boys had confessed about the radio and would be executed the following day. "He had nothing to do with the matter," declared Hannah. "The radio is mine."

This, of course, led to further tortures. She was beaten all over her body, whipped on the soles of her feet and the palms of her hands. During one of the sessions, a tooth was knocked out.

Her interrogators were interested in discovering the British radio code so that they could send out false information, luring Allied bombers into traps. But nothing that they did to her could make her disclose the code, so they brought her to Budapest in a final attempt to make her talk.

CATHERINE SZENES, Hannah's mother, who was still in Budapest, had absolutely no idea why she was being arrested. She was told that she was needed at military headquarters "as a witness." When she was questioned about her children, she informed her interrogator that Hannah was "at an agricultural settlement in the vicinity of Haifa."

She was shattered to learn that her daughter was in the next room. If she did not persuade her daughter to tell everything she knew, she was informed, this would be their last meeting.

Catherine Szenes wrote later:

> Had I not known she was coming, perhaps in the first moment I would not have recognized the Hannah of five years ago. Her once soft, wavy hair hung in a filthy tangle, her ravaged face reflected untold suffering, her large, expressive eyes were blackened, and there were ugly welts on her cheeks and neck.

Hannah threw herself into her mother's arms, crying, "Mother, forgive me!" Mother and daughter were left alone together for a few minutes, during which Hannah confirmed that George was safe in Palestine and reassured her mother that she was not to blame for her return to Hungary. Catherine was then released with the warning that she would be summoned again if her daughter did not confess.

Before long, she was arrested again and imprisoned in the same establishment as her daughter. Also in the prison was Hannah's fellow parachutist, Yoel Palgi, who had entered Hungary separately and had also been captured. Palgi and Catherine both subsequently met Hannah in prison and heard about her from the other prisoners. Both survived the war. From their accounts it is possible to reconstruct Hannah's last months, possibly the most remarkable period of her short life.

HANNAH WAS held in solitary confinement, but she found ways of communicating with her mother and her fellow prisoners. She used to tear out large letters from paper and place them in sequence in her window to transmit messages. To do this, she had to put a table on her bed and a chair on the table; but she persisted, and her window was a sort of information centre, conveying local news and accounts of life in Palestine.

Whenever she was allowed to meet other prisoners, she encouraged them and told them about Zionism and the land of Israel. She also argued fearlessly with her Nazi guards, warning them of the punishment they would receive after their defeat. According to one report, even the prison warden, a notorious sadist, would visit her to argue with her.

Hannah's interrogation continued, but apparently less intensively and far less brutally. In one of their meetings, Hannah told her mother how her interrogators would ask her about her country. After questioning her, they would give her cigarettes and say: "Enough for today. Now tell us about Palestine."

In August and September, the atmosphere in the prison became more relaxed. Three days before Hannah had entered Hungary, the Allies had landed in Normandy. On the eastern front, the Red Army was advancing. The puppet pro-Nazi Hungarian government was overthrown and a new government was formed, charged with preparing to surrender to the Allies.

During this time Palgi met with Hannah before being transferred to another prison. Catherine was placed in a cell next to Hannah's and they would meet during exercise in the yard. Although talking was forbidden, they managed to communicate and send each other presents.

Hannah, who had started making paper dolls for the young prisoners, sent her mother a bouquet of artificial flowers and a special doll for her wedding anniversary. She also sent her well-prepared Hebrew lessons.

One young girl told Catherine that she had heard Hannah asking a German guard what he thought her punishment should be. "If it were up to me I wouldn't punish you at all," replied the guard, "because I've never known a woman as brave as you."

Catherine was transferred to a Hungarian internment camp and then released. Hannah was transferred to a Hungarian prison, and her mother visited her there. She asked for books, particularly a Hebrew Bible, which her mother was not able to find, and for warm clothes. Catherine had meanwhile been contacted by "Geri" (Reuven Dafne), who had reached Budapest. He sent Hannah greetings and an envelope of money.

Catherine's efforts were now concentrated on finding a lawyer to defend Hannah, who was to stand trial for "treason." In her new prison, Hannah gave her cell-mates lectures about Zionism, kibbutzim and the Palestinian Labour movement. She taught illiterate youngsters to read and write, and shared all she had with her fellow prisoners.

The defence lawyer, who expressed admiration for Hannah's achievements, told her mother that she would definitely be found guilty of treason against Hungary, but would only be sentenced to five years. However, during the period of his meetings with her in mid-October, there was a countercoup in Hungary; a new Fascist regime came to power and the Nazis returned to Budapest. Deportations of Jews were resumed at full speed.

The lawyer admitted that now Hannah might receive a much longer sentence, but pointed out that it would only run until Hungary surrendered, which could not be long. She was tried at the end of October, but judgement was postponed for eight days. The general assumption among Hannah's friends was that this postponement was to ensure that judgement would never be passed.

However, in one of the pro-Nazi lurches of the time, Hannah was sentenced to death. There is no account of the court proceedings, but a young Hungarian orderly, on cleaning duty outside her cell on November 7, later told Yoel Palgi how Hannah received news of the verdict. She was told by the prosecuting officer, Captain Simon, that she had been sentenced to death. She would not be permitted to appeal the sentence, but she could request clemency. She insisted on her right to appeal, but refused to ask for clemency: "Clemency—from you? Do you think I'm going to plead with hangmen and murderers? I shall never ask you for mercy."

She was allowed to write letters, but they were never delivered. Captain Simon fled the country when the Red Army occupied Hungary. He apparently took Hannah's letters with him. Before his flight, Simon had told her lawyer that Hannah had remained "rebellious" to the last, and he read him part of a letter that she had written to her comrades: "Continue on the way, don't be deterred. Continue the struggle to the end, until the day of liberty comes, the day of victory for our people." Facing the firing squad, Hannah refused a blindfold.

At a meeting with Catherine Szenes, Simon told her that her daughter had indeed been guilty of treason by joining the British army, serving with the partisans in Yugoslavia and entering Hungary to rescue Jews and British prisoners of war. He added: "I must pay tribute to your daughter's exceptional courage and strength of character both of which she manifested until the very last moment. She was truly proud of being a Jew."

He told Catherine that she could pick up her daughter's letters at the prison, but all she received were her personal effects. In the pockets of two of her dresses she found scraps of paper. One read: "Dearest mother: I don't know what to say — a million thanks and forgive me if you can. You know so well why words aren't necessary. With love for ever, Your daughter."

HANNAH SZENES was buried in the Jewish cemetery in Budapest. In 1950, her remains were taken to Israel, where they lie on Mount Herzl in Jerusalem, with those of the other six parachutists who were killed in carrying out their mission.

Because of the presence of Yoel Palgi and Catherine Szenes in the same prison, the fate of Hannah is better documented than that of her fellow parachutists who fell. Her lively personality, literary talent and the records and memories she left, as well as her bravery under torture, have made her one of Israel's leading heroines. Her poetry and her story are taught in Israeli schools, and she has been the subject of a play by one of Israel's major dramatists.

Above all, she is a symbol. Her mission, reduced to its modest proportions by the British, had no real chance of success. But, in the dark night of terror and murder that was the Holocaust, the bravery and steadfastness of the thirty men and two women who tried to help their fellow Jews stands out like a flaming beacon. Hannah Szenes and the six others who paid with their lives are inscribed in the national memory of the Jewish people. Blessed indeed is the match consumed in kindling flame.

12 🐦

Yigal Allon and the Palmach:
The Youth Movement Army

"With this weapon which has been entrusted to me by the Haganah in the land of Israel, I shall fight for my country against the enemies of my people, without surrendering, without flinching, and with complete dedication."
Oath of the Palmach

Hannah Szenes and her thirty-one comrades parachuted into Nazi-occupied Europe, wearing the uniforms of the British army; but the force that selected them, motivated them and completed their training was the Palmach, the assault force of the Haganah, a military organization unique in the history of warfare.

Including both men and women fighters, minimally armed, without ranks, uniforms, decorations for bravery or normal military discipline, unrecognized, yet accepted as a reality, unpaid, unprofessional, the Palmach was a motivated, idealistic and effective fighting force.

Daring, unorthodox — sometimes rash — it was an army of youth. In focusing on Yigal Allon, who became Palmach commander in 1945, there is no intention of detracting from the decisive contribution made by Yitzhak Sadeh, initiator, founder and first leader of the force. But it was Allon, youthful, imaginative, bold, decisive to the point of ruthlessness, who personified the Palmach.

Allon was later to become an Israeli political figure and cabinet minister, which paradoxically obscured his earlier achievements. Many who were familiar with the politician did not know the extraordinary young man who, before the age of thirty, stamped his distinctive mark on Israel's army and led it in its major and decisive victories in the 1948 War of Independence.

Yeruham Cohen, who served as Allon's intelligence officer during the Galilee campaign that year, recalled how a small Bedouin tribe decided to join the Jewish side at a time when the situation of the Jews "couldn't have been worse." Allon, the regional commander, determined to check the matter out for himself; but, in view of his youthful appearance and lack of visible rank, he decided to present himself to the Bedouin sheikh as the deputy commander.

"Oh, Eegel, my son, you can't fool an old man like me," said the sheikh. "I knew your grandfather. . . . I've known your father for the past seventy-five years. You are the Jewish commander, and it's because I trust you that I'm ready to link the destiny of my tribe with yours."

The story illustrates the way in which the youthful Allon personified the fighting forces of the new state, and at the same time indicates the importance of his individual role in creating confidence and raising morale.

The famous Song of the Palmach declaimed in part:

From Metullah to the Negev, from the sea to the desert . . .
We are always the first, we are the Palmach . . .

It sounds presumptuous, even boastful, but anyone following the turbulent history of the emergence of the State of Israel in the 1940s must be struck by the ubiquity of this unconventional force and its commanders. Wherever the situation was most desperate, wherever the action was hottest, we find the informally dressed youths, with their stocking caps, their Sten guns, their songs and their special youth movement panache.

They were there in the internment camps of Holocaust survivors in Europe, aboard the "illegal" immigrant ships bringing Jews to Palestine, on the beaches carrying refugee children on their backs. In Safed, surrounded and outnumbered by the Arabs, in besieged Jerusalem and in the endangered Negev, it was Palmach commanders and soldiers who played a decisive role.

Of course the Palmach was a relatively small force and could not have won the struggle without the bravery and tenacity of the other fighting units. The Haganah was the backbone of the Jewish defence effort, and the Irgun Zvai Leumi (IZL) and Lohamei Herut Yisrael, or Lehi, the two Revisionist forces, also played a notable role. However, more often than not it was the Palmach that intervened at the decisive moment, or a Palmach officer who set the tone and spirit, which enabled Israel to prevail in 1948.

THE HAGANAH had been formed in 1920, by merging all the local Jewish defence groups under the authority of the newly formed Histadrut Labour Federation. Former members of Hashomer had argued the virtues of an elite force like their own, but Eliahu Golomb, Dov Hos and others had insisted on the necessity of a mass movement embracing the whole country.

The new force was established to meet the threat of anti-Jewish riots in Jerusalem and elsewhere in 1920 and 1921, but there followed several quiet years during which the Haganah was inactive. In 1929, as Jewish immigration started picking up, new outbreaks occurred and Jews were killed in Hebron, Safed, Jerusalem and Motza.

The Haganah was transferred to the control of the Jewish Agency and efforts were made to revitalize the organization and acquire weapons. However, there was another period of relative quiet, and the Haganah again experienced several years of inaction.

In 1936, the Arabs of Palestine launched a co-ordinated series of attacks against British and Jewish targets, followed by a general strike. Several dozen Jews were killed in Jaffa and other towns and villages, and it became increasingly clear that the Jews, by now numbering some 300,000, could not rely on the British to defend their lives and property.

The British mandatory authorities agreed to recruit, train and pay auxiliary Jewish policemen to help defend their communities, and the Jewish Settlement Police (JPS) was established. Members of the JPS, called *notrim* (guards), possessed arms and wore uniforms.

The Haganah, which was organized regionally, was uneven as regards quality and effectiveness. In most villages, every ablebodied man and woman was a member, but this was not always the case in the towns. After the 1936 riots, it was resolved to improve matters. One of those who played a prominent role in revamping the Haganah was a man called Yitzhak Sadeh.

When Joseph Trumpeldor returned to Russia in the latter part of the First World War to recruit pioneers and soldiers for Palestine, one of those whom he met and influenced was Yitzhak Landberg, a former Red Army officer. The Polish-born Landberg was studying philology and philosophy at a university in the Crimea, where he also achieved prominence as a wrestler and weight-lifter.

When he heard of Trumpeldor's death at Tel Hai, Landberg immigrated to Palestine, where he helped to found Gedud Ha'avoda, the Labour Battalion, named after Trumpeldor. The battalion, a mobile commune, performed road and construction work all over Palestine. Apart from his work as a stone-mason, Landberg, who changed his name to Sadeh, also gave military training to members of the mobile workforce. When the rioting erupted in 1936, Sadeh offered his services to the Haganah.

His first action, in the vicinity of Jerusalem, was to organize a mobile patrol, the Nodedet, made up of Haganah volunteers. With this force, which eventually numbered some seventy men, he initiated new tactics. Instead of waiting passively to defend Jewish villages and suburbs, the patrol went out to meet the attackers, setting ambushes near Arab villages which intercepted the gangs as they left their home bases.

At the same time, he took the Nodedet members on tough route

Yitzhak Sadeh, founder and first commander of the Palmach. Russian-born, he came to Palestine in 1920 and, building on General Charles Orde Wingate's groundwork, created the Palmach (*plugot sadeh* — "Field Companies"), which gave him his surname and the Haganah its frontline fighting arm. (*Israel Government Press Office*)

marches, taught them tracking and map-reading and told them stories of Trumpeldor, the Labour Battalion and the Russian civil war.

In 1937, the Haganah leadership, which had originally been cool to the Nodedet, authorized Sadeh to widen the scope of his activities. Drawing on the best of the *notrim,* he formed special field units or flying squads, known as Fosh (Field Companies). Sadeh inspired his young volunteers with his leadership, fostering dedication and comradeship together with physical prowess and enterprise.

Fosh was a nationwide organization, with its own Arabic-speaking intelligence service, topographical unit and educational corps. Always short of money and equipment, financed by a special arms levy imposed on the Jewish community, Fosh nevertheless grew to a membership of 1,000 by 1938.

The young Yigal Allon, who had already seen action against local Arab villagers as a volunteer member of the JPS, was unimpressed by his first sight of Sadeh, who came in 1937 to Kfar Tabor to recruit Galilee youngsters to Fosh. Later Allon was to describe him as "a tall, broad-shouldered, muscular man, a little on the heavy side and bald with a fatty bump on his forehead . . . to complete the dismal picture, he wore glasses." He recalled thinking: "Who is this bald, toothless old man to teach us the art of war?"

Allon was more impressed when the burly Sadeh led them on an exercise that very night, setting an ambush near a local Arab village. Nothing happened, but on their return to Kfar Tabor Sadeh explained around the camp fire:

> If we take to the paths, set up ambushes and fire at their bases, whether we encounter them or not, the Arabs won't be masters of the night any more. We'll cut down on the manpower we need for static defence. If we have the good sense to change our tactics from time to time so that we always have a fresh surprise in store for them, they will be put on the defensive in order to protect their villages. We won't go in for murder or personal terrorism, but we will force them to watch out for themselves. That's our doctrine in a nutshell.

Sadeh's words crystallized their own thoughts, wrote Allon later. "A wonderful feeling took hold of us all and we instinctively knew that this was the man." It was the start of a friendship that was to last until Sadeh's death fifteen years later, a partnership that would have a profound influence on the defence of the Yishuv and the State of Israel.

YIGAL ALLON was the youngest son of Haya and Reuven Paico-vich, founders of Kfar Tabor in Galilee. Haya, the daughter of a Safed rabbi, died when he was only six, and he grew up with his tough, individualistic father. The Russian-born Paicovich had lived and worked in several Galilee villages before going to America for three years to earn money for a plot of land in Kfar Tabor.

A strong man and a gifted farmer, he lived on terms of mutual respect with his Arab neighbours. Allon recalled how his father overpowered two strange Arabs who were grazing cattle on his field. Later he asked him why he had not used his pistol. "The pistol is for when you have no choice," explained Reuven, "when your life is in danger." The young man took this as a lesson in the limitations of the use of force.

When he was thirteen, his father gave him a semi-automatic Browning pistol and told him to go out to guard their field of sorghum. Taking shelter under a large oak tree, the youngster was almost overcome with fear when three men started filling sacks of sorghum at around two in the morning.

Obeying his father's orders, he challenged them in Arabic and fired in the air. The Arabs took up positions and cocked their weapons. The thirteen-year-old was wondering whether he was really going to have to fight, when his father arrived and chased away the intruders.

DURING 1937 and 1938, Sadeh fought for his ideas of "going beyond the fence," which meant "mobile" or "active" defence, the principles of which had been explained to Allon and his comrades around the camp fire; but official Haganah policy was involved in establishing settlements with tower and stockade, which were then defended statically.

The ideas of Sadeh were given a boost by the arrival in Palestine

Yigal Allon (1918–1980). A student of Wingate, he succeeded Yitzhak Sadeh as commander of the Palmach, and was one of the most successful leaders in the War of Independence. The picture shows Allon as commander of the southern front in 1949. (*Jewish Agency Photo Archives*)

Kibbutz Nir David was founded in the Beit Shean valley in 1936. It was one of the first "tower and stockade" settlements, which sprang up literally in one day from dawn to dusk, in critically strategic areas. (*Palphot*)

of Captain Orde Wingate, a British intelligence officer, who was charged with defending the Iraqi Petroleum Company's oil pipeline from Arab acts of sabotage. Wingate, impressed with the Jewish pioneers, particularly in the kibbutzim, quickly became a passionate advocate of the Zionist cause.

He took a special interest in the establishment of Kibbutz Hanita in March 1938 and admired the way its founders remained in place despite the Arab attacks. However, he told the kibbutz members that they were wrong to leave the initiative to the Arabs. They should get out and fight — particularly at night.

Wingate and Sadeh met at Kibbutz Ein Harod, and the two of them immediately hit it off. The burly Jewish pioneer and the ascetic British soldier were very different superficially, but their ideas were almost identical. Wingate was glad to find a Jew who understood his attitude; Sadeh was delighted to have his ideas given the stamp of approval by a professional British soldier.

"We did the same things as Wingate," wrote Sadeh later, "but on a smaller scale and with less skill. We followed parallel paths until he came to us and became our leader."

Major General Charles Orde Wingate, the British officer who was seconded to Palestine between 1936 and 1939. Through his "Special Night Squads" he became mentor to a whole generation of Israeli soldiers, including Moshe Dayan and Yigal Allon. (*WZPS*)

Together the two of them established the Special Night Squads (SNS), joint patrols of British soldiers and Fosh men, who patrolled the pipeline and also defended Jewish settlements. Wingate set a personal example of endurance and stamina, and insisted on strict discipline. At the same time he treated his men as thinking beings, sharing his plans with them and making sure they understood what they were doing.

Despite his careful planning, Wingate also laid stress on improvisation, encouraging his commanders to be independent and to think for themselves. Mobility, surprise and the concentration of maximum force on a major objective were other lessons he taught.

Wingate won the hearts of his Jewish friends, earning the title of *Hayedid,* "the Friend." He pressed ahead with further training courses for Jewish commanders, but the British authorities found him too pro-Jewish. He was transferred out of Palestine and the Night Squads were disbanded. In 1939, the Fosh was absorbed into a new formation of the Haganah called Hish (Field Force), a part-time territorial home guard organized on a regional basis.

In May 1939, the British government published the White Paper on Palestine, which promised to establish a Palestinian state, divided into Arab and Jewish cantons, and limited Jewish immigration to 75,000 to be carried out over the next five years. Bearing in mind the perilous situation of the Jews in Europe, the Jewish community in Palestine saw the White Paper as a betrayal.

Four months later, Britain was at war with Nazi Germany, and the Jews of Palestine were faced with an unbearable dilemma: on the one hand, Britain was standing alone against their deadliest enemy; at the same time, the British were preventing the Jews from escaping annihilation in Europe.

David Ben-Gurion resolved that the Yishuv would "fight the war as if there were no White Paper, and fight the White Paper as if there were no war." (See chapter 14.) This meant that the Jews of Palestine volunteered to serve in the British forces in large numbers; but at the same time every effort was made to bring in Jewish refugees "illegally," despite British attempts to prevent this.

In one incident, Haganah forces blew a hole in the side of the *Patria,* a transport ship in which the British were about to send 257 refugees to the Indian Ocean island of Mauritius, hoping that the delay, caused by damage to the hull, would change their minds. The ship sank in Haifa port and all lost their lives.

Many of the Haganah's best people had joined the British army, but a number of former members of Fosh and the Night Squads were standing by waiting for a Haganah decision on whether to form their own force. Most of the Yishuv's leaders emphasized the importance of service in the British army. The Jews of Palestine, they argued, should be part of the Allied war effort. The British, not wanting to antagonize the Arabs, had initially been reluctant to mobilize the Jews. Now that they had agreed, nothing should be done to halt the flow of volunteers.

However, Sadeh, Golomb, Moshe Sneh and others of the Haganah command argued against "putting all our eggs in one basket." They postulated a worst-case scenario in which the British might withdraw from Palestine, and asked who would defend the Yishuv then. They decided to form an independent, permanently mobilized task-force under the direct authority of the Haganah.

Sadeh was charged with forming the new unit, to be called the Palmach (Assault Companies). He immediately began establishing the force in strict secrecy, recruiting many of his former fighters from Fosh and the SNS, including Yigal Allon and Moshe Dayan, later to become one of Israel's most important military and political leaders. By the summer of 1941, the first nine companies of the Palmach went into training.

Allon, appointed commander of the Palmach's first company, was asked by his proud father: "Yigal, has it ever occurred to you that you are the commander of the first company of the first independent Hebrew army since Bar-Kokhba?"

THE PALMACH had two primary aims: to defend Jewish settlements against Arab bands, and to defend the country against a German-Italian invasion. In the event the Axis forces broke through, the Palmach would engage in sabotage.

In April 1941, Germany had invaded Yugoslavia and Greece and, by the end of May, the British were forced to evacuate Crete, only 500 miles from Syria. Fearing a German invasion of Syria and Lebanon, with the connivance of the Vichy French who controlled those countries, the Allies resolved to pre-empt them.

Unlike the mandatory authorities, who were suspicious of the

Moshe Dayan, Nahalal, 1939, two years before losing his eye in a skirmish with
the Vichy French, here seen with his first wife, Ruth, and her sister Reu'ma, who
subsequently married Ezer Weizman, later to be a commander of the Israeli Air
Force and a Minister of Defence. (*WZPS*)

Jews, the British Special Operations Executive (SOE) was co-operating with the Haganah. It was a strange situation: the mandatory authorities were arresting Jews found with weapons, while the SOE was arming the Jews.

The Palmach was thus being financed by the British, who thought they were paying for 500 men. In fact, because its members received no pay, only a little pocket-money, the Palmach command stretched it to some 1,500.

Although the Palmach was still only in the process of formation and training, it agreed to participate in the invasion of Syria and Lebanon. The first mission of Arabic-speaking Palmach men was sent on an intelligence-gathering mission into the two countries. This operation was a success; but the next mission, the despatch by sea of twenty-three men with a British officer to blow up the Tripoli oil refineries, ended in disaster. The boat disappeared without a trace, and the Palmach lost some of its best members.

Allon then led a small party to the River Litani, returning with four Vichy French prisoners. Recommended for decorations by an Australian colonel, the young Palmach officer demurred, asking instead for the weapons of the four prisoners. The Australian agreed and also allowed them to help themselves to additional arms captured from the Vichy French.

Palmach units penetrated Syria and Lebanon in advance of the Allies, proving adept at scouting, intelligence gathering, sabotage and night fighting. It was on a reconnaissance mission during this period that Dayan lost his left eye.

By mutual consent, the Palmach was not incorporated into the British army. The British looked on their alliance with the Palmach as temporary; the Palmach wanted to remain independent, responsible only to the Haganah. However, the success of the Palmach units prompted the British to agree to the creation of two bases, one near Kibbutz Ginossar by the Kinneret, the other near Kibbutz Beit Oren on the Carmel. The camps lacked even elementary facilities, such as tents and kitchens, and the young soldiers slept in the open.

With Syria and Lebanon occupied by the Allies, the British moved to disband the Palmach; but Sadeh managed to keep it going on a part-time basis, and before very long the British again turned to the force for help. The German army was advancing on Egypt and, with the very real prospect that they might have to evacuate Palestine, the British proposed that the Palmach be trained for sabotage.

A Palmach base was set up at Mishmar Ha'emek in the Jezreel valley, where special Arabic-speaking and German-speaking units were established. The British envisaged that the Palmach would lead an anti-German underground to harry an occupation, but the Haganah had its own plan.

The "Carmel Plan" called for the transfer of the entire Jewish population of Palestine to the greater Haifa area, including Mount Carmel, the valley between Haifa and Acre, the mountains of western Galilee and an airstrip on the coast. There they would hold out for the months — even years — of the Nazi invasion.

Worked out by Sadeh and Professor Yohanan Rattner, a teacher at the Haifa Technion and a member of the Haganah command, the plan envisaged the area's being supplied by plane, submarine and its own agricultural resources. It would be under Jewish military administration and would utilize the arsenals of the Allies. Medical and educational networks would also be established.

The plan, which was approved by the British, proposed not just holding out, but also attacking the enemy from the Mount Carmel base, disrupting communications and serving as a bridgehead for an Allied counterattack.

There was an obvious resemblance to the siege of Masada nearly 2,000 years before. Marches to Masada were part of the Palmach's training programme and the unit's oath was sometimes administered there to new recruits, so that the significance of Masada was not lost on the young fighters. However, Sadeh had put his own activist stamp on the plan and mass suicide was no part of it.

The British victory at El-Alamein removed the danger of Nazi occupation, and the British again lost interest in their erstwhile partners. The question of the Palmach's very existence now arose.

The Haganah leadership realized that, even in the event of an Allied victory, their problems would not be over. If the White Paper remained in force, they would have to confront the British; if it was abrogated, they might well have to fight the Arabs. As Sadeh put it: "The American soldier bears the American rifle; the

Soviet soldier carries Soviet arms; but who will bear arms for the Jews?'' The Palmach, now 1,000 strong, would be needed more than ever.

Early in 1943, the British dismantled the Mishmar Ha'emek camp and took back the arms they had supplied to the Haganah. A few nights later, a Palmach force raided the British arsenal and recaptured the arms without disturbing the British sentries: the alliance was over.

The Palmach now faced a severe economic problem, which was solved by the kibbutzim, the communal farming settlements established over the past three decades, where much of the force's manpower came from. The Palmach members would live on some twenty kibbutzim, spending half the month working and earning their living, and half the month training.

It was not exactly an easy life, but it gave the force its special character and quality. The Palmachniks (as members of the force were called) became a voluntary, committed, egalitarian elite, committed to working on the land, as well as to defending it.

They took pride in taking on the hardest tasks, ploughing the fields, bringing in the harvest, milking the cows, picking the fruit. In the evenings, they would sit around the camp fire, passing an Arab coffee pot from hand to hand, singing songs and telling tales.

From the outset, women were full members of the Palmach, undergoing the same tough commando training as the men. In battle they served as radio operators, nurses, scouts and quartermasters, though a good number fought alongside their male colleagues. The presence of women also contributed to the special atmosphere of the Palmach, turning it into a true army of the people, military but not militaristic. Far from disappearing when the British withdrew their support, the Palmach actually increased in size.

Looking to the future, Sadeh also organized the Palyam, a seaborne Palmach, which trained frogmen in naval sabotage, and other members in the use of naval transports and landing craft. The Palavir, under the guise of a flying club, created an embryo air force, based on light aircraft and gliders.

One last co-operative venture between the Palmach and the British was the despatch of the parachutists into Nazi-occupied

Europe. In September 1944, the British finally assented to the formation of a Jewish Brigade, some 5,000 strong. This unit, which saw action in Italy the following spring, was together with the Palmach and the Haganah to play a vital role in the future Israel Defence Forces.

The Palmach meanwhile continued its very special multi-purpose training programme. Its members received a harsh physical training, with route marches and night exercises. They learned to use a variety of weapons, from knives and grenades, to mortars and explosives. They learned to fight in large and small groups, to plan and to improvise.

The Palmach's doctrine was that the smallest unit was the single soldier with his rifle. The commanders were to "pull" their men after them, rather than "push" them from behind, as illustrated in the command "After me!" It meant that the commanders were exposed to the greatest risks, which could be costly, but it remains the IDF way to this day.

In anticipation of the day when the force could be expanded, large numbers were put through commanders' courses, even though they continued as normal soldiers for the time being. The commanders were taught to decide for themselves, to operate individually and to be unconventional. Originally the company was the basic Palmach unit, but in due course the battalion was introduced, with commanders taught to deploy four companies at a time.

The Palmach was at once the laboratory, the elite, the leadership and the inspiration of the Haganah; but its real test was to come. The Germans had been defeated, but what was to become of the pathetic remains of the Jewish people, the survivors in the death camps all over Europe? What of the future of the Jewish community in Palestine?

For Zionists, the two questions were inextricably linked, and the leadership of the Yishuv prepared to meet the challenge. The political struggle would be waged by the Jewish Agency; the Haganah braced for the military battles ahead. Sadeh, its most imaginative officer, was appointed acting chief of the Haganah General Staff. As commander of the Palmach, he was succeeded by his deputy, comrade and most promising pupil, Yigal Allon, who was appointed shortly before his twenty-seventh birthday.

WITH THE end of the Second World War, the full scale of the Holocaust became generally known: less than a million Jews had survived the Nazi murder machine. Most of them were living in camps for "displaced persons," DPs. The Yishuv hoped for the repeal of the White Paper and the resumption of Jewish immigration, which would enable these survivors to come to Palestine. This hope was reinforced by the results of the British general election of 1945, which brought to power the Labour Party, committed to a pro-Zionist policy.

However, the new Labour government in Britain, more or less continuing the policy of its predecessor, limited Jewish immigration to 1,500 per month. The Yishuv, led by Ben-Gurion, was by now demanding a Jewish state and it adopted a three-point campaign to pressure the British to change their minds, or to force them out of Palestine. The "illegal" immigration, which had proceeded throughout the war, was stepped up; new settlements were established and sabotage was carried out against selected targets.

As the defence organization of the Yishuv, the Haganah was charged with carrying out these operations, which were to lead eventually to the withdrawal of the British and the establishment of the State of Israel.

The IZL, the military arm of the Revisionist Zionists, had already in 1937 resolved to adopt a more activist policy in the wake of Arab riots and terrorist actions. Now the IZL and a more extremist group, Lehi, carried out their own more militant campaigns against the British, independently of the Haganah.

Spearheading the Haganah actions was the Palmach, which took the lead in illegal immigration, settlement and sabotage. Between 1945 and 1947, more than 70,000 Jews were brought to Palestine, despite intensive efforts by the British to prevent them coming. A number of immigrants from Arab countries, where conditions for the Jews were becoming increasingly difficult, were brought in, as well as European survivors of the Holocaust.

In Europe, it had been members of the Jewish Brigade and other Palestinian and Jewish soldiers serving with the Allies who first encountered the DPs. They were quickly reinforced by members of the Haganah, which established a special organization for illegal immigration, called the Mossad Le'Aliyah Bet (Immigration-B).

Each group of would-be immigrants had to be smuggled past

The *Struma,* carrying 769 Romanian refugees to Palestine, sank in the Sea of Marmora off the Turkish coast in February 1942, with the loss of all its passengers except one. *(Zionist Archives)*

European frontier guards to the ports of southern Europe, where they were put on board ramshackle ships which had been acquired by the Haganah. Foreign volunteers, non-Jews as well as Jews, played their part in this extraordinary operation; but it was the Palyam, the naval section of the Palmach, which led and co-ordinated the operation.

The immigrant ships were then forced to run the gauntlet of British naval patrols, which often intercepted and turned back ships containing DPs. Even when they arrived at the shores of Palestine, the immigrants were liable to be arrested by British troops, detained and then deported. Many were sent back to Europe; others were interned on Cyprus.

In one daring action, a Palmach force attacked a detention centre near Athlit. Overwhelming the Arab sentries, they led the new immigrants to freedom.

With the British approaching, the Palmachniks mobilized kibbutz members from the surrounding area, who mingled with the immigrants, exchanging clothes and identity papers with them. British troops and officials, finding it impossible to distinguish

The most infamous refugee ship of them all: the *President Garfield,* renamed *Exodus 1947*. In July 1947, the ship, bearing 4,500 refugees, arrived in Haifa and was refused permission to land. Its passengers were forcibly returned to Germany.

Reunion forty years later. Two of the original American crew members of the *Exodus* meet again in Haifa. (*Nomi Bar-El*)

British soldiers drag "illegal" immigrants off a refugee ship in Haifa port. They were subsequently interned in camps in Cyprus until Israel's independence.

between residents and immigrants, left. This technique was used repeatedly.

Many immigrants were brought overland via Syria and Lebanon. This involved not only passing through hostile territory, but also getting past the British border-guards into Palestine. Here again the field-craft and topographical knowledge of the Palmach were invaluable.

A special organization had been set up by the Haganah to acquire arms. Apart from smuggling arms from Europe and manufacturing them in primitive workshops, considerable quantities were stolen from the British forces stationed in Palestine. One Palmach unit specialized in boarding moving trains and pushing off crates of arms and military equipment. Much of the Haganah's signals and medical equipment was obtained in this way.

A notable clash between the Palmach and the British forces occurred in March 1946, when British soldiers arrested a bus-load of Palmachniks in Galilee. The Palmach men escaped and the British pursued them to the village of Biriya, just north of Safed,

Immigrants are rushed ashore by Palmach and kibbutz volunteers. If caught and interrogated by the British, they were all taught to identify themselves just as "a Jew from Eretz Israel." (*Jewish Agency Photo Archives*)

arresting the entire male population of the village and occupying it.

A few days later, on Tel Hai Day, the day which commemorates the stand of Joseph Trumpeldor and his comrades, youth movement members from all over Galilee marched to Biriya and established a settlement nearby. The British forces dismantled the new settlement also; but, after it had been repeatedly rebuilt by the youthful settlers and other volunteers, eventually agreed that twenty Jews could remain there.

Now openly confronting the British over immigration and settlement, the Haganah joined forces with the IZL and the Lehi in a series of co-ordinated sabotage operations. The Palmach's contribution was the "Night of the Bridges," when the force's sappers blew up ten of the eleven road and rail bridges linking Palestine with Lebanon, Syria and Transjordan. The Palmach lost fourteen of its men in the fighting that accompanied this operation.

The British conducted a massive swoop on twenty-seven settlements, imprisoning thousands of Jews, including much of the leadership of the Yishuv. Most Haganah and Palmach leaders went underground. Less than a month later, the IZL blew up a wing of the King David Hotel in Jerusalem, which housed the secretariat of the mandatory government of Palestine. The blast killed ninety-five people.

The King David operation took place during the period of co-operation between the Haganah, the IZL and Lehi, but it led to mutual recriminations and to the dissolution of the partnership. The IZL and Lehi continued with their operations against the British forces, often against the wishes of the official leadership of the Yishuv, as represented by the Jewish Agency and the Haganah.

IN FEBRUARY 1947, the British asked the United Nations to deal with the Palestine problem, and in the subsequent months, while a UN committee prepared its recommendations, the Jews and Arabs in Palestine marshalled their forces. By now the Haganah had some 43,000 members, but the 3,000-strong Palmach was its only full-time force.

Initially the Palmach bore the brunt of the fighting with the Arab irregulars; but, as time went on, increasing numbers of its

An explosion on February 22, 1948, in Ben Yehuda Street in central Jerusalem took the lives of fifty-two people and wounded another 123. (*Werner Braun*)

officers took command of other units. Thus its contribution to winning the War of Independence was both direct and indirect.

In November 1947, the UN voted to partition Palestine into two separate states with Jerusalem as an international enclave. The Jews accepted the UN resolution; the Arabs rejected it and moved to wipe out the Jewish population. Arab riots and attacks on Jewish settlements, towns and suburbs began at once. The Palmach expanded its forces to approximately 6,000 men and women, organized in three brigades. The Palyam and Palavir were separated from the Palmach and developed into an embryo navy and air force.

The Haganah formed a number of brigades from its own field forces, Hish, and from members of the Jewish Brigade. Jewish volunteers from the United States, Britain and British Commonwealth countries, who came to volunteer their services, were quickly mobilized. Older members of the Haganah were organized on a regional basis as a Home Guard. Teenagers were mobilized as cadets in the Gadna youth defence organization. They served as signallers and couriers.

As the British began evacuating the country, the Haganah held on to the Jewish areas, while extending its control over formerly Arab-dominated areas. Its policy was that no Jewish settlement should be abandoned. By the time the British completed their evacuation on May 14, 1948, and the State of Israel was established, the Jews had consolidated their hold on eastern Galilee and the coastal strip, while the Arabs held western Galilee and most of the central mountain range, Judea and Samaria. Jerusalem was divided and cut off from the other Jewish areas.

By March 1949, the Israeli forces, beating back the forces of five neighbouring Arab states, as well as the local Palestinian Arab irregulars, had held the territory awarded it under the terms of the UN partition plan and improved their position in several sectors. Only the Old City of Jerusalem and the Etzion area south of Jerusalem had been lost.

Space does not permit an account of all the operations in which the Palmach and its officers took part. They played a notable role in many of the thirty-nine separate engagements fought by the Israelis. From Galilee to Eilat, and from the Dead Sea to the

Israel's "secret weapon," a home-made mortar firing an indiscriminate mixture of nails and old scrap metal, but possessing an awe-inspiring noise. Invented by an engineer called David Leibovich, it was dubbed the "Davidka."

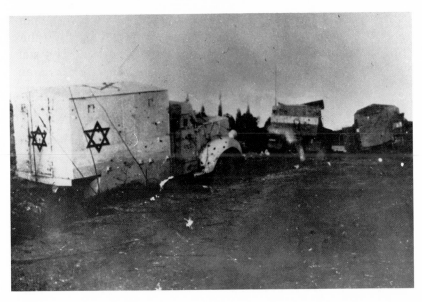

Seventy-seven doctors, nurses and teachers were killed when a medical convoy making its way up to the Hadassah Hospital on Mount Scopus was ambushed in April 1948. (*Zionist Archives*)

A convoy reaches the besieged city of Jerusalem on April 13, 1948. (*Jewish Agency Photo Archives*)

The fallen in the battle of the Etzion bloc, a group of four kibbutzim south of Jerusalem, are laid to rest. The bloc fell on May 14, 1948, the day of the declaration of Israel's independence.

Mediterranean, their contribution was decisive. Here we will content ourselves with brief accounts of the three vital campaigns led by Allon, who emerged from the war as Israel's top field commander.

ON THE eve of the British withdrawal from Palestine, Allon led the Palmach in Operation Yiftah, which took Safed and pushed the Arab forces out of Upper Galilee in four days of desperate fighting from May 6 to 10, 1948.

The small religious Jewish community of Safed had already been under virtual siege in their quarter for some five months, when the British withdrew from the town on April 14. The British forces turned over to the Arabs three major strongpoints: the police station, the ancient citadel in the town centre, and the Teggart fortress, which dominated the city from the top of nearby Mount Canaan. The 2,000 Jews faced the town's 12,000 Arabs, reinforced by 3,000 Arab irregulars and 700 Syrian volunteers.

The night after the departure of the British from Safed, a small Palmach unit broke into the Jewish quarter bringing weapons and food. For the next three weeks, encouraged by the Palmachniks, the Jews of Safed, including women and children, held out, improvising barricades from rocks.

Safed was taken during the night of May 10, in several bold Palmach assaults on the Arab strongholds. But it was not only the tactics that were daring; the strategic concept was courageous in the extreme.

While Allon was concentrating his forces around Safed, other Jewish villages in Galilee were under fierce attack from Arab irregulars and sent appeals for help; but the Palmach commander, taking an enormous risk, concentrated on Safed and left the settlements to fend for themselves.

Later he explained: "I did not agree under any condition to concede the initiative in the Safed area. . . . I believed that consistent pressure on the part of our forces would in the end force the enemy to concede the initiative to us and go over to the defensive."

His gamble paid off: the settlements withstood the attacks, the Arab forces scattered and the Palmach went over to the offensive. At the same time, the Haganah in Operation Ben-Ami, led by Moshe Carmel, took control of western Galilee.

A month later Allon was in charge of Operation Danny, which aimed to wrest Lydda, Ramla and Latrun from Arab control, clearing the approaches to beleaguered Jerusalem. The first two towns were defended by large forces of irregulars, supported by units of the British-officered Arab Legion.

In the hills of Samaria nearby, mobile units of the Legion were deployed, together with Iraqi forces. In concentrating his forces for a powerful blow against the two towns, and not leaving anything in reserve to counter an attack on his flanks from Samaria, Allon was once again taking a risk. But he went ahead and took the two towns.

In the battle for Lydda, Dayan played a key role, leading a jeep-mounted assault. Dayan's lightning attack, which passed straight through the town and out the other side, demoralized the defenders, and Lydda was taken.

By October the Negev had become the important scene of operations and Allon was duly appointed commander of the southern front. Here, deploying larger forces than hitherto, his task was to break through and relieve the Negev kibbutzim, cut off since the Egyptian May offensive.

The two possible assault points were the village of Iraq el-Manshie, and the Huleikat junction farther west. As the latter was more strongly fortified, Allon conducted an attack, supported by air, armour and artillery, on Iraq el-Manshie, but was beaten back with heavy casualties.

Allon proposed switching his entire forces to Huleikat, arguing that the Egyptians would not be expecting an attack. The army command said that such a move would only lead to a costly defeat, but they agreed on condition that Allon took full personal responsibility.

Allon's forces not only broke through at Huleikat, they raced to Beersheba in thirty hours, totally surprising the Egyptian garrison. Subsequently the army won control of the entire Negev, including the southernmost point, Eilat, took the southwestern shore of the Dead Sea in the east and penetrated deep into Sinai in the west.

YIGAL ALLON was undoubtedly the outstanding field commander of Israel's War of Independence. The Palmach, which he commanded, had infused the new army of Israel with its dedication and fighting spirit; but it was also a political force, connected with the kibbutz movement and the left-wing Mapam party.

Against the bitter opposition of Allon and his fellow Palmach officers, Ben-Gurion felt compelled to dissolve the Palmach as a separate force. Previously the IZL and Lehi had also been disbanded as separate forces. The Palmach, the IZL and Lehi were all potentially divisive forces and Ben-Gurion insisted on national unity.

Allon and most of the senior Palmach officers resigned from the IDF, although Allon's deputy, Yitzhak Rabin, stayed on and became Chief of General Staff, leading the IDF to victory in the Six Day War of 1967. Moshe Dayan also remained in the IDF, leading the IDF to victory in the 1956 Sinai Campaign.

ALLON, AND the Palmach forces he led, set standards of dedication, initiative, imagination and courage for the IDF that have been equalled but not surpassed. The legacy of the force is almost entirely positive. The Palmach spirit of volunteerism, daring, comradeship and loyalty has been passed on to the special volunteer units and to the army as a whole. The State of Israel is deeply in its debt.

13 🐦

Dov Gruner and His Comrades:
The Ultimate Sacrifice

🐦 **D**OV GRUNER was hanged at four o'clock in the morning on May 16, 1947, in Acre prison. As he and three other members of the Irgun Zvai Leumi were executed one after the other, they sang "Hatikva," the Jewish national anthem. The other Jewish prisoners in the massive fortress joined in "so that the four would not die alone."

After a while, the other prisoners stopped and listened. The singing was not so loud. Half an hour later, only two voices could be heard, and later still a single voice. After a pause the prisoners sang "Hatikva" once more in tribute to the four who had died:

> Our hope is not yet lost,
> Our hope of two thousand years,
> To be a free people in our land,
> The land of Zion and Jerusalem.

That day, her voice choked with tears, the Hebrew radio announcer read the official communiqué announcing the hanging of Gruner and his three fellow IZL members.

Despite the controversy in the Palestinian Jewish community regarding the policy and actions of the IZL, the announcer's grief was universal. Dov Gruner, the twenty-eight-year-old immigrant from Hungary, had won the admiration even of his British adversaries.

"The fortitude of this man, criminal though he be, must not escape the notice of the House," Winston Churchill told the British parliament in a speech otherwise condemnatory of the IZL struggle against the mandatory authorities.

Major Dare Wilson, who served in Palestine with the Sixth Airborne Division, later wrote in a memoir: "Although it might be described as fanaticism, his conduct throughout his year in custody, four months of which was spent in the condemned cell, was that of a very brave man."

Gruner had been captured a year previously during an IZL arms raid on the British police station in Ramat Gan, near Tel Aviv. An IZL man, dressed as a British sergeant, drove up in an army lorry with ten colleagues disguised as Arab prisoners. After gaining admittance to the station, they overpowered the police inside, blew open the iron door of the armory with an explosive charge and started loading weapons and ammunition onto their lorry.

Guards on the roof of the station realized what was happening and started firing at the IZL men. Reinforcements were summoned from nearby Petah-Tikvah, and a half-hour battle ensued in which three IZL men and an Arab policeman were killed; the lorry, loaded with arms, got away.

Gruner, who had been providing cover with a Sten gun, had his jaw blown off. Major Donelly, the man who shot him, staunched the blood with a handkerchief. Gruner managed to mumble his thanks.

Because of his wounds, he was not able to stand trial until the following January, by which time the struggle between the IZL and the British authorities had escalated considerably. Among the many actions carried out by the underground organization in the meantime had been the King David Hotel blast in July 1946.

Dov Gruner, an IZL member, was captured in a raid against the British at Ramat Gan police station. Severely wounded, he was sentenced to death and, despite international calls for clemency, was hanged in Acre prison on May 16, 1947.

Gruner, who had served in the British army for five years during the Second World War and had been wounded twice during his service, refused to accept the authority of the British military court to try him.

The British had no right to be in Palestine, he told the court, because they had betrayed the trust of their mandate by turning the country into a military base and trying to steal it from the

Jewish people. British rule now rested on the principle of brute force, he maintained, and the laws drafted by "the bearers of the bayonets" were contrary to the rights of man, the wishes of the local population and international law.

Gruner declared:

> When a regime in any country becomes a regime of oppression it ceases to be lawful. It is the right of its citizens — more it is their duty — to fight against it and overthrow it. That is what the Jewish youth is doing and will continue to do until you evacuate this country and return it to its lawful owners, the people of Israel. For this you ought to know: there is no force in the world that can break the link between the people of Israel and its one and only country.

Sentenced to death by the court, Gruner responded by singing "Hatikva." The sentence was confirmed and a date set for execution; but the IZL captured a British intelligence officer and a judge, threatening that if Gruner died so would the hostages. Gruner's execution was "indefinitely postponed to enable him to appeal to the Privy Council," and the hostages were set free.

In point of fact, Gruner refused to appeal to the Council. A Jerusalem lawyer, hoping to save his life, persuaded him that the IZL wanted him to appeal, when this was not in fact the case. He signed a power of attorney for an appeal to be made in his name, but later tore it up when he discovered that the IZL was leaving the decision to him. He simply refused to accept the jurisdiction of a British court — even when his life depended on it.

A fellow prisoner described Gruner as "calm and in wonderful spirits." He never asked anything for himself, but was constantly asking about the "the fighting family" (his IZL colleagues). In a letter to IZL commander Menachem Begin, Gruner wrote:

> Of course I want to live. Who does not? But if I am sorry that I am about to finish, it is mainly because I did not manage to do enough. I too could have let the future fend for itself, taken the job I was promised, or left the country altogether and lived securely in America. But that would not have given me satisfaction as a Jew and certainly not as a Zionist. . . .
>
> The right way to my mind is the way of the Irgun, which does not reject political effort but will not give up a yard of our country

because it is ours . . . that should be the way of the Jewish people
in these days: to stand up for what is ours and be ready for battle,
even if in some instances it leads to the gallows. . . .

I write these lines forty-eight hours before the time fixed by our
oppressors to carry out their murder, and at such moments one does
not lie. I swear that if I had the choice of starting again I would
choose the same road, regardless of the possible consequences for
me.

Your faithful soldier, Dov

Although he himself refused to appeal to the Privy Council, two
appeals were made to the Council on his behalf, one by Gruner's
uncle, a citizen of the United States, the other by the Tel Aviv
Municipality. Both were rejected — the second after the execution
had already been carried out.

Shortly before his execution Gruner and his fellow death-cell
prisoners celebrated the Passover *Seder* with a rabbi. Two guards
were present and Gruner, with his customary politeness, repeatedly offered them his seat. Despite the circumstances he treated
them as his "guests."

Gruner and his comrades were hanged with almost indecent
haste after being transferred from Jerusalem to Acre prison. His
sister Helen Friedman, who had come specially to Palestine to see
him before his death, was not even informed of his impending
execution.

However, when the guards came to summon him to execution,
he refused to stand up to hear the sentence confirmed and was
dragged struggling to the scaffold.

THE IZL (National Military Organization) was first established
when the nonsocialists split off from the Jerusalem branch of the
Haganah in 1931; but it was in 1937, when Jabotinsky split from
the rest of the Zionist movement to form his Revisionist movement, that the IZL became an active force.

Rejecting the Haganah policy of restraint in the face of Arab
attacks on Jews, dissatisfied even with the more activist policies of
Yitzhak Sadeh and Eliahu Golomb, the IZL carried out retaliation
for Arab attacks, killing Arabs whenever Jews lost their lives.

The IZL split in its turn in 1939, when Jabotinsky suspended military activity and announced full support for the British war effort, backed by IZL leader David Raziel. Avraham Stern, who thought that the struggle against the British should continue despite the war, split from the IZL to form Lohamei Herut Yisrael, Lehi (Fighters for the Freedom of Israel), often referred to as the Stern Gang.

Raziel was killed when on a mission for the British in Iraq, and under its new leader, Menachem Begin, the IZL resumed the struggle against the British in 1944, after the British had continued to bar the gates of Palestine to Jews fleeing from the Holocaust, and when an Allied victory against Germany had become certain. The actions of the IZL and Lehi against the British continued until the departure of British troops from Palestine in May 1948.

In 1945, when the British Labour government made it clear that it would continue with the policy of restricting Jewish immigration to Palestine, the Haganah, the IZL and Lehi combined in a joint campaign of resistance against the British authorities. For several months, from October 1945 to July 1946, the united resistance operated, carrying out numerous, effective acts of sabotage; but incidents like the King David Hotel blast eventually brought their cooperation to an end.

The IZL and Lehi continued their operations against the British, sometimes against the active opposition of the Jewish Agency, the embryo Jewish government in Palestine. They made things very uncomfortable for the British troops stationed in Palestine, who were forced to live behind barbed-wire fortifications and move about in heavily armed convoys.

Despite the continuing controversy regarding the actions of the two small Jewish underground groups, IZL and Lehi, there is universal admiration for their courage and dedication. In particular, Dov Gruner and the other underground fighters who were sentenced to death by the British military courts conducted themselves with great personal bravery.

This account, focussing on these remarkable young men, who were willing to pay the ultimate price for their principles, pays tribute to their courage and their devotion to the cause of Israel. They were true heroes of the Jewish people.

Yitzhak Shamir, today Israel's Prime Minister. As Yitzhak Yezhernitsky he was one of the leaders of the Lehi underground movement (called the Stern Gang by the British). (*WZPS*)

Menachem Begin, commander of the IZL, in 1947: the picture is taken from a British police "Wanted" poster of the time. Begin became Prime Minister of Israel in 1977, resigning in 1983 in the wake of the Lebanon War.

TEN JEWS were hanged during the period of the British Mandate; two others avoided execution by committing suicide in the death cell. Others were sentenced to death and had their sentences commuted to life imprisonment. Two of the latter were rescued by the action of their fellows in the underground.

The first hanging was in 1938. During the previous two years, there had been Arab attacks on Jews all over the country. The IZL organized some reprisals, but on the whole the reaction was restrained. In Galilee, following the ambushing of a Jewish taxi on the Acre-Safed road and the murder of its five occupants in April 1938, three young members of the Betar Revisionist youth movement from nearby Rosh Pina planned revenge.

Shlomo Ben-Yosef, a young immigrant from Poland, and two friends acquired a pistol and an old hand grenade and ambushed the Safed-Tiberias bus. Their shots missed and the grenade was a dud, so nobody was hurt, but the three were arrested and brought to trial. One was judged mentally unbalanced, but the other two were sentenced to death.

Ben-Yosef's companion had his sentence commuted, because he was under age; but, despite world-wide protests and appeals, which cited both the provocation that preceded the act and the fact that Ben-Yosef had not killed anyone, his sentence was confirmed.

To a group of journalists who visited him in Acre jail, Ben-Yosef declared: "Do not console me. I need no consolation. I am proud to be the first Jew to go to the gallows in Palestine. In dying I shall do my people a greater service than in my life. Let the world see that Jews are not afraid to face death." On the way to his execution, he sang the Betar anthem; just before he died, he cried: "Long live the Jewish state! Long live Jabotinsky!"

Yehezkel Ben-Hur, who killed an Arab boy in a similar incident near Jerusalem the following November, was also sentenced to death; but his sentence was commuted, thanks to the intervention of Jabotinsky with the Queen of the Netherlands, who appealed to King George VI.

By 1944, the IZL had joined Lehi in hitting British targets in Palestine, due to the British policy of preventing Jewish immigration from Nazi Europe. The Lehi leadership focused its anger on Sir Harold MacMichael, the High Commissioner for Palestine, who was seen as personally responsible for closing the gates. An assassination attempt organized by Lehi failed, and a new High Commissioner, Lord Gort, in due course replaced MacMichael.

Lord Moyne, Britain's Minister of State in Cairo, was perceived as being a strong opponent of Jewish immigration to Palestine. A story widely believed at the time quoted his reaction to the proposal to save a million Hungarian Jews threatened with extinction: "What would I do with a million Jews?" It has not been established that he made this remark, and subsequently evidence has emerged that Lord Moyne was not hostile to Zionism.

However, in the highly charged atmosphere of the time, with Jews being massacred by the Nazis in Europe, and the world as a whole showing a callous indifference, the story had an explosive effect on some of the Jews of Palestine. Lehi determined to assassinate Moyne, not in revenge for his policies and statements, but to shock the British authorities into a change of policy.

In November 1944, Eliahu Hakim, a twenty-year-old member of Lehi born in Beirut, and Tel Aviv–born Eliahu Beit-Tsouri, three years older, shot Lord Moyne in the Gezira suburb of Cairo. They made their escape on bicycles, but were captured by Egyptian policemen, whom they refused to injure on the grounds that, unlike Moyne, the policemen were not guilty of anything.

On January 11, both men were sentenced to death in Cairo. They had not denied the charge, but stated: "We fight for our freedom . . . if we have turned to the gun, it is because we were forced to the gun." Before his execution, Hakim wrote from prison: "I am absolutely calm and my conscience settled because I have the feeling I have done my duty."

The Chief Rabbi of Egypt, who spent the last night with the two men, said they remained calm and composed to the end. Hakim described his red, burlap, hanging tunic as "the finest suit of clothes I have ever worn in my life." The two men were hanged on March 23, 1945.

A year later, two IZL men, Michael Ashbel and Yosef Simhon, were captured during an arms raid on the Sarafand military camp near Tel Aviv. After they were sentenced to death, the IZL captured six British officers, one of whom escaped. The IZL announced it would hang the others if its own men were executed, and the sentences against Ashbel and Simhon were commuted.

Meanwhile, Dov Gruner had been captured, but he was still too ill from his wounds to be brought to trial. In December, two IZL prisoners, sentenced to eighteen years in jail for illegally carrying arms, were sentenced to flogging. When one of the men was flogged, the IZL flogged four British servicemen in retaliation; but three of the IZL people involved, Mordechai Alkoshi, Yehiel Drezner and Eliezer Kashani, were captured.

The three, who were savagely beaten up by British troops after their arrest, were sentenced to death by a British military court. However, when the IZL took its hostages and secured the postponement of Gruner's sentence, the executions of Alkoshi, Drezner and Kashani were also postponed.

The four men were being held in Jerusalem, but were suddenly transferred to Acre under heavy guard on April 14, 1947. There they were hanged two days later. There were no final requests, no rabbi, no last visitors, no warning. Their bearing at their execution has already been described.

By the time of their execution, two other men, Meir Feinstein of the IZL and Moshe Barazani of Lehi, were also under sentence of death. Feinstein had been captured — and had lost his arm — during an IZL attempt to blow up the Jerusalem railway station the previous October. Barazani was caught throwing a hand-grenade at a British officer's car in March of that year.

The two men were being held in Jerusalem and the IZL managed to smuggle a grenade into the jail hidden in a scooped-out orange. Their plan was to blow themselves up, taking their executioners with them; but it was foiled by the dedication of a rabbi, Rabbi Jacob Goldman, the private secretary of Chief Rabbi Isaac Halevi Herzog.

Spending several hours with the two men on the night before their execution on April 21, 1947, on the instructions of the Chief Rabbi, Goldman also insisted he would be present at the hanging on the following morning. The two men did their best to discourage him, but nothing could dissuade him from doing his duty. Not wanting to kill or injure Rabbi Goldman, Feinstein and Barazani embraced in the cell that night with the grenade between them. The muffled explosion was heard by the guards, who rushed to the condemned cell, but the two men were dead. Their plan to kill their executioners had failed, but they had cheated the gallows.

THAT SUMMER, the IZL mounted its most spectacular operation, blowing a hole in the seemingly impregnable Crusader wall of the Acre fortress and freeing 251 prisoners, 131 Arabs and 120 Jews, including many IZL and Lehi men. It was a brilliantly coordinated action, involving prisoners inside the fortress as well as the attackers from outside, but fifteen IZL men were killed and fifteen captured.

Three of them, Avshalom Haviv, Meir Nakar and Ya'acov Weiss, were put on trial for their lives. Haviv lectured the court, comparing the situation in Palestine with that in Ireland, and quoted Bernard Shaw to the effect that Irish fighters were prisoners of war and would become martyrs if hanged. He continued: "You tyrants will never understand the spirit of free men, going to their deaths,

British soldiers examine the point in the walls of Acre prison from where the IZL prisoners made their dramatic escape in May 1947.

as Dov Gruner and his three comrades went, with a song springing from their hearts.''

Nakar termed British rule as ''bankrupt,'' and poured scorn on a government ''which spends half its budget on police purposes, and yet remains helpless in the face of the anger of a people in revolt.''

Weiss, a survivor of the Holocaust, told the court: ''We know there will be one outcome of this fight: our people will attain its freedom and its enslaver will disappear from the land . . . there can be no greater happiness than to give our lives for a great ideal, and to know that we are among those bringing about its fulfillment.''

When the three men were sentenced to death, the IZL captured two British sergeants from the intelligence corps. Within hours of the executions of Haviv, Nakar and Weiss on July 29, 1947, the British sergeants, Clifford Martin and Mervyn Paice, were hanged by the IZL. The hangings of the British sergeants were widely condemned, but no more Jews were hanged by the British in Palestine.

Like their predecessors, Haviv, Nakar and Weiss went to their deaths singing "Hatikva."

MENACHEM BEGIN, who became Prime Minister of Israel in 1977, wrote in *The Revolt,* his account of the underground struggle against the British, about the special type of courage required by a man sentenced to death:

> He has no enemy in front of him. His enemy lurks beyond the locked door, awaiting his prey. There is no glorious battle, no storming assault. There are only thoughts — thoughts of the time that is running out with every tick of the clock. And thoughts beyond time. The days are long, the nights longer. There is too much time to think. There is something and somebody that crops up. The voice of an old mother, the voice of a young betrothed, distant yet clearly heard. . . .
>
> Here there can be no swift subjugation of the instinct of self-preservation. The sickening struggle with it is continuous. It begins all over again every morning, every hour, every minute, when he lies down and when he gets up, and as he paces the locked and lonely cell. Not everybody — not even a very brave soldier — is capable of passing this test.
>
> The soldiers of the IZL endured it calmly.

ON FEBRUARY 14, 1982, Prime Minister Begin informed the Israeli cabinet that a set of stamps had been issued commemorating "the martyrs of the generation of the establishment of the State of Israel." Half of them were in memory of the IZL and Lehi fighters who made the ultimate sacrifice for the Zionist cause.

Five years later, in July 1987, forty years after the final executions in Acre, the author of this book, in his capacity as President of Israel, dedicated a memorial sculpture in Ramat Gan's Dov Gruner Square, and eulogized the ten IZL and Lehi fighters and four others who had been hanged for loyalty to the cause of Zionism.

Selfless dedication and courage transcend earlier differences, and all the people of Israel commemorate those who were willing to pay the supreme sacrifice in order to create a free Jewish state.

14 🐦

David Ben-Gurion:
The Courageous Decisions

🐦 N̲O̲ ̲O̲N̲E̲ had a greater under-
standing of the peril facing the Jewish community of Palestine in
early May 1948 than its leader, David Ben-Gurion. He had been
the first of his colleagues to realize that the 650,000 men, women
and children of the Yishuv, already engaged in a desperate battle
for their lives, would have to face not only the million-strong Arab
community in Palestine, but also the regular armies of seven Arab
states.

More than anyone else, he perceived the weakness of the Yishuv's position, its lack of a properly organized army, its paucity of
weapons and its extended defence lines, reaching from Tel Aviv to
Jerusalem, Galilee, the Jordan valley and the Negev. Outnumbered and ridiculously outgunned, the physical survival of the
Jews was in considerable doubt.

No less a figure than U.S. Secretary of State George Marshall,
a former general and distinguished military expert, sent Ben-
Gurion's colleague Moshe Sharett from Washington to Tel Aviv

with a dire warning to agree to a ceasefire and to postpone the declaration of the Jewish state, with the expiry of the British Mandate and the withdrawal of British forces.

"I think he's right," Sharett told Ben-Gurion, when they met in Tel Aviv. The sixty-one-year-old leader persuaded his colleague not to put forward this opinion at the fateful meeting of his Mapai Party Central Committee the following day. He asked Sharett to give the committee a full and precise account of his talk with Marshall, but to omit the words, "I think he's right."

Sharett's account was not the only sombre news that the committee heard that day. Golda Meir returned from secret talks with King Abdullah of Transjordan to report that he was no longer able to give assurances that he would stay out of an Arab-Jewish war; in fact, his British-led Arab Legion attacked the following day — even before the British had left — besieging the Etzion Bloc of settlements south of Jerusalem.

Haganah Chief of Operations Yigael Yadin, reporting on the military situation, described the Yishuv's chances as about even. He then added: "To be more frank, I would say that they [the enemy] have a considerable advantage." Israel Galili noted the overwhelming Arab superiority in heavy weapons.

The news from the battle fronts was far from encouraging: the Etzion Bloc was being overwhelmed, western Galilee was cut off, Jerusalem was besieged, with water and food running out, and a heavy battle loomed on the road to Jerusalem. The pressure in favour of postponing the proclamation of the state was intense.

Conceding that the situation was "very perilous," Ben-Gurion rallied his colleagues with the assurance that more arms and equipment, "rifles, cannon, bazookas, warplanes," were on the way, and secured a majority in the party and in the People's Administration (the provisional government of the Yishuv) for proclaiming the state.

Ben-Gurion worked into the early hours of the morning of May 14, 1948, finalizing the wording of the Declaration of Independence. Shortly before 4 P.M., he arrived with his wife Paula at the Tel Aviv Museum, where the leaders of the Yishuv were gathered. Spontaneously, they rose and sang "Hatikva." Immediately afterwards, the small stocky man, his pugnacious face framed with the

Ben-Gurion declares the independence of the State of Israel, May 14, 1948, beneath a photograph of the visionary of the Jewish state, Theodor Herzl, who wrote, "If you will it, it is no dream." (*Werner Braun*)

famous wings of white hair, read out the Declaration of Independence in a firm, clear voice.

UNDOUBTEDLY Ben-Gurion's most important decision, the Declaration of Independence was only one of a series of courageous resolutions made before and after May 14, 1948, resulting in the creation and survival of the State of Israel, the re-establishment of Jewish sovereignty in the land of Israel, after a break of nearly two millennia.

Ben-Gurion's determined and inspiring leadership places him with Joshua, King David and Judah the Maccabee — and in our own time with Churchill, Roosevelt and de Gaulle — as a powerful and charismatic leader, with sufficient vision to see several steps ahead and to grasp the basic issues facing the nation, with sufficient courage to lead it against the most impossible odds and to demand the most extreme sacrifices from his people.

He was endowed with the personality and power of leadership to weld together elements of different outlooks and philosophies to one common purpose. He had the necessary historic vision and understanding to appreciate already in 1945 that there was no chance of an agreed settlement with the British and that, therefore, the Jews in Palestine must prepare for the creation of a national army and for a full-scale war.

Had he not grasped the significance of the new developments, events would have overtaken the Jews of Palestine and found them completely unprepared, both politically and militarily. While Ben-Gurion's colleagues and political opponents were thinking in terms of commando raids and small unit warfare, Ben-Gurion realized that there would be no compromise and that he would have to go the whole way.

Above all, he knew what he wanted and was unwilling to compromise — hence his insistence at all stages on preparation for an all-out war, and his understanding of the meaning of statehood, which at times clashed with the confusion and contradictions of some outdated Zionist ideologies. He made mistakes, but his faults were those of a very great man. Without his foresight, imagination and determination, it is doubtful whether the State of Israel would have come into being.

ARRIVING IN Jaffa from Russian Poland in 1906, at the age of twenty, David Gruen (as Ben-Gurion was still called) immediately resolved to proceed to the Jewish agricultural settlement of Petah-Tikvah, which he was sure would be more to his liking than the mercantile, urban port. He set out on foot in the late afternoon, with thirteen comrades and a donkey, arriving at 10 P.M. and staying up talking into the small hours.

It was a significant decision: having determined to immigrate to the land of Israel, he would participate in the physical redemption of the land. His first job, as a day labourer, spreading manure in the citrus groves, was strenuous and exhausting, requiring "great patience and devotion from those who have never worked before," as he wrote to his father in Plonsk. He found it difficult to work with blistered hands in the summer heat, but he was determined to stick it out.

He joined the other Jewish pioneers in despising the First Aliya immigrants for employing Arabs to do their hard work, convinced that a Jewish renaissance could only come about through Jewish labour. However, struck down with malaria a few weeks after his arrival, he was advised by the local doctor to return home to Poland, a suggestion he rejected out of hand. Weakened by frequent bouts of malaria, he worked only an average of ten days a month, with the result that he was frequently hungry.

Before long the young Gruen became involved in politics. A member of the Marxist Poalei Zion party back in Poland, on arrival in Jaffa he found himself closer to the rival workers' party Hapoel Hatzair, with its greater emphasis on Zionism and Hebrew. Almost at once he resolved to work for the unity of the two Labour parties. Labour unity, as a preliminary stage to national unity, became a cause to which he remained dedicated in various forms all his life.

A strong socialist, he nevertheless developed a pragmatic approach, adapting his socialism to the Zionist task which was most important to him. For some time he remained in a minority in his party, trying unsuccessfully to encourage more use of the Hebrew language. Although elected a member of the party's central committee, he was unable at that time to prevent its drift to the left and its continued espousal of Yiddish.

After working in a number of settlements in the coastal plain,

Gruen decided to go north to Galilee to be in the forefront of the Jewish pioneering endeavour. He settled at Sejera, the first Jewish agricultural settlement in Lower Galilee, where he was delighted to find that all the work was done by Jews. Here was the land of Israel he had dreamed about.

Gruen was, however, lonely in Sejera, the more so after the arrival of the secretive Bar-Giora group (the predecessor of the Hashomer guard organization) from which he was excluded, although he did stand guard at the settlement, and on one occasion proved his bravery in the face of a hostile crowd of local Arab villagers.

After working at a number of other settlements in Galilee, Gruen was asked by Yitzhak Ben-Zvi, the leader of Poalei Zion, to come to Jerusalem to work on the party's newspaper, *Ahdut* (Unity). Adopting the Hebrew name Ben-Gurion, he forged a strong friendship with Ben-Zvi and persuaded him of the importance of Hebrew and of placing Palestine at the centre of Zionist affairs. At a time when most Jews — and most Zionists — were outside the land of Israel, Ben-Gurion insisted that the Zionist movement must be run from Palestine and that its main task must be to build up the Jewish community there.

Ben-Gurion was disappointed with the initial failure of the Second Aliya, the second wave of immigration to Palestine, and he once said that nine out of every ten immigrants who arrived in the early years of the century eventually left the country; but he was undeterred, determined to remain and build a Jewish nation.

Convinced that this could best be achieved in co-operation with the Ottoman authorities ruling Palestine at the time, Ben-Gurion and Ben-Zvi resolved go to Constantinople to study law. In view of his sister's marriage to a wealthy merchant, Ben-Gurion felt able to appeal to his father to finance his studies, which were preceded by a year learning Turkish in the Greek port of Salonika, where there was a large Jewish community, and where the port was run by Jewish stevedores.

If he had been disappointed by the initial failure to create a large Jewish working class in Palestine, Ben-Gurion was reassured by the Jewish port workers of Salonika, who proved that Jews were capable of being labourers. After completing their studies in Constantinople, Ben-Gurion and Ben-Zvi returned to Jaffa, to discover that the First World War had meanwhile broken out.

THE TWO men still believed in co-operation with the Ottomans and consequently when Turkey joined the war on Germany's side, they obtained permission to recruit a Jewish militia to defend Palestine. However, the new Turkish commander, Jemal Pasha, took ruthless action against both Arab nationalists and Zionists, and Ben-Gurion and Ben-Zvi were deported to America.

As soon as they arrived, the two set about organizing Hehalutz, a movement of Jewish pioneers for Palestine. They traveled all over the United States, but their success was limited. At the same time, Jabotinsky was trying to raise a Jewish fighting force in London. Ben-Gurion, who believed in Jewish labour and self-defence, but was doubtful about military conquest, wrote: "A homeland is not possessed by gold or conquered by the power of the fist; it is built by the sweat of the brow . . . the Land of Israel will be ours when a majority of its workers and guards shall be of our people."

Ben-Gurion won a considerable name for himself by debating fiercely and effectively against anti-Zionist Jews, but he and Ben-Zvi only managed to recruit about a hundred pioneers. The year 1917 brought the Balfour Declaration, in which Britain pledged to support a "National Home" for the Jews in Palestine; it was also the year of the Russian revolution. The Poalei Zion movement split into those who still aspired to a Jewish revival in Palestine and others who favoured returning to Russia to build a socialist society there. Ben-Gurion threw himself into the struggle for the Palestinian cause and became converted to the idea of a Jewish fighting force within the British army. He and Ben-Zvi joined the Committee for a Jewish Legion in the Land of Israel.

Although he obviously welcomed the Balfour Declaration, Ben-Gurion was far less euphoric about it than his colleagues. Many Zionists saw the declaration almost as the coming of the millennium; but Ben-Gurion cautioned them that only the Jews themselves could win their independence, and they could only achieve it through hard, unremitting labour.

In 1918, Ben-Gurion signed up for the American battalion of the Jewish Legion, which was to be a unit of the British army for service in Palestine. He had meanwhile married Paula Munweis, an American Jewish nurse; but, despite her entreaties, he set out for the battalion's training camp in Canada. After rigorous training and promotion to lance corporal, Ben-Gurion set sail for England and then Egypt, where he became sick with dysentery.

As he lay in a Cairo hospital, he read in the journal *Ba'avodah*, published by the agricultural union in Palestine, an article by Berl Katznelson on the central role of the Palestinian-Jewish workers as "the true vanguard of Zionism." As soon as he recovered, he went to the camp of the Palestinian battalion, where he met Katznelson and proposed the union of the Labour movements in Palestine.

When they arrived back home in Palestine, Ben-Gurion persuaded his Poalei Zion party to support unification; but the other party, Hapoel Hatzair, turned down the proposal. Undeterred, Ben-Gurion and Katznelson called a "general conference of all the workers in the Land of Israel" and formed Ahdut Ha'avodah, the unified Labour movement, which called for "international guarantees for a Jewish state in the Land of Israel."

Although Hapoel Hatzair refused to join the new party, it did eventually combine with Ahdut Ha'avodah in a General Federation of Hebrew Workers, known to this day as the Histadrut. Ben-Gurion held fast to his aim of a unified Jewish community, led by the Labour movement.

Not himself religious — he had married Paula in a civil ceremony — Ben-Gurion was acutely aware of Jewish tradition and resolved to forge an alliance with at least part of the religious Jewish community of Palestine. To this end he found common ground with Rabbi Yehuda-Leib Fishman of the Mizrahi religious movement, making compromises to bring Mizrahi into an Elected Assembly of Palestinian Jewry. The assembly became an embryo parliament, and the alliance between Ben-Gurion's Labour movement and Mizrahi was to last more than fifty years.

In the 1920s, Ben-Gurion concentrated on building up the Histadrut, the headquarters of which he moved to Jerusalem, and in finding employment for new immigrants. Even then he was a unique combination of visionary and man of action, combining unusual breadth of vision with a single-minded sense of purpose.

Although his Histadrut wage was meagre, and he had to send money to his wife, who was then on a long visit to his family in Plonsk, he spent more than he could afford on books. Despite his energetic organizational work for the Labour movement, he found time to study Judaism, Christianity, Arab history, the ancient history of the Middle East, socialism and Zionism.

He also consolidated the power of the Palestinian Labour-Zionists in the World Zionist Movement. Crusading among the Jewish communities in Eastern Europe, he clashed with the anti-socialist Revisionists of Jabotinsky, facing down angry crowds which pelted him with stones and eggs. Back home he campaigned energetically against limitations on Jewish immigration by the British Mandate authorities. In response to the Jewish immigration after the war, the local Arabs became increasingly violent, notably in 1920, 1921 and 1929, when bloody riots broke out, causing the British to try to curb the Jewish influx.

A forceful personality, who was prepared to clash with others when fighting for his principles, Ben-Gurion nevertheless always strove for unity. Although he regarded the pro-British stance of Chaim Weizmann with suspicion, he forged an alliance with him to ensure British support for Jewish immigration, with Weizmann in charge of the London end of the campaign.

In 1935, Ben-Gurion became chairman of the Jewish Agency Executive and undisputed leader of the Palestinian Jewish community. From then on, he ran the Zionist movement in tandem with Chaim Weizmann, president of the World Zionist Organization.

Despite bitter clashes with Jabotinsky, Ben-Gurion held a series of meetings with the Revisionist leader to try to hammer out a common policy. In point of fact, the two men reached an agreement, but their respective movements refused to ratify it, and the two movements remain locked in political conflict to this day. His alliance with Weizmann fared better, although in time the two leaders were to clash, as Ben-Gurion adopted a more activist stance in contrast to Weizmann's cautious approach.

Ben-Gurion was firmly opposed to dispossessing the local Arabs from their lands, contending that Jewish development in Palestine could be confined to untilled lands. For many years, he believed that there was an identity of interests between the Jewish workers and the Arab peasants; but after the 1929 Arab riots, he became increasingly aware of the existence of an Arab national movement and concluded that there was no alternative to the creation of a Jewish majority in Palestine, which would be capable of defending itself militarily.

Despite this conclusion, Ben-Gurion always realized that Jews and Arabs would have to live together in Palestine and the Middle East, and he made a number of attempts to reach an understanding with Palestinian and other Arab leaders. On more than one occasion there was some progress, but events were to overtake these attempts at diplomacy. In 1935, Hitler's Germany adopted the Nuremberg race laws, savagely discriminating against the Jews. Immigration from Europe increased to an unprecedented extent, and new Arab violence broke out in 1936.

Faced with a nationwide Arab strike, coupled with acts of terror against the Jewish population, Ben-Gurion stuck firmly to two principles, largely against the views of his colleagues: restraint in self-defence, and maintenance of good relations with the British. He spoke out in favour of "the moral and political principles which guide Zionism and the Yishuv . . . if attacked, we must not exceed the bounds of self-defence." At the same time he worked for Jewish economic self-sufficiency and redoubled immigration.

If he had opposed the right in insisting on moderation and good relations with the British, he was no less determined in opposing the left represented by Weizmann, who was inclined to accept a suspension of Jewish immigration. This was to be the pattern throughout Ben-Gurion's career: vigorous promotion of a pragmatic policy, attempting to achieve maximum consensus, while rejecting extremism of both left and right. It was one of the most important characteristics of his successful leadership.

Ben-Gurion's relations with Weizmann reached breaking-point with the arrival of the British Peel Commission, which came to Palestine to examine what was to be done in the light of the continuing Arab rebellion. He was pleased with Weizmann's public statement to the commission, but furious with his later *in camera* testimony, which he termed "a political catastrophe."

Weizmann had told the committee that he thought a million Jews could be brought to Palestine over "twenty-five or thirty years."

However, the Peel recommendation to partition Palestine into a Jewish and an Arab state found him once more agreeing with Weizmann not only against Jabotinsky's Revisionists, but against most of his own Labour colleagues. Jabotinsky still believed in a Jewish state on both sides of the River Jordan, and even the Labour-Zionists were not prepared to waive their claim to all of western Palestine.

Ben-Gurion saw it differently, believing that the prospect of a sovereign Jewish state far outweighed any question of what its borders might be. The Peel Commission's partition plan would have awarded the Jews only Galilee, the Jezreel valley and the coastal plain; but Ben-Gurion argued that, with their own state, however small, the Jews of Palestine could advance their cause. "A partial Jewish state is not the end, but only the beginning," he wrote to his son Amos.

Nevertheless, he never committed himself categorically to the specific partition proposals. One of his ideas was that the Negev desert should remain under British Mandate control, which would leave open the option that it could later become part of the Jewish state. However, he forced the Jewish Agency Executive to agree to discuss the partition proposals. In later years Golda Meir, one of his colleagues opposed to partition, admitted that Ben-Gurion had been right and that immediate acceptance of partition might have enabled the Yishuv to rescue at least some of the European Jews who perished in the Holocaust.

When the British themselves dropped the partition plan, Ben-Gurion changed his attitude towards them, resolving that if Britain tried to abandon its commitments, "we too shall withdraw our support of Britain and build up our own military strength, so that we can if necessary fight the British as well."

Ben-Gurion, who had been strongly convinced of the importance of the British link, became progressively disillusioned with Britain after it backed down from the Peel partition plan, and he began looking towards the United States, with its large Jewish community, for support.

In May 1939, the British government published its infamous White Paper, which pledged to turn Palestine into an independent Arab state with a Jewish minority. Jewish immigration was severely restricted, and Jews were only permitted to continue to buy land in five percent of Palestine's area. All this at a time when the Jews of Europe, in mortal danger from Hitler, needed their national home more than ever before.

Ben-Gurion was determined to defeat Britain's new policy. However, as war between Britain and Germany approached, he found himself in a dilemma. On the one hand, Britain was preventing the rescue of the Jews of Europe, but at the same time it was unthinkable not to support Britain against Hitler. With his colleagues, he worked out a dual policy, which he expressed in one sentence: "We shall fight the war as if there were no White Paper, and the White Paper as if there were no war."

Ben-Gurion inspired the Jewish community with his fiery speeches against the White Paper, but he did not content himself with mere rhetoric, organizing the Jewish Agency — and in particular the Haganah — to defy Britain and bring European Jews to Israel "illegally." However, his colleagues were concerned at the adoption of such a strong anti-British policy, and he failed to carry his views in the Jewish Agency.

Furious, Ben-Gurion resigned as chairman of the Jewish Agency Executive, but his resignation was rejected. As war swept over Europe, he came to acknowledge that the war against Hitler had to take precedence over the war against the White Paper. In London during the summer of 1940, Ben-Gurion was overwhelmed by the courage of the British during the bombing of London. Later in 1948, while considering the pros and cons of declaring Israel's independence, he would say: "I have seen what a people is capable of achieving in the hour of supreme trial. I have seen their spirit touched by nobility . . . this is [also] what the Jewish people can do."

In London, he campaigned for the establishment of a Jewish army. Returning to Palestine, he resolved to work for "the transferring of millions of Jews to Palestine and establishing it as a Jewish commonwealth." He flew to America and, at a national conference of American Zionists, the "Biltmore Programme" was adopted, calling for the opening of Palestine to Jewish immigration, the development of unpopulated and uncultivated areas and the establishment of a Jewish commonwealth. This was by far the most radical Zionist stance ever adopted by the movement outside Palestine, and it is noteworthy that it was adopted in America, hitherto the bastion of the gradual approach. It was a reflection of the menacing situation of the Jews in Europe, but also a result of the force of Ben-Gurion's personality and sense of urgency.

During the war Ben-Gurion's conflicts with both left and right continued unabated. He clashed repeatedly with Weizmann, who was not in his view sufficiently militant in prosecuting the cause of Jewish immigration to Palestine. On the other hand, when the dissident Revisionist organizations launched anti-British attacks in 1944, he opposed them and even ordered the Haganah to co-operate with the British in curbing them.

As soon as the war was over in 1945, Ben-Gurion looked ahead, beyond the confrontation with the British, to what he saw as the inevitable struggle with the Palestinian Arabs, whom he foresaw would be backed by the Arab states. In July 1945, he met secretly in New York with eighteen Jewish millionaires, who pledged to finance the purchase of huge quantities of arms.

One of them, Rudolf Sonneborn, founded the Sonneborn Institute, ostensibly for shipping medicines and hospital equipment, but in fact for supplying both weapons and ships for the "illegal" immigration of Jews to Palestine. The Institute, in which all the millionaires participated, was to play a vital part in ensuring that the Jews of Palestine had the equipment to ensure their survival.

Ben-Gurion continued to clash with Weizmann, stating openly that, if Britain continued with the policy of the White Paper, "we in Palestine will not fear, nor retreat in the face of Britain's great power, and we shall fight against her." When the newly elected British Labour government, despite earlier promises to the contrary, maintained White Paper policy, Ben-Gurion ordered the Haganah to launch an armed uprising against the British.

The British government resolved to send an Anglo-American commission of inquiry to Palestine to determine whether there was room for the Jewish survivors of the Holocaust, and the

insurrection was temporarily halted. When the commission recommended the establishment of a trusteeship for Palestine, abol-
ishment of both the White Paper and the restrictions on Jewish
land purchase in Palestine, as well as the immediate admittance of
100,000 Jews to Palestine, Weizmann welcomed it, whereas Ben-
Gurion was disappointed.

Britain had promised to carry out the recommendations, but
went back on its word and refused to permit the immigration of
the 100,000, upon which Ben-Gurion ordered the renewal of the
armed insurrection. However, following the blowing up of the
King David Hotel by the IZL in July 1946, he agreed to the suspension of the armed struggle.

One of the Zionist leaders, Nahum Goldmann, now proposed
that the Jewish Agency accept the idea of "a Jewish state in a
sufficient part of the Land of Israel" — in other words, partition.
Ben-Gurion supported the idea, although he abstained in the actual vote in the Jewish Agency Executive. Late in 1946, the Zionist
Congress met in Basel and approved the principle of partition.
Although Ben-Gurion and Weizmann were in agreement on this,
they clashed fiercely on the question of "resistance." After a prolonged dispute, Ben-Gurion prevailed. He was elected to head an
"activist" executive; no one was elected president. Ben-Gurion
also secured for himself the defence portfolio.

RETURNING TO Palestine, Ben-Gurion concentrated his formidable intellect on military affairs, interrogating the Haganah commanders down to the smallest details, visiting units and reading
everything about military matters that he could lay his hands on.

He discovered that the Haganah had neither the equipment nor
the plans for war against regular armies. Operational planning
was based on the assumption that the worst danger facing the
Yishuv was an uprising by the Arabs of Palestine. Furthermore, he
found that there was a split between commanders who had served
in the British army, and Haganah and Palmach members who had
remained in Palestine to defend the Yishuv during the war.

Ben-Gurion set himself to unify these two elements, making
Yisrael Galili, of the kibbutz-Palmach leadership, chief of Haganah
National Command, and Yaacov Dori, who had served with the

British in the First World War, chief of staff of the new Israel Defence Forces. His other main task was to acquire heavy equipment, tanks, halftracks, cannon, heavy mortars, warplanes and patrol boats. It was no less important to convince the Haganah commanders, who had hitherto been leading a guerrilla force, of the importance of such equipment.

He sent his agents to Europe to buy arms and equipment and mobilized the funds for the purpose. At the same time he instructed the local manufacturers of arms and equipment to order raw materials and gave them the necessary budget.

During this period he also laid down the strategic principle that no Jewish settlement would be abandoned, which meant that the Haganah had to disperse its forces and maintain lines of communication all over the country.

To this end, Ben-Gurion created military districts or commands astride the possible invasion routes of the Arab armies and established brigades on a territorial basis. The Golani Brigade operated in the Jordan valley and eastern Galilee; the Carmeli Brigade covered Haifa and western Galilee; the Alexandroni Brigade the coastal plain; the Etzioni Brigade Jerusalem; and the Kiriyati Brigade Tel Aviv. In addition the Palmach disposed of three brigades — Negev, Yiftach and Harel.

The Jewish population was concentrated in long strips of farming villages in eastern Galilee, across the Jezreel valley and down the coast to Tel Aviv and farther south. Particularly vulnerable were the communications with the outlying settlements of Galilee and the Negev and the link between Jerusalem and the coast — not to mention the links between Jerusalem and its surrounding Jewish villages.

In November 1947, the United Nations voted in favour of partition of Palestine into a Jewish and an Arab state. The Palestinians and the Arab governments rejected the UN resolution and the opportunity to establish a Palestinian state. The Palestinians launched a guerrilla war, which escalated as the months passed, and the Arab armies prepared to invade as the British Mandate came to an end. Their declared aim was to destroy the proposed Jewish state before it could be established and to drive the Jews into the sea.

As the Haganah defended Jewish settlements and fought to keep open its lines of communication, and the local Arabs, on occasion supported by British troops who were still in the country, launched numerous raids on the Jewish towns and settlements, Ben-Gurion stepped up his search for arms and despatched Golda Meir to the United States to raise money.

During the winter of 1947–48, the struggle continued, with the Arabs concentrating their attacks increasingly on the convoys that were supplying Jerusalem and the Jewish settlements in Galilee and the Negev. The battle for the roads went badly and Jerusalem, western Galilee and the Negev were frequently cut off.

Setting up a thirteen-member provisional government, called the People's Administration, Ben-Gurion also ordered the Haganah to concentrate an unprecedentedly large force to break through to Jewish Jerusalem, which was becoming increasingly short of food and water. The Haganah command proposed 500 men; Ben-Gurion angrily demanded 2,000, which involved withdrawing arms and men from the already inadequately defended settlements.

Hitherto the Haganah's actions had all been on a company level. Now Ben-Gurion was demanding a brigade-size operation. Operation Nahshon called for opening a corridor to Jerusalem by occupying the high ground and the Arab villages bordering the road. Before the operation was launched, the Haganah carried out two key actions, blowing up the headquarters of Hassan Salameh, area commander of local Palestinian forces, and taking the Kastel, an Arab village dominating the road to Jerusalem.

During Operation Nahshon, the Kastel changed hands a number of times, but was finally taken by the Jewish forces when local commander Abdel Kader el-Husseini was killed. The road to Jerusalem was opened, enabling supplies to be brought in before the road was again cut. At the same time some of the arms acquired in Europe started reaching the Yishuv.

Although it only afforded Jerusalem temporary respite, Operation Nahshon was a turning-point in the struggle, with the initiative passing to the Jews for the first time. It was Ben-Gurion's first major strategic decision, and it confirmed him as the military leader of the Yishuv, as well as its political leader.

Subsequently, the Haganah carried out Plan D, which involved further reorganization and seizing key areas to enable the Yishuv to hold the areas allotted to the Jewish state by the UN partition vote, plus Jewish settlements outside it. One of the notable parts of Plan D was Operation Yiftah to liberate Galilee, led by Yigal Allon (see chapter 12).

At the same time, Ben-Gurion initiated contacts with King Abdullah of Transjordan, in an attempt to forestall his participation in the coming war. This attempt was ultimately unsuccessful, and Transjordan's British-led Arab Legion and Frontier Force proved to be the most effective soldiers opposing the Jews in the War of Independence.

Even before the proclamation of the state, the Arab Legion attacked the Etzion Bloc of settlements south of Jerusalem, and the Egyptian army attacked the Negev in overwhelming force. In this situation, with Jerusalem again cut off and the Yishuv besieged on all sides, Ben-Gurion decided, after a fierce debate in the provisional government, to issue the Declaration of Independence. The State of Israel was born again after 2,000 years and all over Palestine the Jews celebrated. The one exception was Ben-Gurion, who wrote in his diary: "I feel like the bereaved among the rejoicers."

WHEN THE armies of Lebanon, Syria, Transjordan, Iraq and Egypt attacked the new State of Israel, it did not yet possess a national army. The Etzion Bloc had fallen even before the state was proclaimed, many of its inhabitants massacred, others taken prisoner. The Arab Legion improved its positions in Jerusalem, cutting off Mount Scopus, site of the Hadassah Hospital and the Hebrew University, which were to remain isolated for nineteen years. (Jerusalem itself was again isolated from the coastal plain.) The Egyptians bombed Tel Aviv's central bus station, inflicting heavy casualties, and continued to advance in the Negev; in the north, although the situation was less dangerous than in Jerusalem and the south, there were fierce battles against the Syrians and Lebanese.

Most of the arms purchased in Europe had not yet arrived, and after the fall of Etzion, many questioned Ben-Gurion's strategy of holding every Jewish settlement. The demands came pouring in to evacuate besieged villages. Doggedly, courageously, Ben-Gurion fought for time, refusing evacuation demands, yet unable to promise assistance.

It is true that the Arab invasion plan was less a co-ordinated attack than a division of Palestine into the areas to be occupied by the respective Arab armies, and that each army looked to its own interests rather than co-ordinating its operations; but the Israelis, who disposed of what was no more than a partisan force with a wide range of light arms and virtually no air force, heavy arms, armour or artillery, were, on the face of it, no match for the Arab invaders.

As the fighting proceeded, the IDF was fashioned into a co-ordinated fighting force that could move units from one front to another via internal lines of communication. Above all, the Israelis knew they were literally fighting for their lives and the lives of their families. This, despite mistakes and some internal bickering, brought about their remarkable victory in the 1948 War of Independence.

If the Israeli soldiers fought with heroism and tenacity, and the Palmach soldiers demonstrated particular flair and panache, it was the sixty-one-year-old Ben-Gurion, a military autodidact without an army background or military experience, who made the important decisions, directed the strategy and quite simply refused even to consider retreat or withdrawal. He had played a crucial role in preparing his people for an all-out conflict; now he was the central pillar in the actual conduct of the war.

AS THE Syrian army attacked the Jordan valley settlements, a delegation came from Degania, the first kibbutz, to Ben-Gurion in Tel Aviv demanding troops and equipment. "There aren't any," Ben-Gurion told them. "The whole country is a front line; we are unable to send reinforcements." One of the delegation burst into tears, asking whether the Jordan valley was going to be abandoned. Only many years later did Ben-Gurion disclose how badly he felt about refusing help, but there was nothing he could promise.

Chief of Operations Yadin told the Jordan valley defenders that they would have to let the Syrian tanks approach within thirty yards of the settlement and attack them with petrol-bombs. This tactic was employed successfully at Degania. When some ancient cannon (French guns dating back to the turn of the century) finally arrived, Ben-Gurion consented to their being despatched to the Jordan kibbutzim — but only for twenty-four hours; afterwards they were transferred to the central front at Latrun.

At the end of the first week, things were going badly: the Arab Legion continued to take Jewish suburbs in Jerusalem and held the Latrun police fort that controlled the road to Jerusalem. The Egyptians were driving towards Tel Aviv and the Iraqis threatened to cut the coastal plain in half. The situation appeared to be hopeless; but then the first Messerschmitt aircraft arrived from Czechoslovakia, and a ship bearing rifles and cannon arrived.

Within days of facing defeat, Ben-Gurion demanded offensive action on the northern and central fronts, while holding the line in the south. As he had previously, he placed maximum emphasis on relieving besieged Jerusalem. He thought that the Arab Legion was the most dangerous force facing his troops, and determined to smash it; but, even more important, he saw Jerusalem as the symbol of Jewish independence and was determined not to let it fall. In the past Ben-Gurion had insisted on the centrality of Jerusalem, moving both the Histadrut offices and the Zionist executive there; now his commitment to King David's eternal capital was even more dramatically expressed.

There were stormy arguments between Ben-Gurion and Yadin, who saw a greater danger from the Egyptians, but Ben-Gurion insisted on an immediate attack against Latrun with a newly formed brigade, reinforced with new immigrants straight off the ship. Yadin pleaded for a postponement, insisting the brigade was not ready for battle. Ben-Gurion ordered: "Attack, whatever the cost."

The repeated unsuccessful attacks on Latrun were viewed by many at the time as a military mistake, but Ben-Gurion's dogged insistence on relieving Jerusalem ensured that the historic Jewish capital — or at least its western half — became part of Israel. The Latrun battle also forced the Arab Legion to concentrate forces there, preventing it from overrunning western Jerusalem. Sir John Bagot Glubb (Glubb Pasha), the British commander of the

Arab Legion, wrote in his memoirs that the battle of Latrun necessitated concentrating forces there and prevented the Legion from taking all of Jerusalem.

However, despite a heroic house-to-house battle, the outnumbered, outgunned Israelis defending the Jewish Quarter of the Old City ran out of ammunition, and a surrender was negotiated with the Arab Legion at the end of May.

Shortly afterwards, a route to Jerusalem by-passing Latrun, Israel's "Burma Road," was discovered, and the author of this book was a member of the team that reconnoitred the route and brought Ben-Gurion the plan for reaching Jerusalem along it. Ben-Gurion immediately ordered the mobilization of hundreds of civilians to pave as much of the secret route as possible. By the time of the first United Nations – sponsored truce on June 11, the first convoys had got through and Jerusalem was no longer cut off.

In Galilee, Syrian and irregular forces had been pushed back, and the Arab invasion in the north had been successfully blocked. In the coastal plain, Iraqi forces had been repulsed.

In the south, the sparsely defended Jewish settlements of the Negev put up a fierce resistance to the overwhelming Egyptian attacks, forcing the Egyptian army to by-pass many of them. Even on this front, the Israelis scored a number of successes and kept the road open for a time, but by the time of the first truce the Egyptians had succeeded in cutting off the Negev.

The first truce was a welcome respite for the Israelis, particularly for Jerusalem, where food and water had almost run out. The UN organized some convoys under Arab Legion inspection, but further supplies and military equipment were brought in via the "Burma Road."

Both sides used the truce to strengthen their positions. The Israelis absorbed artillery and a hodge-podge of tanks and armoured vehicles acquired from all over the world. Apart from the mortal danger to Israel posed by the Arab invasion, Ben-Gurion was also faced with the problem of the dissident Jewish fighting forces.

The IZL attempted to bring in the *Altalena,* a vessel loaded with armaments, but negotiations with the Haganah regarding the disposal of the equipment aboard the *Altalena* broke down, and in one of his most controversial decisions Ben-Gurion ordered the Haganah to sink the ship. His decision is a subject of internal dispute in Israel until today. Ben-Gurion's critics still criticize his action; his admirers cite it as an example of his single-minded courage. Ultimately Ben-Gurion took his stand on the imperative of unity, insisting that there could only be one government in Israel, one army, and one commander of that army. After the sinking of the *Altalena,* there seemed to be a danger of civil strife among the Jews, but the dissident leadership backed down; subsequently the IZL ceased to exist as a separate force and its members joined the IDF.

Ben-Gurion's authority was also under attack from the left, from the Palmach commanders, who accused him of bias against them in favour of officers who had served in the British army. It was a fact that Ben-Gurion, while acknowledging the bravery and ingenuity of the Palmach men, felt they were more guerrilla fighters than regular soldiers, and lacked experience in commanding the larger formations now being deployed in a full-scale war.

The Palmach members of the General Staff submitted their collective resignations in protest against Ben-Gurion's plans to reorganize the IDF command. Ben-Gurion retorted that they were guilty of a political mutiny. When he failed to get backing from his cabinet, he submitted his own resignation as Prime Minister and Defence Minister. Despite harsh criticism of Ben-Gurion, his cabinet colleagues eventually realized that they could not manage without him and asked him to come back on his own terms.

The Palmach, like the IZL, was subsequently disbanded and ceased to exist as a separate entity within the IDF. Once more Ben-Gurion insisted on national unity and on his own authority as leader and commander-in-chief. Again, Ben-Gurion had hewn a strong path down the centre, rejecting the proposals of both left and right.

After the truce, which lasted four weeks, Israel, armed with its additional equipment, took the initiative, occupying much of Galilee and widening the corridor from the coastal plain to Jerusalem. Israeli forces extended their control in the area of Jerusalem, but an attempt to break into the Old City failed. Israeli aircraft bombed targets in Egypt and Syria. Ben-Gurion's strategy of holding on in as many locations as possible had justified itself.

The first commanders of the Israel Defence Forces: Yigal Allon, Yaacov Dori, Yigael Yadin, with David Ben-Gurion and Reuven Shiloah. (*Fred Csasnik*)

This round of fighting, which only lasted ten days, transformed the situation in Israel's favour, and the Arab side was glad to agree to an unlimited truce; but Ben-Gurion realized that the task had not been completed and he was concerned that the military victories would not be reflected in a political settlement.

The UN peace envoy, Count Folke Bernadotte, had already suggested removing the Negev from Israel and giving Jerusalem to the Arabs, with the Jewish population having autonomy. Now he reiterated his plan for the Negev, while suggesting that Jerusalem be placed under international control. Bernadotte's plan was rejected by both sides; but the day after he presented it, he was assassinated in Jerusalem by members of the Lehi group. Incensed, Ben-Gurion ordered the arrest of dissidents throughout the country, but Bernadotte's murder had given his anti-Israel plan a certain moral force.

Taking advantage of constant violations of the ceasefire by the Arab side, Ben-Gurion proposed the conquest of Judea, the part of the West Bank south of Jerusalem, but it was turned down by his cabinet colleagues. Undeterred, Ben-Gurion proposed a plan to liberate the Negev, still cut off by Egyptian forces.

A supply convoy to the Negev was attacked by the Egyptians, upon which Operation Ten Plagues went into effect. When the UN called for another ceasefire, Ben-Gurion managed to delay Israel's reply until the road to the Negev was opened and Beersheba had been captured. In the north, there were also ceasefire violations, which enabled the IDF to complete the conquest of Galilee.

Israel was now in possession of more than it had been awarded by the UN partition plan; but Ben-Gurion, who had been prepared to accept partition, pointed out that the plan had been invalidated by the concerted Arab invasion, which had almost destroyed the Jewish state. When Egypt refused to obey the UN Security Council call to negotiate an armistice with Israel, Ben-Gurion ordered the final campaign of the war, which took the IDF to Eilat and into Sinai. Warned by the United States that Britain would enter the battle on Egypt's side under the terms of the Anglo-Egyptian defence treaty, Ben-Gurion ordered his forces to withdraw from Sinai.

In the War of Independence, the very existence of Israel hung in the balance. It was saved by the great and historic leadership of Ben-Gurion, who led a nation determined to survive and prepared to make every sacrifice to achieve that end. That sacrifice was made in 1948, but it would continue to be exacted in the years to come.

At this point Ben-Gurion the realist took over from Ben-Gurion the visionary. Foreseeing problems with an Arab majority, conflicts with the UN and the great powers, he gave up his plan to take Judea and Samaria (the West Bank) and even the eastern half of Jerusalem. Israel now had work for many years, he pointed out, there was plenty to do.

Even while the war was raging in the second half of 1948, 100,000 new immigrants arrived in the new state, which somehow managed to find them homes and jobs. Ben-Gurion now set himself a new task: the ingathering of the exiles.

IN HIS early years Ben-Gurion had worked on the land. Subsequently he became a leader of the Labour-Zionist movement,

Raising the flag of Israel at the United Nations building, Lake Success, New York, May 14, 1948. *Center:* Abba Eban, and *right:* Moshe Sharett, shortly to become Foreign Minister of the new state. (*Zionist Archives*)

Rhodes, April 3, 1949: Moshe Dayan adds his signature to the Armistice Agreement with Jordan. At his left is Reuven Shiloah, the head of the Israeli delegation. (*Jewish Agency Photo Archives*)

Prime Minister David Ben-Gurion takes the salute on the first anniversary of Israel's Declaration of Independence, May 14, 1949. (*Krongold, London*)

turning it into the main instrument of national renaissance. He had then taken over the leadership of the Zionist movement, waging the political struggle for Israel's independence. When the main task had become a military one, Ben-Gurion turned himself into a military leader, preparing his people for war and directing the struggle.

He remained very involved with security matters, but he now turned his hand to persuading his colleagues of the feasibility of a seemingly impossible task: doubling the nation's population in four years. In the years 1948–51, almost 700,000 new immigrants flooded into an Israel still beset by murder and infiltration across its borders from the Arab states, which, although they had signed armistices, refused to recognize it. The immigrants came mainly from Germany, Romania, Bulgaria, Turkey, Iraq, Yemen, Morocco, Algeria and Tunisia.

The economic and social problems were formidable, and many of his colleagues urged that immigration be held back, but Ben-Gurion insisted that they come. At one stage some 200,000 people were living in tents, and ugly immigrant camps were thrown up all over Israel. Israeli officials made frantic efforts to secure loans and credits from Western nations and donations from Jews all over the world, but there was never quite enough. Often the country waited for a single ship with food supplies to come in, literally on the verge of starvation; but Ben-Gurion refused to consider holding back the immigration.

Although the main task in those early years was the absorption of the immigrants and the establishment of an economy, Israel's political problems were far from over. The UN General Assembly passed a resolution calling for the internationalization of Jerusalem. Ben-Gurion had been prepared to give up on Judea and Samaria, and even to accept a divided Jerusalem, but that was as far as he was prepared to go. "Israel has and will have only one capital: Jerusalem the eternal," he told the Knesset. The Knesset and all but two government ministries were quickly transferred to Jerusalem, amidst an international furore.

At the same time, Ben-Gurion maintained secret contacts with King Abdullah of Transjordan, but the King's British advisers discouraged him. Nevertheless, agreement in principle was reached

The early years of the state were taken up with absorbing a million and a half immigrants from more than seventy different countries. Children from Kurdistan in a ma'abara (immigrant camp) at the Kastel, near Jerusalem, 1952. (*Werner Braun*) A young mother from Morocco in the new town of Dimona, 1957. (*David Rubinger*)

with Abdullah; but the Jordanian monarch's assassination in 1951 in the Al-Aksa Mosque in the presence of his grandson, the present King Hussein, put an end to the process.

However, economic problems remained paramount and Ben-Gurion, although he understood little of economics, took two steps to secure finance for his struggling nation. No one could object to his first move: at a rally in New York's Madison Square Garden, he launched the Israel Bonds campaign, which over the years was to contribute significantly to the country's development. His other proposal once again brought him into a savage conflict with both left and right: a claim to West Germany for compensation for Jewish property looted by the Nazis.

After the Holocaust, in which six million Jews — more than a million of them children — had been massacred under conditions of incredible barbarity, the matter of Germany in the Jewish state engaged the deepest and strongest emotions. Many Jews, particularly survivors whose families had been wiped out, found difficulty even in hearing the name of Germany. A distinguished visiting musician had been physically attacked for playing the works of composers regarded as close to the Nazi regime and ideology.

Into this emotional powder-keg came the question of German compensation payments to Israel. Many were genuinely hurt and outraged, and even the political opposition from both right and left could not be dismissed lightly. Menachem Begin's Herut nationalists, no less than the socialists of Mapam, were giving voice to genuine and deep-rooted feelings.

Ben-Gurion was entirely consistent in approving an application for compensation. His entire life had been dedicated to one purpose: the revival, survival and prosperity of the Jewish people in their ancestral homeland. More than most of his colleagues and opponents he had seen the dangers looming in Europe. No one had urged Jewish immigration more passionately than Ben-Gurion; no one had fought the British Mandate regime more tenaciously for the right of Jews to enter their land. He had even been prepared to defy his own colleagues and accept the Peel partition plan in the hope that even a minuscule Jewish state would be able to save at least some of Europe's Jews.

After the war, when touring the death camps of Europe, he had delivered one message to the survivors: come home! He had been —and remained—obsessed with creating a strong Jewish sovereignty, where nothing like the Holocaust could ever happen again.

Now again in the matter of reparations from Germany he was guided by one overriding principle: the survival and welfare of the State of Israel. Everything else was subordinate to that.

Nahum Goldmann had become chairman of the Jewish Agency, and it was to him that Ben-Gurion turned to negotiate the reparations agreement. The two agreed that the basic claim would be for $1,000 million. Goldmann put the matter to West German Chancellor Konrad Adenauer, who accepted this figure as the starting-point for negotiations.

The country was in an uproar when Ben-Gurion brought the matter to the Knesset. Left and right united against Ben-Gurion with huge protest demonstrations, and Knesset members arriving for the session had to make their way through police barriers and barbed wire.

Explaining his decision to the Knesset, Ben-Gurion agreed that there could never be any compensation for the deaths of millions of Jewish men, women and children. However, he pointed out, apart from the murder and torture, Jewish property had also been plundered by the Nazis. The German people were still benefiting from this pillage of Jewish factories, businesses, shops and homes.

"The government of Israel considers itself bound to demand from the German people restitution for this stolen Jewish property," declared Ben-Gurion. "Let not the murderers of our people also be the beneficiaries of its property."

Down the road in Jerusalem's Zion Square, Menachem Begin was also making a speech. Telling the crowd (inaccurately) that the police possessed grenades "which have gas made in Germany —the same gas that was used to kill your fathers and mothers," Begin went on to declare: "We are prepared to suffer anything, torture chambers, concentration camps and subterranean prisons, so that any decision to deal with Germany will not come to pass."

He then marched to the Knesset to take part in the debate. An angry crowd stormed the Knesset, breaking through the barbed-wire barriers, overturning cars and throwing stones. Ninety-two policemen and thirty-six civilians were injured and the army had to be called in to restore order.

Ben-Gurion was particularly incensed by what he perceived as a threat to the Knesset's sovereignty. He broadcast to the nation that, "The state possesses sufficient forces to protect Israel's sovereignty and freedom, and to prevent thugs and political assassins from taking control."

After a stormy debate lasting several days, the Knesset backed Ben-Gurion, and a month later West Germany undertook to provide Israel with goods and services worth $715 million over a period of twelve years. A further $107 million was to be paid to world Jewish organizations.

The German reparations payments made a major contribution to Israel's industrialization and the stabilization of its economy during the 1950s and 1960s. Once again it had been Ben-Gurion the pragmatist who had prevailed over both doubting colleagues and determined opponents to ensure the prosperity of his nation.

The early years of the state were marked by a continuing political duel between Ben-Gurion and his opponents from both left and right, which reached a climax in the dispute over German reparations. But if the aging leader had disagreed violently with Begin on many matters, the two men found common ground when Ben-Gurion resumed his role as the nation's military leader in 1955.

IN NOVEMBER 1953, Ben-Gurion resigned the premiership and retired to Sde Boker, an isolated kibbutz in the heart of the Negev. Worn out by his unrelenting military and political struggles, the sixty-seven-year-old statesman decided to take a well-earned rest. However, he was also concerned to set a personal example.

Since his earliest days, Ben-Gurion had seen the importance of pioneering settlement, which he saw as the basis of the Jewish renaissance in its ancient land. He might have returned to Galilee, of which he had fond memories, but he was convinced that the future development and prosperity of the nation lay in settling the uninhabited Negev. His pragmatic vision realized that this was the one large area where the Jews would be allowed to expand and develop.

He had fought hard, both diplomatically and militarily, to ensure that the Negev was included in the State of Israel, but he was disappointed at the slow rate of development. Only a few kibbutzim had been added to already existing settlements, and the area's three development towns and Eilat were struggling. Many wept when Ben-Gurion retired to the Negev. He sternly told them not to weep but to follow.

At Sde Boker, Ben-Gurion worked as a shepherd, replied to hundreds of letters and studied classical Greek. However, it was difficult for such an authoritative leader to be suddenly divorced from the reins of power, and the stream of political and military leaders to the tiny kibbutz was almost uninterrupted. This was all the more so as Israel's security situation was deteriorating, as the Arab states stepped up their murderous campaign of infiltration and sabotage.

In Egypt, a military junta had ousted King Farouk, and the new leaders adopted a far more radical anti-West and anti-Israel policy. When Gamal Abdel Nasser, the behind-the-scenes leader of the coup, became President of Egypt, this became even more pronounced, and raids against Israel were increased.

The pressure mounted on Ben-Gurion to return, particularly after a security mishap in Egypt led to the resignation of Pinhas Lavon, who had succeeded him as Defence Minister.

In February 1955, Ben-Gurion returned to the Defence Ministry, serving under Moshe Sharett, who remained Prime Minister and Foreign Minister. Sharett had always espoused a political stand closer to that of Ben-Gurion's old rival Chaim Weizmann, but as long as he had been the subordinate, the two worked well together. Now that the roles were reversed, it became increasingly difficult.

Ben-Gurion demanded an activist policy of retaliation to infiltration and cross-border raids; Sharett believed in restraint. Ben-Gurion was convinced that, if Israel replied vigorously to Egyptian provocations, a wider conflict could be avoided. As the raids escalated Ben-Gurion went further, presenting a plan to drive the Egyptians out of the Gaza Strip. Sharett — and a majority of the cabinet — rejected the proposal, leading to an open rift between the two men.

When elections were held later that year, Ben-Gurion resumed the leadership of his party and formed the new government: once again he was both Prime Minister and Defence Minister. Challenges were not slow in coming. While Ben-Gurion was still forming his administration, the Egyptians signed an agreement in Prague whereby they began to receive unprecedented quantities of arms from the Soviet Union via Czechoslovakia. This totally upset the tenuous arms balance in the Middle East, and Israel made unsuccessful diplomatic efforts to foil the deal.

Furthermore, President Nasser declared openly that the acquisition of the weapons was a major step towards the decisive battle for the destruction of Israel. Egypt had never allowed Israeli shipping through the Suez Canal, but now Nasser blockaded the Straits of Tiran in southern Sinai, preventing vessels from reaching Israel's southern port of Eilat.

Acting on instructions from Ben-Gurion, IDF Chief of Staff Moshe Dayan proposed a plan to strike against Egypt and capture the southern part of the Sinai peninsula to free the Straits of Tiran. However, Ben-Gurion decided on delaying the operation to enable Israel to try to acquire weapons to match the Egyptian build-up.

Negotiations with the United States for an American guarantee to Israel and arms supplies continued into 1956, but were unsuccessful. Britain too was unwilling to help; but France, engaged in a bitter war in Algeria, proved more amenable. Shimon Peres, Ben-Gurion's Director-General of the Defence Ministry, forged a friendship with Paris, which turned France into Israel's chief supplier of modern weapons for a decade. In April 1956, the first Mystère-4 fighter-planes arrived in Israel.

Buoyed up by Nasser, the Arabs stepped up their pressure. In the north the Syrians shelled Israeli fishing boats on Lake Kinneret; tension increased along the Jordan, as pro-Nasser elements gained influence in Jordan; and there were mounting clashes along the Gaza Strip border with Egypt.

Ben-Gurion eased Moshe Sharett out of the Foreign Ministry into a position in the World Zionist Organization and appointed the more activist Golda Meir, as a preliminary step to forging an even more comprehensive alliance with France. Apart from massive arms supplies, the French moved towards the idea of joint action with Israel against Nasser's Egypt, which was giving arms and support to the rebels fighting the French in Algeria.

The turning point came on July 26, two days after the first major shipload of French arms arrived in Israel: Nasser nationalized the Suez Canal, which had been jointly owned by France and Britain. These two nations immediately began planning military action against Egypt, but they were deterred by the United States. In September the French began actively planning military co-operation with Israel against Nasser.

BEN-GURION was extremely cautious about the various plans put forward by the French and British, particularly the British proposal for an "Israeli pretext," which would involve Israel first attacking Egypt, and only afterwards Britain and France occupying the Suez Canal Zone to separate the combatants. He was suspicious of British intentions and objected to Israel being used by the two powers for their own ends.

He wanted to ensure full partnership and foresaw international condemnation if Israel acted alone. He was also concerned about the reactions of the United States and the Soviet Union, and about the possible bombing of Israel's towns by Egypt's newly acquired bombers.

On October 20, 1956, Ben-Gurion flew to France for secret meetings with French and British government representatives. Ben-Gurion was still suspicious of the British; but Egypt, which had formed a joint military command with Syria and Jordan, was increasing its terror attacks against Israeli civilians across the border, and Ben-Gurion felt there was no alternative to wiping out the terrorist bases from which the attacks came. He was also mindful of the fact that Israel had managed to form an alliance with a Western power, France.

The plan was for the IDF to drop paratroops at the Mitla Pass, west of the Suez Canal, and shortly afterwards to cross the border, attacking terrorist bases in Gaza and driving south to liberate the Straits of Tiran. France would supply aerial cover for Israel's cities. The British and French would deliver an ultimatum to Israel and Egypt to withdraw to positions ten miles east and west of the canal.

If the Egyptians refused, as anticipated, they would start attacking the canal zone.

Ben-Gurion was by now seventy years old, and he felt the tension keenly. After a cabinet meeting, he developed a high temperature and was confined to his bed. There he received the leaders of Israel's political parties and informed them of the plan. His old rival Begin, leader of the largest opposition group, pledged his full support.

President Eisenhower was tied up in his campaign for re-election and the Russians were involved with problems in Poland and Hungary. Nevertheless, Ben-Gurion came under heavy pressure from the United States, which had learned about the Israeli mobilization, and feared that Israel was about to attack Jordan, from where some of the largest terrorist attacks were coming. The American Ambassador brought Ben-Gurion two personal messages from President Eisenhower, warning him against action "which would endanger the peace and growing friendship between our two nations."

Ben-Gurion replied, noting the "ring of steel" around Israel's borders resulting from the joint Arab command, and pointing out Nasser's expansionary policies. "My government would be failing in its responsibilities," he wrote, "if it were not to take all necessary measures to assure that the declared Arab aim of eliminating Israel by force should not come about."

For Ben-Gurion, October 30 was a tense day. The IDF had dropped paratroops at the Mitla Pass and its forces were advancing in Sinai and Gaza, but the French and British were late in starting their bombing raids on the canal zone. Nevertheless, Ben-Gurion vetoed a request from the commander of the Israel Air Force to bomb Egyptian targets, saying that as long as the Egyptians did not bomb Israel, the Israelis must not hit Egypt from the air.

By November 5, the IDF had taken Gaza and Sinai down to the Straits of Tiran; its forces were positioned east of the Suez Canal; the terrorist bases had been destroyed and the Egyptian army had been dealt a devastating blow. However, the political battle with the United States, the United Nations and the Soviet Union was about to begin.

At the outset of the fighting Eisenhower had sent a message

Lieutenant General Moshe Dayan was Commander of the IDF in 1956 during "Operation Kadesh," otherwise known as the Sinai Campaign. (*WZPS*)

stating that, if the IDF contented itself with destroying the terrorist bases and then withdrew, he would issue "a declaration of profound admiration and warm friendship" for Israel. As the battle raged, the UN Security Council was called into session to demand a ceasefire, but France and Britain wielded their veto. The UN General Assembly then adopted a resolution calling for a ceasefire and Israeli withdrawal.

On November 4, the Soviet Union completed its crushing of the Hungarian revolt and entered the Middle East fray, despatching threatening notes to Britain, France and Israel, implicitly threatening the use of nuclear weapons and accusing Israel of "sowing hatred of the State of Israel among the Eastern peoples, such as cannot but leave its mark on the future of Israel and places in question the very existence of Israel as a state."

Britain and France had started the actual invasion of the canal zone, but they backed down under international pressure without completing their operation.

Tending the wounded, Sinai, 1956. (*"Bamahaneh"*)

Rising from his sickbed to address the Knesset, Ben-Gurion termed the Sinai Campaign "the greatest and most splendid military operation in the chronicles of our people." He pronounced the armistice signed with Egypt in 1949 "dead and buried," but offered peace with Egypt and all the other Arab nations. He indicated Israel's intention of keeping at least part of Sinai, when he declared that Yotvat (Tiran) would become "a part of the Third Kingdom of Israel."

Ben-Gurion was not overly concerned when the UN General Assembly voted for a resolution ordering Israel to withdraw unconditionally, with only Israel voting against. However, when the newly re-elected President Eisenhower despatched an extremely sharp message, and the United States reeled off a series of threats, ending by making it quite clear that the Americans would not protect Israel against Soviet intervention, he was deeply concerned.

As the threats and condemnations poured in from all over the world, several cabinet ministers urged an immediate unconditional withdrawal. Ben-Gurion agreed to the principle of withdrawal, even without a peace treaty; but he bargained with the Americans to make it conditional on the entry of an international peace-keeping force.

Ben-Gurion was still hopeful that the Israelis could hold on to Gaza and southern Sinai, and he delayed the pullback as long as possible. However, after sharp confrontations with Eisenhower, Ben-Gurion concluded that he would have to withdraw completely. He put his faith in a French proposal that the UN would take over full powers of military and civilian administration in the Gaza Strip until a peace settlement could be concluded.

He was concerned that if Israel rejected the French plan, its only supply of weapons would be cut off. He was somewhat reassured when the Americans appeared to back the idea, but despite this the Egyptian military government was restored in Gaza in a matter of days.

The return of the Egyptians led to a period of violence in Gaza, during which Gazans suspected of "collaboration" with Israel were summarily executed. The UN forces were deployed at the southern tip of Sinai and along the Sinai and Gaza borders with

Israel; but Israel was to experience a decade of comparative quiet, with shipping moving freely through the Straits of Tiran and Eilat developing into an important port.

Ben-Gurion, who had found the courage to launch the Sinai Campaign, showed equal bravery in bowing to the inevitable. The Sinai Campaign removed from Israelis the sense of insecurity about their very existence. In the words of Ben-Gurion: "There is no power in the world that can reverse your great victory. . . . Israel after the Sinai Campaign will never again be the Israel before this mighty operation."

And indeed Israel's foreign relations were boosted by the campaign, as Asian, African and Latin American countries turned to the Jewish state for agricultural and military assistance. Israel's relations with France prospered and the French continued to be Israel's main arms supplier.

More than anything else, the Sinai Campaign increased Israel's self-confidence. There had been concern in some quarters that the Israel of the 1950s, which had absorbed hundreds of thousands of new immigrants, many of them from developing countries, was not as tough as the Yishuv that had won the War of Independence. The new Israel had proved that it was the equal of the 1948 generation, if not more than that. Ben-Gurion, who had led his people to independence and in the fight for their very existence, had consolidated his achievement.

The Old Man's task was not over and he continued to serve his nation for several years, building a "peripheral alliance" with Turkey, Iran and Ethiopia, beyond the ring of Arab hostility, and presiding over Israel's agricultural development and remarkable technological achievements. He also made strenuous efforts to bring new young leaders, such as Moshe Dayan, Abba Eban and Shimon Peres, into the leadership of his party and the nation, but here he was less successful in the face of opposition from his colleagues.

In 1965, Ben-Gurion broke with his party colleagues over the so-called "Lavon Affair," insisting on the establishment of a judicial committee of inquiry to investigate a security mishap in the 1950s. He subsequently led a revolt of young Labour party members and formed Rafi, the Israel Workers' List.

On the eve of the Six Day War in 1967, his old rival Begin proposed that he return to lead the government in face of the threatening situation; but it fell to one of his protégés, Dayan, to become Defence Minister at that time.

After the Six Day War, a majority of his Rafi party rejoined the Labour party, but Ben-Gurion continued to lead a small four-member opposition party in the Knesset, before finally retiring to Sde Boker.

He played no part in the remarkable victory of the Six Day War of 1967, or the amazing recovery in the Yom Kippur War of 1973. Nor did he live to see the visit to Jerusalem of Egypt's President Sadat in 1977, and the subsequent Israel-Egypt peace treaty; but the Israel of these achievements was the Israel he had built.

Ben-Gurion, with his dogged sense of purpose, his remarkable vision and his indomitable courage, is the towering figure of modern Jewish history. No less remarkable a quality was his clear-sighted pragmatism: his ability to judge realistically what he could attain and go all out for it.

By his courageous decisions, from the time he resolved to come and be a pioneer in Palestine to the declaration of the State of Israel, the fighting of the War of Independence, the ingathering of the exiles, the establishment of Jerusalem as Israel's capital, the development of the Negev and the consolidation of the nation's security in the Sinai Campaign, he set his stamp on Jewish history and shaped the modern Jewish nation. Thanks to Ben-Gurion, Israel has a national army, the IDF, above politics and subject to the civil authority, and a national education system.

For sixty-five years, from when he joined Poalei Zion in Warsaw, until 1970, when he retired from the Knesset, he was involved in the forefront of Jewish and Zionist public affairs. From the time he was elected chairman of the Jewish Agency Executive in 1935 to his relinquishing of the premiership of the State of Israel nearly three decades later, he was the supreme leader of his people and nation. The very embodiment of courage and tenacity, he is worthy to take his place in the pantheon of Jewish history among the historic figures of the past.

15 ⟣

The Yom Kippur Defenders:
Courage in the Face of Disaster

⟣ "**Y**OU HAVE saved the people of Israel!" This emotional message delivered over the radio network of the Seventh Armoured Brigade of the IDF at the end of the fourth day of the 1973 Yom Kippur War was entirely uncharacteristic. The speaker, Major General Rafael Eitan, is not an emotional man, and certainly not given to rhetoric. Years later, assuming the position of Chief of General Staff of the IDF, his speech lasted fully nineteen seconds.

What had prompted the gratitude of the normally taciturn Eitan was a battle of epic proportions, during which the Seventh Brigade with 100 tanks had blocked for four days and three nights a Syrian advance by five times that number.

Farther south, the Barak Armoured Brigade, with only fifty-seven tanks, had been almost totally wiped out by the advance of Syrian forces backed by 600 tanks. There the Syrians had broken through, but they had been delayed long enough for the IDF's hastily mobilized reserves to arrive.

It was a display of courage and stamina that has rarely been equaled, well worthy of comparison with the battles of Judah the Maccabee, Bar-Kokhba or even the ghetto fighters.

The IDF also fought bravely on the southern front; but, despite the enormous forces deployed by Egypt in crossing the Suez Canal, and despite their initial success, it was the Syrians, arriving at the very borders of Galilee, who threatened Israel itself, and it was the few defenders on the Golan Heights who held them at bay until sufficient reserves arrived to turn the tide of battle.

In selecting some of the men of the Seventh and Barak Brigades, who participated in the savage armour battles on the Golan in the Yom Kippur War, there is no intention of downgrading or diminishing the bravery of the soldiers of the many other units who defended Israel on both northern and southern fronts in 1973. On the contrary, the telling of their story is a tribute to all the Yom Kippur defenders, whose grit and tenacity saved the State of Israel from defeat at the hands of Egypt and Syria.

The IDF also fought with courage and effectiveness in the Sinai Campaign of 1956, in the Six Day War of 1967 and the War of Attrition in 1969–70; but in the Yom Kippur War Israel faced mortal danger and, battling with incredible bravery and self-sacrifice, won an astounding victory. The inherent strength and resilience of the people of Israel was revealed in the stark and tragic days at the outset of the war, when, fighting back against overwhelming odds, they overcame the initial setbacks.

Haganah means defence, and the pre-state Jewish military organization was given that name deliberately. When the Israeli army was established, the name was retained in the Israel *Defence* Forces. In point of fact, however, both the Haganah and the IDF were usually forced to take the initiative and to go on to the attack against their enemies.

Until 1973, the main characteristics of the IDF were its speed, mobility, boldness, initiative and improvising ability. Some doubted its stamina.

In the Yom Kippur War, a classic war of defence, the soldiers of Israel, facing an onslaught from combined forces far larger than its own, exhibited raw courage, tenacity and awesome staying power.

The Six Day War of 1967: Jerusalem under bombardment.

They also proved that, even in an era of electronic warfare, using guided missiles and push-button technology, the human element is the decisive one. The saga of the Yom Kippur War prompts a sense of deep humility. The State of Israel and the Jewish people owe an unpayable debt to the Yom Kippur defenders.

The IDF, based largely on its reserves, is truly an army of the people. In 1973 it had to pay the price for the mistakes and misjudgement of the country's political and military leadership. It passed the perilous test magnificently and its success was ultimately to lead to the peace process with Egypt.

ISRAEL'S 1948 War of Independence established the Jewish state, but did not bring it peace. By the 1960s, however, it seemed that Israel was gradually gaining a reluctant acceptance in the Arab world. The borders were relatively quiet; Tunisian President Habib Bourguiba spoke of recognizing the reality of the Jewish state; and the Egyptians had much of their army bogged down in a civil war in distant Yemen.

However, the Soviet Union was pouring weapons into Egypt and Syria, President Nasser was pursuing an aggressive pan-Arab policy that included war against Israel and a number of renewed border attacks and counterstrikes escalated into a confrontation. Nasser sent Egyptian troops into Sinai, expelled the UN peace-keeping troops stationed there and closed the Straits of Tiran. Israel had long made it clear that closing these straits was a casus belli, so that Egypt was in effect declaring war.

The guarantees that Israel had received in 1956 after withdrawing from Sinai and Gaza, notably those promising freedom of shipping in the Red Sea, were shown to be worthless. For several weeks Israel, which had mobilized its forces to meet the Egyptian threat, tried the diplomatic option, but to no avail. Egypt signed agreements with Syria and Jordan, completing the armed encirclement of the Jewish state. Egyptian forces massed in Sinai and Arab forces mobilized all around Israel, including 2,500 tanks and 600 frontline planes. Nasser promised the annihilation of Israel.

On June 5, 1967, Israel launched a pre-emptive strike against

Israeli Centurion tanks advancing across the Golan Heights, June 1967. (*"Bamahaneh"*)

A burnt-out Syrian tank at Tawfiq on the Golan Heights, June 1967. The picture graphically indicates how the Syrian strategic positions threatened the Huleh valley and northern Israel.

Egyptian, Syrian, Jordanian and Iraqi airfields, destroying the bulk of Egypt's air force and seriously damaging most of the important airfields in a few hours. More than 400 enemy aircraft were put out of action in two days, most of them on the ground. The Jordanian army invaded West Jerusalem and attacked targets in Israel. The IDF took Gaza and Sinai even more swiftly than in 1956, occupied the West Bank of the Jordan, captured East Jerusalem and drove the Syrians back from the Golan Heights east of the Sea of Galilee, from where they had been shelling settlements for nineteen years.

It took just six days to complete the astounding victory, and at the end of it Israel was in possession of areas considerably larger than its own. Differing attitudes were subsequently to emerge in Israel concerning the future of these territories; but on June 19,

Entering the Lions' (St. Stephen's) Gate, the Old City of Jerusalem, June 7, 1967. *Left to right:* Major General Uzi Narkiss, Commander of the central front; Moshe Dayan; Lieutenant General Yitzhak Rabin, Commander-in-Chief of the IDF.

The return to the Western Wall, June 1967: the photograph that became a worldwide symbol of Israel at war and the reunification of Jerusalem. (*David Rubinger*)

1967, the National Unity Government voted unanimously to re-turn Sinai to Egypt and the Golan Heights to Syria in return for a peace agreement. The Golan would have to be demilitarized and special arrangements would be negotiated for the Straits of Tiran. The government also resolved to open negotiations with King Hussein of Jordan regarding the eastern border.

The Israeli decision was conveyed to the Arab nations by the United States, but unfortunately it met with a negative response. Meeting in Khartoum shortly after the war, an Arab summit con-ference resolved that there would be no peace, no recognition and no negotiations with Israel.

THE ORIGINS of the Yom Kippur War of 1973 can be traced back to the conclusion of the Six Day War, seven years earlier. Although Egypt and Syria planned and launched the Yom Kippur War, the Israeli political and military leadership cannot entirely escape responsibility for its outbreak.

Israel's overconfidence in the superiority of its armed forces enabled Egypt and Syria to surprise it on October 6, 1973, and gain spectacular initial successes. Egyptian forces crossed the Suez Canal and destroyed the Bar-Lev Line, Israel's fortifications along the canal. The Syrians virtually wiped out an entire Israeli ar-moured brigade and were poised to invade Galilee.

The defence concept of Israel is dictated by its inability to main-tain a large standing army. Its intelligence services are supposed to give advance warning of an attack, permitting the speedy mobili-zation of the reserves. The small regular army is supposed to block the initial attack, assisted by the air force, which has a large regu-lar component. In the Yom Kippur War, the intelligence assess-ment was erroneous.

Despite clear indications of preparations for war on the part of Egypt and Syria, Israel's military intelligence assumed that, as had happened the previous May, the enemy would go to the brink, without actually attacking.

This specific failure of intelligence was backed by far wider, more general misconceptions. Lulled by the strategic depth and more defensible borders gained in the 1967 war, Israel's leaders, notably Defence Minister Moshe Dayan, were convinced that

The Yom Kippur War of 1973 took the country totally by surprise. *Center:* Lieutenant General David ("Dado") Elazar, Commander-in-Chief of the IDF. *To his left:* Major General Shmuel Gonen ("Gorodish"). Both officers had to resign following a court of inquiry after the war. (*Army Spokesman*)

Israel's situation had never been better. They predicted that it would be many years before the Arab nations would be in a position to wage war effectively.

Prime Minister Golda Meir, whose courage and resolution were to prove vital during the war, cannot be absolved from responsibility for failure to prevent it. Her doctrinaire, inflexible approach to problems and to government contributed to the failure, because of the lack of proper staff work and alternative evaluations of the political and military situation. She had little idea of orderly administration, with the necessary checks and balances, preferring to work with her closest colleagues, her so-called kitchen cabinet.

In addition to this, overconfidence after the Six Day War victory had caused laxity in the IDF. Semitrained reservists were manning the Suez Canal forts at a time when a maximum state of alert was called for. The lack of discipline was reflected in the high rate of traffic and training accidents, many of them fatal. The slovenly

Prime Minister Golda Meir during the first days of the war.

turnout of the individual soldier and the sloppy maintenance of camps and equipment were an indication of a deeper malaise.

All these factors had an effect when the armies of Egypt and Syria launched their assaults in overwhelming strength on Yom Kippur, the Day of Atonement, when the nation was for the most part fasting and at prayer. In some ways this made mobilization easier, as a majority of the population was at synagogue or at home. Thus the reserve soldiers rushed to their units and assembly points, exchanging prayer shawls for uniforms and weapons: Israel was once again fighting for its existence.

THE GOLAN HEIGHTS was captured by the IDF from the Syrians in the last two days of the 1967 war. It is a plateau, some forty-five miles long by fifteen miles wide, extending from 9,000-foot Mount Hermon in the north to 600 feet above the Yarmuk valley in the south. To the east, the rough, boulder-strewn surface rises

Golda Meir addresses the troops on the Golan Heights, October 1973. *To her right:* Moshe Dayan and Major General Yitzhak Hofi, Commander of the northern front in the Yom Kippur War.

Suez Canal, 1973: an Israeli army pontoon bridge crossing from west to east. (*IDF*)

gently toward Damascus. To the west, the plateau drops sharply to the Hula valley and Lake Kinneret (the Sea of Galilee).

The Syrian onslaught began with a massive air and artillery attack, under cover of which its armour advanced. At the same time, a helicopter-borne commando force took the vital Israeli reconnaissance position on Mount Hermon.

In the northern sector of the Golan Heights, the Seventh Brigade with its 100 tanks was attacked by Syrian infantry supported by some 500 tanks. Farther south, the main Syrian thrust, supported by 600 tanks, was launched at the Barak Brigade, which had fifty-seven tanks at its disposal.

General Yitzhak Hofi, GOC of the northern front, left Major General Eitan, a veteran paratroop officer popularly known as Raful, in command of the division holding the Golan Heights with orders to block the Syrian advance for as long as possible. Raful's headquarters were in Nafekh.

A number of incidents and personalities have been picked out to illustrate the heroic blocking action of the IDF on the Golan, but

Supplies are brought to the surrounded Egyptian Third Army cut off by the encircling Israelis. Clearly visible is the breach in the Bar-Lev line caused by high-velocity water hoses. (*David Rubinger*)

the overall credit must go to the steady determination, faith and courage of Raful, who directed the defence operation.

As the Barak Brigade, commanded by Colonel Yitzhak Ben-Shoham, clung tenaciously to its positions opposite Rafid, the Syrian armour was held up by a hastily improvised unit of four tanks called "Force Zvika." Its commander was Lieutenant Zvi Greengold (Zvika), a member of Lohamei Hagetaot, a western Galilee kibbutz founded by former partisans and ghetto fighters. He was on leave at his kibbutz, before starting a company commanders' course, when war broke out. Hitch-hiking to Nafekh on the first day of the war, he volunteered his services and was put in charge of four tanks, three of which had been damaged in the battles and repaired. One of the main Syrian thrusts was coming through the Tapline route, the maintenance road which runs alongside the Tapline oil pipe, which goes from Saudi Arabia via the Golan Heights to Lebanon. At 9 P.M. Force Zvika advanced to meet it.

After moving south, Zvika deployed his tanks by the side of the road, waiting for the Syrian advance. The enemy column appeared and Zvika's first shot at short range set the lead Syrian tank alight, but the explosion put his communications system out of order. Zvika signalled to his nearest tank to come alongside and changed positions with its commander.

He now had a tank with a communications system and he told the commander of the other tank to follow and imitate everything he did. A few hundred yards down the road, he found that he had lost his accompanying tanks and was on his own. Coming over the hill, he sighted three Syrian tanks and destroyed them.

He took up a new position and waited. Half an hour later, he saw a line of some thirty Syrian tanks and trucks approaching along the road. Putting the lead tank out of action at a range of twenty yards, he then proceeded to play hide-and-seek with the Syrian force, popping up from behind a hill, firing and disappearing. In this way he knocked out ten more tanks. The Syrians, presumably thinking they were confronting a sizable force, withdrew.

The first force of reserves had by now arrived at Nafekh. Lieutenant Colonel Uzi, with seven tanks, now took Zvika under his command. Uzi advanced southwards along the Tapline route with five tanks, while Zvika with three tanks drove parallel to him between the wire fences protecting the pipeline.

Fire was opened on them from both sides and, at around one o'clock in the morning of October 7, after holding the Syrians for several crucial hours, Uzi's force was wiped out. Uzi's own tank was hit and he was thrown out of it, seriously wounded. He lost his sight and his left arm.

Zvika's three tanks had meanwhile pulled back; but they were also hit by Syrian gunfire and burst into flames. Zvika and his crew managed to jump clear with their clothes on fire, rolling themselves in a ditch by the side of the road to extinguish the flames.

On the other side of the wire fence, Zvika joined up with three other Israeli tanks. Taking over one of them, he donned a helmet and announced over the radio, "Force Zvika." Shortly afterwards his burns began to take effect and he started to pass out; but the calm voice of Ben-Shoham coming through his earphones woke him up, and he managed to keep going.

By the morning of October 7, the Barak Brigade, which had fought valiantly against incredible odds, had been almost completely destroyed. Ben-Shoham, his deputy, David Yisraeli, and their operations officer advanced along the Tapline route with their few remaining tanks.

Ben-Shoham's tank knocked out five Syrian tanks and several armoured personnel carriers. He continued to give instructions to his deputy, who relayed them to the other tanks. In the midst of the battle, Yisraeli's tank ran out of ammunition. In a last desperate gesture, Yisraeli ordered his tank to charge the Syrians, while firing his machine gun; but he was killed when his tank was hit and destroyed.

Exposed in the turret of his tank, not knowing the fate of his deputy, Ben-Shoham continued to advance towards Nafekh, passing a disabled Syrian tank lying in the ditch. He barely glanced at it, but a Syrian soldier in the tank killed him with machine-gun fire as he went past. By noon, ninety percent of the officers of the Barak Brigade had been killed or wounded. The last remaining officer of the Brigade holding field rank was the intelligence officer.

At 1:15 P.M. that day the Syrians advanced on the divisional command headquarters at Nafekh. After the Syrians had by-passed the headquarters on both sides, Eitan finally moved his headquarters to a point some three miles north along the Tapline route.

Advancing into the Nafekh camp, the Syrians met fierce resistance from the few infantry remaining there. As the infantry fought desperately, a lone tank appeared, firing at the leading Syrian tank. It was Zvika, who was just ahead of the lead tanks of a new reserve brigade, which had just reached Nafekh.

That morning Zvika had joined Ben-Shoham's deputy, Yisraeli. But, after Yisraeli had been killed, he decided not to continue along the Tapline road. Instead, he cut across country towards Nafekh. There he joined up with another tank commanded by a reserve lieutenant. The two of them worked together, with Zvika firing at everything in sight.

The driver was in a state of shock, incapable of responding to orders, and somehow Zvika acquired a fresh driver and followed the new reserve unit which had come to relieve Nafekh. Twenty hours after it had set out, Force Zvika drove back into Nafekh. All around were the burnt-out Syrian tanks and armoured vehicles.

Wounded and bloody, his clothes burnt, his blond hair scorched, Zvika painfully pulled himself out of the tank. He fell into the arms of Major Dov, the surviving intelligence officer of the Barak Brigade. "I can't go on," he whispered. He was evacuated to hospital, but a week later he had returned to the front. Zvika Greengold was later awarded the Order of Courage, the IDF's highest decoration.

ZVIKA'S INCREDIBLE twenty-hour campaign, much of it conducting a lone battle, is only one of the many stories of heroism of the Barak Brigade, which delayed the Syrians on the southern sector of the Golan. Farther north, an equally remarkable struggle was being waged by the Seventh Brigade, under the command of Colonel Avigdor Ben-Gal.

The Brigade held out during four days and three nights of unrelenting fighting. By Tuesday afternoon, the Syrians had broken through and Ben-Gal's force, reduced from 100 tanks to a mere seven, was preparing to withdraw, when it was relieved by a reserve unit of thirteen tanks. The combined force launched a counterattack, and the Syrians, who had lost some 500 tanks and armoured vehicles, withdrew across the ceasefire line.

The battle of the Seventh Brigade began at 1 P.M. on the first day of the war, when massive Syrian armour advanced towards them. The Syrians had been supplied with sophisticated infra-red night-fighting equipment by the Soviet Union, far in advance of anything the Israelis had. Taking this into consideration, Ben-Gal ordered his men to wait until they reached a range of 800 yards before opening fire, to minimize the advantage of the infra-red devices.

The Syrians attacked in waves, losing large numbers of tanks and other vehicles. The Seventh Brigade, deployed in a more concentrated formation than the Barak Brigade had been able to manage farther south, defended with deadly effectiveness, knocking out tank after tank.

When a Syrian column started advancing north towards Kuneitra, Ben-Gal realized he would be outflanked. Accordingly, he ordered Captain Meir Zamir, nicknamed "Tiger," to move towards the fortifications south of the town. Tiger spaced his tanks at intervals along the road, while sending his deputy with a force parallel to the Syrian column.

The deputy was now behind the Syrian column and he opened fire, setting five tanks alight. The Syrians panicked and their tanks started crashing into one another. Tiger's tanks on the road now started picking off the Syrian tanks. He then moved them south-wards into positions of cover overlooking the road.

At dawn the Syrians regrouped and started moving down the road, straight into Tiger's ambush. He then rolled up the surviving Syrian forces towards Kuneitra, destroying many tanks on the way and attacking an approaching Syrian supply column. Ben-Gal refused his request for permission to pursue the column.

The valley opposite the Seventh Brigade, north of Kuneitra, which was to be named the "Valley of Tears," was already strewn with burning Syrian tanks, trucks and personnel carriers on the morning of October 7. But the Syrians launched a new advance along a two-and-a-half-mile front under cover of an intense artillery bombardment.

Ben-Gal directed the battle backed by Rafael Eitan. His Fifth Battalion was fighting an entire brigade; his First Battalion, farther north, was attacked by two Syrian armoured battalions, backed by infantry in armoured personnel carriers. He moved the Seventh Battalion, under the command of Lieutenant Colonel Avigdor Kahalani, into the central sector overlooking the Valley of Tears.

After the first day's fighting, Ben-Gal never had more than forty-five tanks at his disposal, but with them he was holding off some 500 Syrian tanks, backed by infantry and artillery. With their infra-red fighting equipment, the Syrians were able to get very close that night.

The Syrian infantry, equipped with RPG anti-tank bazookas, was knocking out many Israeli tanks; but at 1 A.M. on the morning of October 8, the battle died down, only to resume at 4 A.M. The Seventh Brigade was desperately trying to repair, rearm and refuel its tanks.

At dawn some 130 destroyed Syrian tanks and many other

Two of the heroes of the Yom Kippur War: Colonel Avigdor ("Yanush") Ben-Gal and Lieutenant Colonel Avigdor Kahalani. Two hundred sixty Syrian tanks were destroyed in a desperate battle that held on to the Golan Heights. Major General Rafael Eitan told them, "You have saved the people of Israel!"

burnt-out vehicles littered the Valley of Tears, many of them between — or even behind — the Israeli positions. All through the day of October 8, the brigade fought off concentrated Syrian attacks. On the southern flank, Tiger, with seven tanks, held off Syrian attempts to break through, destroying some thirty Syrian tanks and twenty personnel carriers with infantry. On the northern flank, casualties mounted, as Syrian artillery identified the Israeli positions and rained down their barrage.

After three days and two nights of almost continuous fighting, Ben-Gal's forces were exhausted. There was no time to eat or sleep and the commander realized that the effectiveness of the tanks was dropping. The brigade had lost fifty dead and many others were wounded. It was only the resourcefulness of the ordnance unit that kept some forty tanks functioning. Despite their enormous losses, the Syrians were continuing to advance.

On the night of October 8, the Syrians launched an advance on the northern flank, and Ben-Gal brought Tiger round from the south to attack them from the rear. With seven tanks, Tiger broke the advance of a Syrian armoured company backed by infantry.

Tuesday morning saw the heaviest artillery barrage yet, with the firing of Katyusha rockets, and MiG-17 planes bombing the battered Seventh Division. Thousands of shells pounded the IDF positions, and a Syrian column of 100 tanks, backed by infantry in armoured personnel carriers, advanced.

The Israelis opened fire at maximum range, but the Syrian advance continued, despite heavy losses. The IDF tank commanders, as usual exposed in the turrets of their tanks, were suffering a high rate of attrition. Ben-Gal ordered the tanks back out of range of the Syrian artillery.

Kahalani now arrived with his Seventh Battalion, consisting of six tanks, which had been held in reserve. Coming through the smoke, he found Syrian tanks in the former Israeli positions. Rapid orders, faithfully executed, resulted in the destruction of four Syrian tanks at point-blank range in the space of a minute and a half.

Part of the Syrian force withdrew, and the Brigade advanced again to the high ground; but the Syrian advance still continued in most sectors. The commander of the First Battalion was killed and Ben-Gal ordered Kahalani to take command of the remnants of his force.

Kahalani now faced the armoured force of the Assad Republican Guard, an elite Syrian unit, which, however, proved less effective than many other forces. Manoeuvering on the high ground around the Valley of Tears, the Seventh Battalion destroyed the Assad unit.

Ben-Gal now put Kahalani in charge of the central sector. "Don't worry, I'm a black panther, they won't get past me," said the young battalion commander of Yemenite origin confidently; he then set about reviving the spirits of the exhausted men under his command.

In the early days of the State of Israel, David Ben-Gurion liked to look forward to the days when the Jews, who came from over seventy different countries, would be fully integrated into one nation. On one occasion he predicted that the children of Jews who had emigrated from Yemen would fill senior IDF command positions. Kahalani, today an IDF general, is the fulfilment of his prophecy.

Already a hero of the Six Day War, where he won the medal of Exemplary Conduct, Kahalani bore scars on his hands as a result of burns received in that conflict. Because of this he had acquired the nickname *Avigdor Hasaruf,* "Charred Avigdor."

Later Kahalani was to recall that the exhausted men simply did not react when he addressed them over the communications network. "They did not hear me, or they didn't understand," he said. He tried an appeal to their pride: "How can we allow them to advance, while they retreat?" he demanded. "Knocking out a Syrian tank isn't much of a problem." He did not, he admitted later, really believe himself; but somewhere, somehow, his message got through.

The citation awarding Kahalani the Order of Courage reads in part: "By his quality of leadership and personal example, Lieutenant Colonel Kahalani set a personal example to his men, reviving their spirits which were at breaking-point. He was the first to storm the enemy positions, accompanied by a subordinate officer. The entire force followed him and succeeded in retaking the Syrian positions which proved to be the key strategic points in the entire sector." Interviewed after the war, Kahalani remarked, "I don't know why I was cited [for the award]. I can think of two operations in which my battalion functioned well."

The Syrians had by now surrounded the Seventh Brigade, which was fighting off attacks from all angles of the compass. The tanks had become indistinguishable and mixed up with one another, as each individual tank fought for its survival.

The men had been fighting continuously for four days and three nights, and the tanks were down to an average of three to four shells each. Ben-Gal turned to speak to his operations officer, but he was fast asleep on the floor of the personnel carrier. Up to this point it had not occurred to Ben-Gal to retreat, but now he told Raful that he doubted whether they could hold out. Raful pleaded for one more hour.

Tiger's forces to the south were down to two shells per tank, but Ben-Gal asked him to hold on for ten minutes. Tiger, who had now run out of shells completely, filled his pockets with hand-grenades and prepared to withdraw. Before he gave the order, he was

The famous tripartite hand grasp and the beginning of a new era: President Anwar el-Sadat of Egypt, President Jimmy Carter and Prime Minister Menachem Begin, the White House, Washington, March 26, 1979. (*Israel Government Press Office*)

President Sadat addressing a press conference at Sharm el-Sheik, Sinai, June 1981. He was assassinated in Cairo four months later. (*IPPA*)

relieved by the aforementioned force of thirteen tanks, which had been repaired at brigade headquarters. Colonel Yossi Ben-Hanan, who had rushed back to Israel from his honeymoon in the Himalayas, organized the thirteen repaired tanks, manned them and led them into battle.

A report came from the southern sector of the Valley of Tears: the Syrian supply columns were turning round and withdrawing. Their forces broke and began retreating in panic. The Seventh Brigade had held out just long enough.

With their reinforcements, the Seventh now had twenty tanks, and with them they pursued the fleeing Syrians. In the Valley of Tears there were over 500 destroyed Syrian vehicles — 260 of them tanks — and countless destroyed Israeli vehicles. It was at this point that Raful told the survivors of the Seventh: "You have saved the people of Israel!"

Later he was to say: "That was a terrible night; there were moments when it hung by a hair."

MUCH MORE could be told: the Seventh Brigade, reinforced and redeployed, played a major part in the subsequent advance into Syria. Even more incredibly, the Barak Brigade was reconstituted and also played its part. Later the IDF had to take on units from Morocco, Iraq and Jordan, as well as the regrouped Syrian forces; but the war ended with the IDF within artillery range of Damascus.

Nevertheless, the decisive hours were those at the outbreak of war, when the defenders of the Golan quite literally put their bodies between Israel and its enemies. Many paid with their lives; many more were seriously wounded and permanently disabled; but their sacrifice led ultimately to the peace process in the Middle East.

The Yom Kippur War convinced Egyptian President Anwar Sadat that Israel could not be defeated on the field of battle and, in due course, he made peace with the Jewish state. The Israeli-Egyptian peace treaty was a watershed in the development of the Middle East conflict, signalling the beginning of Israel's acceptance in the region. It came about as a result of the bravery and tenacity of the IDF, which was never better demonstrated than it was on the Golan in October 1973.

16 ⤳

Entebbe Rescue: Wherever
Jews Are in Danger . . .

⤳ ON JULY 3, 1976, the IDF res-
cued 105 hostages being held in Uganda in a spectacular operation
that inspired the free world. It was an action both bold and brilliant, unexpected and almost unprecedented. It showed that the
community of nations need not stand helpless in the face of terror-
ism and extortion; but can hit back effectively, turning the tables
on the men of blood and violence, who threaten the very fabric of
modern civilization.

The Entebbe rescue was accomplished with breathtaking speed.
The Israeli force spent less than 100 minutes at Entebbe — only
some fifteen seconds elapsed between the first shot fired and the
elimination of the four terrorists who threatened to massacre the
hostages — and the entire operation was completed in a single
night. The gathering of intelligence, selection of the rescue force,
planning and rehearsal were accomplished in the space of a week;
but Entebbe was no flash in the pan: it was the result of years of
training and preparation, of dedication and discipline.

In making the decision to mount the rescue, one of the most daring and risky operations ever carried out, the government of Israel knew that it possessed one of the most formidable and competent fighting forces in the world: the volunteer elite of the IDF.

THE GENESIS of the IDF's special units goes back to the tradition of the Fosh, the Special Night Squads and the Palmach, which specialized in daring, unorthodox tactics. With the necessary dissolution of the Palmach, its members were distributed throughout the IDF to its considerable benefit, but at the same time some of the boldness and imagination of the force was lost.

In the early 1950s Israel was the victim of continuous incursions across its borders. In 1952 alone there were some 3,000 incidents of murder, infiltration, sabotage and theft. Morale was at a low ebb and the IDF command, hoping to revive the spirit of the Palmach, formed a special volunteer force called Unit 101.

Commanded by Ariel Sharon, then a young major, Unit 101 struck back at the infiltrators, carrying out a series of bold and effective actions deep in Arab territory. The force only had some forty-five members and operated for a mere five months, but its exploits became legendary, reviving the fighting spirit of the IDF. It was soon merged with the newly formed paratroop battalion, and the paratroops continued to launch daring and successful raids, setting new standards for the whole army.

Sharon, backed by IDF Chief of General Staff Moshe Dayan, established certain principles. The paratroop actions were minutely planned, based on precise data from the target area. They had to be completed whatever the cost, and no comrades were ever left behind, whether wounded or dead. The force operated on the old Palmach principle of the commander leading his men.

One of the most famous leaders of Unit 101 and the paratroops was Meir Har-Zion, who led many of its most daring operations. Brought up on a kibbutz, Har-Zion, a fearless, adventurous youth, ventured on dangerous field trips while still in his teens. Often he crossed the border into enemy countries, and one hike ended when he and his sister were taken prisoner by Arab forces and thrown into a Syrian jail.

Unit 101 was set up in 1953 as a volunteer unit mainly to undertake commando operations across Israel's borders. Its commander was Ariel ("Arik") Sharon. (*WZPS*)

Meir Har-Zion, considered by many to be the finest of Israel's commandos, was a member of the elite Unit 101. (*"Bamahaneh"*)

Lieutenant General Rafael Eitan ("Raful"), commander of the IDF during the Lebanon War. He had a distinguished military career in each of Israel's wars and is a recipient of Israel's highest military award, the Medal of Courage. (*Werner Braun*)

Joining the army in 1953, Har-Zion was soon perceived as a natural leader. His bravery was phenomenal. Almost nightly, he led dangerous and difficult raids into enemy territory, inspiring his men with his special brand of cool courage, often engaging in hand-to-hand combat.

Finally, he was critically wounded in a raid on a Jordanian police station, and his life was saved by an emergency tracheotomy, performed with a penknife. Dayan wrote that Har-Zion's "courage and fighting instinct set an example for the entire army." Sharon wrote that he was "the fighting symbol not only of the paratroops, but of the entire Israel Defence Forces."

Apart from Har-Zion and Sharon himself, such figures as Rafael Eitan and Yitzhak Hofi, GOC of Northern Command in the Yom

Israeli commandos dressed as mechanics storm the hijacked Sabena Boeing 707,
Lod airport, May 1972. (*David Rubinger*)

Kippur War, and Mordechai Gur, Chief of General Staff at the time
of Entebbe, were among the early paratroop officers.

Inspired by their example, the best young recruits to the IDF
began to volunteer for the paratroops and other special reconnaissance units that were formed, so that there were always many
more candidates than the units could absorb.

It was the members of these units who carried out many of the
IDF's most exciting operations. When Arab terrorists hijacked a
Belgian airliner and forced it to land at Lod airport, holding the
passengers hostage in May 1972, a special unit disguised as mechanics stormed the plane, killed the gunmen and rescued the
ninety-seven passengers.

In 1974, special units broke into a school in northern Israel,
where children were being held hostage, and killed the terrorists;
but on that occasion, twenty-two of the children also lost their
lives.

Numerous other actions, from an apartment house in Beit
Shean to the Savoy Hotel in Tel Aviv, proved that Israel was not

prepared to give in to terrorist blackmail, when there was a military option, in which its volunteer units could be deployed.

WHEN THE news reached the Israeli cabinet on Sunday, June 27, 1976, that an Air France plane, with large numbers of Israelis on board, had been hijacked by four terrorists—two Palestinians, two West Germans—who had boarded with their weapons at Athens airport, and forced to land at Entebbe in Uganda, it seemed at first that there was no military option.

Israel's special forces had operated with notable success as far away as Beirut in Lebanon and Naja Hamadi in Upper Egypt, but Uganda was over 2,000 miles away. The 256 passengers and twelve crew members were being held hostage by the four hijackers and colleagues who joined them in Entebbe, supplemented by Ugandan troops.

The day after the hijack, Mordechai Gur ordered a paratroop force to be mobilized. His idea was that the unit would be dropped on Entebbe, or cross Lake Victoria, kill the terrorists and guard the hostages until arrangements could be made with the Ugandan government for their release. The plan was rejected by Prime Minister Yitzhak Rabin, himself a former Chief of General Staff, as impractical.

Idi Amin, President of Uganda, was vindictively hostile towards Israel and, from the moment that the plane landed, he co-operated fully with the terrorists. France had troops stationed in Djibouti, within striking distance of Entebbe; but not once during the week-long crisis did that country show any desire to mount a rescue mission.

On Tuesday, June 29, Uganda Radio made known the demands of the hijackers: the release of fifty-two convicted terrorists—forty from Israel, five from West Germany, six from Kenya and one from Switzerland—in return for the release of the hostages. The non-Israelis were separated from the others and flown back to France.

There are differing versions concerning the separation. One of the hostages, Sarah Davidson, is convinced that the terrorists made every effort to keep all the Jewish passengers in Entebbe. One of the German hijackers told them that the hall where they were being detained was overcrowded, so that some were being moved to an adjacent hall. All at once, recalled Davidson, she realized the names that were being called out: Rosenberg, Aaronovich, Brodsky . . .

Another, Ilan Hartuv, maintains that Jews were also released, once the terrorists were convinced that they were not Israeli citizens. There was confusion, according to Hartuv, regarding passengers with both Israeli and foreign passports, who were suspected of being intelligence agents and were consequently maltreated. The other Israeli hostages threatened a hunger strike and the "interrogations" were stopped.

The Israeli government set up a negotiating procedure, using intermediaries, while still considering the military option. On his own initiative, Major General Dan Shomron (at the time Chief Infantry and Paratroop Officer, today the IDF Chief of General Staff) ordered his staff to start planning a rescue operation.

Later Rabin was to recall that he had been under tremendous pressure to negotiate with the terrorists from the relatives of the hostages in Israel. The pressure lessened only slightly when the negotiating process got under way.

In Entebbe, the hostages themselves were standing up to the pressure rather better than their relatives back home. Faced with a personal demand by Idi Amin to write a letter to their government demanding the release of the terrorists in exchange for themselves, they agonized for an entire day over its composition.

"It had to be acceptable to Amin," recalled Sarah Davidson, "but we were determined to include nuances that would be understood by the government of Israel, indicating that we were not asking for surrender to the hijackers' demands."

By the evening of Wednesday, June 30, Shomron's staff had prepared a rescue plan, involving landing in Entebbe, killing the terrorists, releasing the hostages and flying them back to Israel. The initial strike would be directly at the terrorists who were holding the hostages at the old terminal of Entebbe airport, in order to prevent them killing their prisoners. The air force confirmed that its Hercules transport aircraft could reach Entebbe, but would need additional fuel for the return journey. It was resolved to refuel at Entebbe airport.

The overall commander of the Entebbe operation, Brigadier General Dan Shomron (today Chief of Staff of the IDF), at a press conference with foreign journalists. (*IPPA*)

On Thursday, July 1, while the negotiating process proceeded, Shomron was invited to present his plan to the IDF General Staff. Defence Minister Peres was present at this meeting with the army's top command. Shomron suggested a landing at Entebbe at 11 P.M. on Saturday, July 3. There would be a dry run using a full-scale model on the Friday.

Peres asked for the views of all those present, and in the ensuing discussion Shomron stated that, provided the landing could be carried out successfully, there was a 100 percent chance of success. Peres indicated that he was in favour and ordered the General Staff to go ahead with preparations, subject to cabinet approval.

Peres and Gur put Shomron in command of the operation and gave him authority to pick his team. At the same time, the negotiations were continuing for the release of terrorists in exchange for the hostages. The hijackers had set a deadline for Sunday, July 4, after which they said they would start "selective executions" of the hostages.

Two hundred crack troops from a number of the IDF volunteer units were selected and began training for the operation. There were to be five forces: one to secure and illuminate the runway; one to occupy the old terminal and release the hostages; one to take control of the new terminal; one to secure the airfield and destroy the Ugandan fighter aircraft stationed there; and one to evacuate the hostages from the terminal to the waiting aircraft.

Many Israelis had served in Uganda years before, when it was still friendly towards Israel. Several IDF personnel had assisted in the training of Ugandan troops, and their knowledge was now utilized. Photographs of the airport were scanned and a "home movie," which showed Idi Amin arriving in a black Mercedes limousine escorted by a Land Rover, gave the planners a new idea.

At the same time Israeli agents were despatched to Paris, where they debriefed the non-Israeli passengers, now back in the French capital, who gave full information about conditions at the airport. The interrogators were able to discover the daily routine at the airport, where the passengers were held, where the terrorists slept, the number, nature and character of the terrorists and the location of the Ugandan soldiers. More information became available from a television film of Entebbe airport by a foreign correspondent.

Gur, who had become convinced of the feasibility of the plan, decided that he would be in overall command from his General Staff headquarters; Chief of Operations Yekutiel Adam and Air Force Commander Benjamin Peled would be an advanced command headquarters in a plane flying over the airport; and Shomron would command the operation on the ground.

The vital part of the plan was the storming of the old terminal, the killing of the terrorists and the release of the hostages. To lead this operation Shomron selected Lieutenant Colonel Jonathan ("Yoni") Netanyahu, one of the IDF's most promising young officers.

YONI WAS born of Israeli parents in New York, arriving in Israel at the age of two in 1948, when the War of Independence was still raging. At the age of sixteen he returned to America with his parents and completed his high school studies there.

Back in Israel in 1964, he joined the paratroops, where his record was outstanding. In due course he became a battalion commander, with a reputation as a strict disciplinarian and somewhat of an eccentric. His soldiers were baffled by a commanding officer who read Plato in his spare time.

One of his soldiers wrote later: "He wasn't a martinet. He was a super-martinet. But, if he made us jump into the water, he jumped into the water. If he sent us on a run, he ran with us. And when we had to run with stretchers, he ran with stretchers."

On his way to study mathematics, physics and philosophy at Harvard, he cancelled his trip when the Six Day War broke out. He fought with distinction in Sinai and on the Golan Heights, where he was hit in the elbow. In great pain, he crawled to the medical tent under fire, arriving just before he passed out. He recovered, but lost the full use of his left arm.

After the war, he married and returned to the United States to study; but he was back in Israel after a year, continuing his studies at the Hebrew University of Jerusalem. He wanted to rejoin the army, writing to his wife: "I believe I can be important to the army now. Anyone who can contribute anything should do so. I believe that the question of Jewish existence depends on us, our abilities and our spirit."

Lieutenant Colonel Jonathan ("Yoni") Netanyahu, field commander of the Entebbe rescue, was killed during the course of the operation.

Despite his disability, he was accepted to a crack reconnaissance unit because of his past record, and was soon in action on the borders. He proved himself a brilliant soldier and a superb commander, but he never grew accustomed to the brutality of war. One of his letters from this time reads: "This sick world doesn't do anything. Everyone is steeped in his own wars, including Israel, including me. And me? I feel I can thrust away the end as far as Israel is concerned. How do I do it? By learning war!"

He resumed his studies in the United States, but the autumn of 1973 saw him leading a force on the Golan in the Yom Kippur War with typical bravery. A fellow officer later recalled how Yoni's personal example helped him overcome his fear on encountering a Syrian commando unit: "Yoni lifted himself up very quietly, as if we weren't under fire. He waved to the men to get up with him and began to advance as though in an exercise. He walked upright, throwing orders right and left.''

After the tide of battle on the Golan turned and the IDF was advancing, one of the armoured units was badly mauled by the Syrians and its commander Yossi Ben-Hanan was wounded. An initial attempt to extricate him failed; but, under cover of darkness, Yoni led his paratroop unit through Syrian-controlled territory, evacuating Ben-Hanan from under the noses of Syrian artillery and armour.

After the Yom Kippur War, Yoni was given command of a tank battalion, which had almost been wiped out, reconstituting it successfully. His address to the battalion before being reposted expresses clearly the best tradition of leadership in the IDF and has been reproduced in military manuals. In it, among other things, he talks of the responsibilities of command, stresses the importance of attention to detail and the vital necessity of demanding the best possible results. "I want the men of the battalion always to be slightly worried—in case perhaps there is something else we could do, we could improve and we haven't done it."

YONI HAD just finished gruelling manoeuvres in the desert, when he was called into service for Entebbe; but he threw off his exhaustion and started rehearsing his men with characteristic thoroughness.

Over and over again, the tired soldiers repeated the attack, shaving seconds off the time needed to disembark from the plane and reach the old terminal. Speed was absolutely vital if a massacre of the hostages by the terrorists was to be avoided.

Before finally approving the plan, Gur was determined to test a ''blind landing'' in a Hercules to prove to himself that it could be accomplished. Having made this final test, he asked each of the commanders involved for their opinions. All were in favour and he decided to approve the operation.

On the morning of Saturday, July 3, Gur presented his final plan to Peres and then the two of them presented it to Rabin. The Prime Minister gave his approval and the soldiers received their final briefing.

The plan was as follows. The first aircraft would land and disembark a paratroop unit, which would be responsible for securing the runway and providing additional emergency lights. The same plane would then taxi towards the terminals, where two more units — one for each terminal — would disembark.

Yoni's force would proceed to the old terminal, where the hostages were being held, in a black Mercedes, like that used by Idi Amin and his senior officers, escorted by two Land Rovers. A second force would seize control of the new terminal. Shomron would also disembark with his advanced headquarters staff.

A second aircraft, landing seven minutes after the first, would disembark additional forces with armoured cars to secure the area around the terminals. The second plane would also carry Shomron's command jeep.

A third plane, landing immediately after the second, would have two more armoured cars for Yoni's force and a unit of the Golani Brigade, which would control the area between the two terminals and also act as a reserve. The Golani men were also to assist the passengers to reach their plane from the old terminal.

The fourth aircraft would bring a van for evacuating wounded, further reserves, a medical team and a refuelling team. The fourth plane would be the one to take the hostages back to Israel.

At 3:20 P.M. on Saturday, the cabinet was still discussing the plan; but the takeoff was approved for 3:30. If the cabinet decided against, there was still time to recall the planes. The plan was duly approved as the planes were already on their way.

After a flight of seven hours, the aircraft were approaching Entebbe, and the first plane landed, coming in directly behind a British cargo plane that had received permission to land.

The plane touched down and the men of the first unit jumped off while it was still moving. They placed emergency lights, ready to provide alternative illumination in case the Ugandans switched off the runway lights.

The plane reached a dark, unlit corner of the airfield and the Mercedes and two Land Rovers drove off. The noise of the British cargo plane drowned out any noise made by the Israeli force, and the three vehicles drove towards the old terminal with their headlights on.

July 4, 1976, Israel's two hundredth birthday gift to the United States: the successful storming of the hijacked Air France airbus at Entebbe airport, Uganda. The IDF Chief of Staff, Lieutenant General Mordechai ("Motta") Gur, gives details at a press conference the day after the operation. (*Israel Government Press Office*)

About a hundred yards from their objective, two Ugandan soldiers appeared in the headlights. One of them pointed his rifle at the Mercedes and ordered it to stop. Yoni and another officer fired at him with hand-guns equipped with silencers, wounding him.

The soldiers jumped from the vehicles and raced on foot to the old terminal. One entrance was blocked, so the entire force entered by the other, instead of by the two entrances as planned. One force broke into the hall where the hostages were. A terrorist on the right of the hall opened fire and was shot dead. Two more terrorists, one of them a German woman, were on the left of the hall and were also killed. A fourth terrorist, at the end of the hall, was shot.

Only fifteen seconds elapsed between Yoni's first shot at the Ugandan soldier and the deaths of the four terrorists guarding the hostages. The hostages were confused, despite instructions from the soldiers in Hebrew and English to lie down. One of them, who stood up, was also shot.

Yoni, who was standing by the entrance, was shot from the control tower and hit in the neck. He was evacuated, but died of his wounds.

The three additional aircraft landed on schedule and the troops conducted mopping-up operations, killing the remaining terrorists and any Ugandan troops who attacked them. Two European terrorists tried to slip away from the old terminal, but were identified and shot.

Ugandan troops were still firing from the control tower, but were neutralized by heavy machine-gun fire and rocket-propelled grenades. The Golani men began evacuating the wounded and the other hostages.

The second force stormed the new terminal, taking control of it fifteen minutes after the start of the action. Ugandan soldiers were allowed to flee; those who surrendered were locked in a room. Paratroop Sergeant Sorin Herscu was shot in the mouth at close range by a Ugandan soldier and gravely wounded.

The captain of the lead aircraft now asked Shomron for permission to take off without refuelling, planning to refuel in nearby Kenya, where a plane equipped as a field hospital had already landed. Flying above Entebbe, the IDF Chief of Operations and the Commander of the Air Force authorized this.

A little less than an hour after the initial landing, the first Hercules, loaded with the hostages, took off for Nairobi, the capital of Kenya. The Israeli cabinet, realizing that Kenya would be bound to refuse, had not asked permission either for the landing of the field hospital or for the refuelling; but it was calculated that the Kenyans, no friends of the Ugandan regime of Idi Amin, would co-operate if a forced landing was made. This turned out to be correct; the Kenyan government even waived payment for the fuel.

Forty-two minutes after the first aircraft left, the final plane took off with Shomron on board. Before leaving, the soldiers had set fire to eight Ugandan MiG aircraft with machine-gun fire.

The hostages, including the French air crew, were flown back to

Passengers, crew and soldiers return to Israel after the successful conclusion of "Operation Yonatan" in Entebbe. (*David Rubinger*)

a tumultuous welcome in Israel; but a tragic postscript remained to be acted out. One of the hostages, seventy-three-year-old Dora Bloch, had choked while at the airport and been evacuated to Kampala hospital. She was dragged from her bed and brutally murdered by Amin's security men.

THE ENTEBBE rescue operation had to be carried out with no safety margin. On the battlefield, an attack can be remounted, another force can be thrown in, artillery or air support can be called up. None of these options existed at Entebbe: the operation had to succeed the first time, and to be carried out with lightning speed. The slightest error or miscalculation could have led to disaster.

Three of the hostages lost their lives in the operation, and, in Yoni Netanyahu, the IDF lost one of its most promising commanders. Sergeant Sorin Herscu, wounded high up in the spine, became a quadriplegic, paralyzed in all four limbs.

Herscu, an immigrant from Romania, was nearing the time of his release from the IDF, when he volunteered for the Entebbe action. Today he is confined to a wheelchair and needs constant attention to help him function. Nevertheless, he leads a full life, earns his living as a computer operator and contrives to practise target-shooting at Beit Halohem, the disabled soldiers' recreation centre in Tel Aviv.

AT THE United Nations Security Council debate, in which an unsuccessful attempt to condemn Israel for carrying out the action was made, the author of this book, representing Israel, said:

> We come with a simple message to the Council: we are proud of what we have done because we have demonstrated to the world that a small country, in Israel's circumstances, with which the members of this Council are by now all too familiar, the dignity of man, human life and human freedom constitute the highest values. We are proud not only because we have saved the lives of over a hundred innocent people — men, women and children — but because of the significance of our act for the cause of human freedom.

Apart from this message to the world at large, the IDF action at Entebbe delivered a special message to the Jewish people, telling them clearly and dramatically that, as in the time of the Maccabees, they are not alone. Throughout the two millennia of exile and persecution — and particularly during the dark night of the Nazi Holocaust — the Jews had been helpless and isolated, with no one to protect them.

Sarah Davidson said later that the most important thing for her and her fellow hostages was the knowledge that their people and government were worrying about them day and night. "I know we don't seem to be a good people sometimes," she said. "We are crude and impolite; but after Entebbe I know that there is a wonderful Israel beneath the surface and I am madly in love with it."

The lesson of Entebbe is that, as opposed to the situation in the past, wherever Jews are in danger, they know that someone is worrying about them. They may sometimes find themselves living in fear, but never again do they have to live without hope.

INDEX

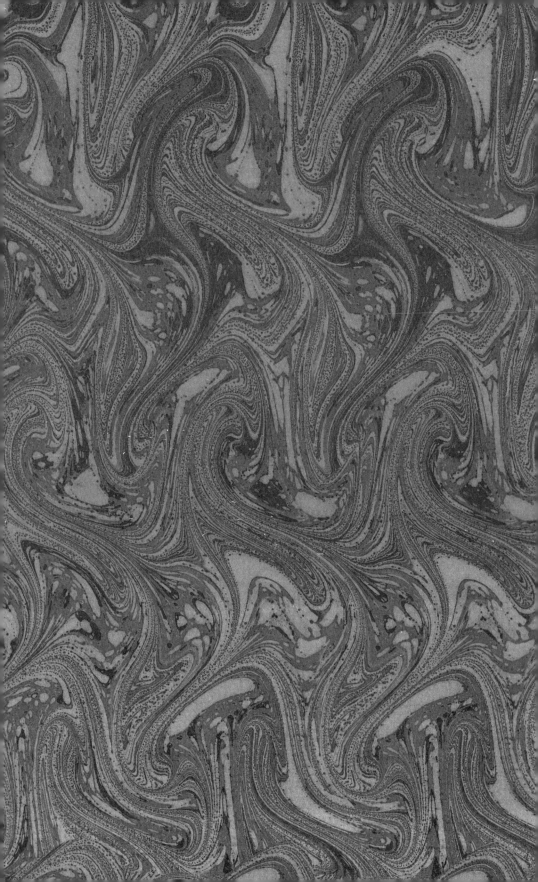